Praise for
The Meritocracy Myth, Fourth Edition

"I don't think there is a competitor that accomplishes what this book does—summarize the sociology of inequality in a clear, interesting, and succinct-yet-thorough fashion. *The Meritocracy Myth* provides a coherent perspective on the world. Many textbooks are a long mishmash of theories and facts; this one has a compelling message and point of view."

—**Scott Harris, Saint Louis University**

"In the land of opportunity, hard work and playing by the rules pays off and merit is rewarded by success. The wide-awake sociology of McNamee shines the bright light of reality on the myth to show that birth counts more and education less, and while luck is important, no one can count on it, and those who play by the rules often benefit least."

—**Paul Durrenberger, Pennsylvania State University**

"*The Meritocracy Myth* exposes the deceptive American rhetoric that hard work, talent, and virtue are all that is necessary to make it to the top. With inequalities at the core of sociology, *The Meritocracy Myth* makes a valuable contribution to the field by closely examining the contributing mechanisms that perpetuate class disparities. For sociology students, reading *The Meritocracy Myth* is a great application of important sociological concepts and theories to explain how all of our lives are influenced by socioeconomic class arrangements. The fourth edition is as relevant as ever in highlighting the importance of cultural myths that justify the exceedingly inequitable distribution of wealth in our modern society."

—**Beth Davison, Appalachian State University**

"American cultural explanations of success and failure—with their outsized emphases on the roles of hard work and smart choices—offer only a partial understanding of people's fortunes. This makes it difficult for Americans to fully understand social problems like inequalities based on race, class, and gender. Stephen McNamee's important book, *The Meritocracy Myth*, gives students and citizens alike a much deeper and more complete understanding of why some people succeed and some people fail. McNamee expertly explains how individuals are entangled in a web of forces that interact to shape their fortunes—from the impact of families and schools, to larger economic and political forces beyond our immediate environments and control. The fourth edition includes an additional section on marriage and mobility. To solve our most pressing problems, we need informed, engaged, and responsible citizens—this book is essential reading in that pursuit. "

—**Lawrence M. Eppard, Shippensburg University**

The Meritocracy Myth

Fourth Edition

Stephen J. McNamee
University of North Carolina Wilmington

ROWMAN & LITTLEFIELD
Lanham • Boulder • New York • London

Executive Editor: Sarah Stanton
Assistant Editor: Carli Hansen
Senior Marketing Manager: Kim Lyons

Credits and acknowledgments for material borrowed from other sources, and reproduced with permission, appear on the appropriate page within the text.

Published by Rowman & Littlefield
An imprint of The Rowman & Littlefield Publishing Group, Inc.
4501 Forbes Boulevard, Suite 200, Lanham, Maryland 20706
www.rowman.com

Unit A, Whitacre Mews, 26-34 Stannary Street, London SE11 4AB, United Kingdom

British Library Cataloguing in Publication Information Available

Library of Congress Cataloging-in-Publication Data Available

ISBN 978-1-5381-0339-5 (cloth : alk. paper)
ISBN 978-1-5381-0340-1 (pbk. : alk. paper)
ISBN 978-1-5381-0341-8 (electronic)

♾™ The paper used in this publication meets the minimum requirements of American National Standard for Information Sciences—Permanence of Paper for Printed Library Materials, ANSI/NISO Z39.48-1992.

Printed in the United States of America

To the memory of
Robert K. Miller, Jr.,
colleague, coauthor, and friend

Contents

Preface to the Fourth Edition

In the first edition of this book, published in 2004, my coauthor Robert K. Miller, Jr., and I set out to challenge the commonly held assertion that in America, people get out of the system what they put into it, based exclusively, or primarily, on their individual merit. We did not suggest that individual merit is a myth, or that it has nothing to do with who gets ahead and who falls behind. Instead, we made the case that the presumption that the system as a whole fundamentally operates on the basis of merit in determining who gets what and how much is a myth.

According to the meritocracy myth, America is a land of unlimited opportunity in which individuals can go as far as their individual talents and abilities can take them. We identified the characteristics most frequently identified with individual merit—innate talent or capacity, hard work, having the right attitude, and playing by the rules, or having high moral character and virtue—and examined the empirical evidence of the impact of these factors on prospects for social mobility. We then identified a variety of nonmerit factors, including inheritance, social and cultural capital, differential access to educational opportunities, reduced rates of self-employment, luck, and discrimination that tend to neutralize, suppress, or even negate the effects of individual merit. We concluded that the overall evidence suggests that Americans tend to overestimate the effects of merit factors and underestimate the effects of nonmerit factors in terms of how the system actually operates.

Since the publication of the first edition, nonmerit factors have become even more important. These changes are described and analyzed in the current edition. Economic inequality has increased, along with consolidation of privilege, especially at the top of the system. The gap between the rich and the poor has widened, making it more difficult for those at the bottom of the system to close the gap. Consolidation of power and privilege especially has allowed those at the top of the system to more easily pass on nonmerit economic, social, and cultural advantages to succeeding generations. The continued decline of self-employment and increasing dominance and power of existing large corporations has further eroded the entrepreneurial pathway to social mobility, creating barriers for entry and making it more difficult for individuals to move up in the system by striking out on their own and creating new enterprises. Globalization, deindustrialization, and de-unionization have compromised opportunities for millions of working-class Americans through no fault of their own. Finally, the increasing capacity of propertied interests to disproportionately influence political outcomes has further consolidated power and privilege at the top of the system. To the extent that propertied interests prevail rather than the interests of the general public, the system gets further tilted, or "rigged," in favor of the already privileged.

NEW TO THE FOURTH EDITION

In the current edition, data, tables, and figures have been updated and descriptions of new research on these topics have been incorporated. A concerted effort was made to streamline the presentation of evidence throughout. The current edition takes a more explicitly life-cycle approach as an organizing scheme. As in previous editions, the first chapter describes the origins and prospects of the American Dream. Chapter 2 assesses the key factors associated with the formula for success based on individual merit. Subsequent chapters describe various nonmerit barriers to mobility, organized roughly by the stage of the life cycle in which they are typically encountered. Chapter 3 discusses the effects of initial class placement at birth on future life chances. Chapter 4 describes the informal advantages of social and cultural capital, resources typically initially acquired in childhood and extended throughout the life course.

Historically, the primary pathways of upward mobility in America have been through education and entrepreneurial activity. Chapter 5 describes the effects of unequal access to formal educational opportunities, beginning with K–12 and extending through higher education. Following the completion of formal education, the next stage of the life cycle for most Americans is to enter the full-time labor force. Chapter 6 describes the declining prospects for upward mobility through self-employment and the ascent of large-scale corporations. Chapter 7 describes the impact of luck on economic outcomes, especially with regard to the nonmerit effects of what kinds of jobs are available in the labor force that individuals enter into, how much they pay, and how many people are pursuing them—independent of personal characteristics.

After completing formal education and getting established in the labor market, the typical next stage in the life cycle for most people is marriage. Chapter 8 discusses the prospects for social mobility not directly based on one's merit or achievement, but through marriage or partnering. Chapter 9 discusses the nonmerit factor of discrimination in all of its forms as they relate to economic outcomes. Depending on the type involved, discrimination can be encountered throughout the life course, as in the case of race or sex discrimination, or it may be encountered at later stages in the life course, such as with age discrimination. The concluding chapter summarizes the main points in the book and presents policy options regarding how issues of economic inequality might be addressed. Transition statements at the end of each chapter have been added to assist the reader in placing each chapter in relation to the next.

Chapter 8 (Mobility through Marriage: The Cinderella Effect) is new to this edition. The tendency toward class endogamy, especially within the upper class, was discussed in prior editions, but the increasing importance of the consolidation of privilege through marriage among the affluent and the passing on of nonmerit economic, social, and cultural privilege to children warranted a separate discussion in this new edition. Because men have historically controlled access to power, wealth, and status, this particular form of upward mobility has generally been more available to women. As women have more recently increased their levels of educational attainment and labor-force participation, however, the prospect for men to marry up has also increased. Marrying for money as the primary motivation for marriage is a type of social climbing that is generally not considered socially acceptable, and would not be viewed as a legitimate part of the American Dream. The strong tendency for homogamy and concentration of wealth at the top of the system increases the capacity for "power couples" to pass on nonmerit economic, social, and cultural advantages to children, increasingly creating "divergent destinies" for succeeding generations.

Finally, in prior editions we presented brief biographical vignettes on presidents, including George W. Bush and Barack Obama, as examples of how economic, social, and cultural factors shaped their rise to prominence. In the current edition, I have included a biographical vignette on Donald Trump and his family in this regard.

Acknowledgments

Several people facilitated the completion of this fourth edition. I thank the editors at Rowman & Littlefield, especially Sarah Stanton, Carli Hansen, and Jehanne Schweitzer, for their support and assistance in shepherding this edition along. I also acknowledge the intellectual debt I owe to my stratification teachers and mentors, including John Murray, Norbert Wiley, Reeve Vanneman, and William Form. I also thank my students, who over the course of my career have deepened and sharpened my understanding of the processes of inequality.

In addition, I am grateful to anonymous reviewers who provided useful suggestions for revision for this edition. I am grateful for the institutional support provided by the University of North Carolina Wilmington. To my colleagues in the Department of Sociology and Criminology, I extend my appreciation for their ongoing encouragement and support.

I am especially thankful to my daughter, Dr. Catherine McNamee, coauthor of chapter 8, "Mobility through Marriage," for lending her expertise to this project. Cate is a lecturer in sociology specializing in family demography in the School of Social Sciences, Education and Social Work at Queens University in Belfast, Northern Ireland. I also wish to acknowledge my wife, Christine, for her generous understanding, patience, and helpful advice in completing this edition.

I am especially grateful to Dr. Robert K. Miller, Jr., my coauthor for the previous three editions of this book, and to whose memory this edition is dedicated. For more than thirty years, Rob and I collaborated on a number of projects. We spent countless hours deliberating on the topics and issues discussed in this book. His voice is very much still present in these pages, and words alone cannot express my intellectual indebtedness.

1

The American Dream

Origins and Prospects

> The reason they call it the American Dream is because you have to be asleep to believe it.
>
> —George Carlin, *Brain Droppings*

In the image of the American Dream, America is the land of opportunity. Presumably, if you work hard enough, play by the rules, and are talented enough, you can overcome any obstacle and achieve success. No matter where you start out in life, the sky is ostensibly the limit. According to the promise implied by the American Dream, you can go as far as your talents and abilities can take you.

Although most Americans enthusiastically endorse this image in abstract terms (Longoria 2009; McCall 2013), the lived experiences of many Americans tell them that factors other than merit also make a difference: "it takes money to make money" (inheritance); "it's not what you know, but who you know" (social capital); "what matters is being in the right place at the right time" (luck); "the playing field is not level" (discrimination); and "he or she married into money" (hypergamy).

Americans are ambivalent about economic inequality and often simultaneously hold contradictory principles about how income and wealth should be distributed (Longoria 2009; McCall 2013). While many Americans, for instance, proudly proclaim the virtues of "getting out of the system what you put into it" (meritocracy), they also steadfastly defend the right of individuals to dispose of their property when they die "as they personally see fit" (inheritance). These beliefs, however, pose a fundamental contradiction between freedom of choice at the individual level and equality of opportunity at the societal level. Simply put, to the extent that income and wealth are distributed on the basis of inheritance, they are not distributed on the basis of merit.

While "merit" is a characteristic of individuals, "meritocracy" is a characteristic of societies as a whole. Meritocracy refers to a social system as a whole in which individuals get ahead and earn rewards in direct proportion to their individual efforts and abilities. The term *meritocracy,* coined by British sociologist Michael Young in his dystopian novel *The Rise of the Meritocracy, 1870–2033: An Essay on Education and Equality* (1961), is closely linked with the idea of the American Dream. Although Young envisioned a fictional and futuristic society operating as a meritocracy, the opportunity to achieve the American Dream implies a society that in fact already operates on those principles.

The term *American Dream* was first popularized by historian James Truslow Adams in his 1931 best-selling book, *The Epic of America.* Adams defined it as "that dream of a land in which life should be better and richer and fuller for every man, with opportunity for each according to his ability or achievement" (1931, 404). In a general way, people understand the idea of the American Dream as the fulfillment of the promise of meritocracy. The American Dream is fundamentally rooted in the historical experience of the United States as a nation of immigrants. Unlike European societies dominated by hereditary aristocracies, the ideal in America was that its citizens were "free" to achieve on their own merits. The American Dream was the hope of fulfillment of individual freedom and the chance to succeed in the New World. As Thomas Jefferson (1813) put it, America would replace the European aristocracy of birth with a new American "natural aristocracy of talent and virtue."

In *Facing Up to the American Dream* (1995), Jennifer Hochschild identifies four tenets of the American Dream: 1) who—everyone regardless of origin or station; 2) what—reasonable anticipation or the hopefulness of success; 3) how—through actions under one's individual control; and 4) why—because of the association of true success with virtue in various ways; that is, "virtue leads to success, success makes a person virtuous, success indicates virtue, or apparent success is not real success unless one is also virtuous" (Hochschild 1995, 23).

Together, the tenets of the American Dream comprise an ideology of inequality. Ideologies provide socially acceptable explanations for the kind and extent of inequality within society. Ideologies are ultimately based on persuasion as a form of social power. Persuasion entails not just making claims but getting society's members to go along as well. It is not enough for some simply to have more than others. For a system of inequality to be stable over the long run, those who have more must convince those who have less that the distribution of who gets what is fair, just, proper, or the natural order of things. The greater the level of inequality, the more compelling and persuasive these explanations must appear to be.

The type of justification or ideology varies depending on the type of inequality. In feudal societies, for instance, the principle of "birthright" and the idea of "the divine right of kings" were used to justify the power and privilege of the nobility over commoners and peasants. In slave societies, slave owners used ideas like "the spoils of victory" or "innate superiority" to justify the ownership of other human beings. In traditional Indian caste societies, inequality was justified by a Hindu belief in reincarnation; that is, one's place in this life was based on one's performance in past lives. In some forms of early Calvinist belief, salvation was seen as "preordained," and success in this life was taken as a sign of God's approval of the "elect." Currently in the United States inequality is "legitimized," or "explained," predominantly by an ideology of meritocracy. America is seen as the land of opportunity where people get out of the system what they put into it. Ostensibly, the most talented, hardest-working, and most virtuous get ahead. The lazy, shiftless, and inept fall behind. In this formulation, you may not be held responsible for where you start out in life, but you are responsible for where you end up, because the system is "fair" and provides ample opportunity to get ahead.

An important aspect of ideologies of inequality is that they do not have to be objectively "true" to persuade those who have less to accept less. Racism, for instance, is predicated on the false assumption of innate racial superiority. Racism involves a double falsehood: that there are biologically distinct categories within the human population (a view that modern biology soundly rejects), and that these "races" are innately and hierarchically ranked. Americans, including people of color, were long persuaded to accept these myths, and it took centuries of struggle to begin to counter them. Likewise, women long accepted a definition of themselves as inherently inferior to men. The women's movement challenged these definitions, and they too are now largely rejected.

Racism and sexism rest ultimately on biological assumptions of innate superiority and inferiority that can be demonstrated empirically to be false. From the point of view of those in power, however, an ideal ideology is one that cannot be proven either true or false, such as reincarnation or the divine right of kings. People do not act on the world as it is but as they perceive it to be, and as they make sense of it. For ideologies of inequality to "legitimize" particular social arrangements, it is not necessary that the ideology be objectively true or even falsifiable; what matters is that people accept and act on it.

Acceptance of meritocracy in America then is predicated not on what "is," but on the belief that the system of inequality is "fair" and it "works." According to the ideology of meritocracy, inequality is seen to be fair because everyone presumably has an equal (or at least an adequate) chance to succeed, and success is determined by individual merit. The system supposedly works because it is seen as providing an individual incentive to achieve what is good for society as a whole; that is, those who are most talented, the hardest-working, and the most virtuous get, and should get, the most rewards.

INDIVIDUALISM AND THE ORIGINS OF THE AMERICAN DREAM

The American Dream has at its core an emphasis on the individual (Collero 2009). According to the ideology of the American Dream, we are "masters of our own fate."

We "go our own way" and "do our own thing." The American emphasis on individualism is not a historical accident but is firmly rooted in the religious, political,
economic, and cultural experience of America as a nation of immigrants.

Religious Origins

A key source of American individualism is the religious backgrounds of the first
English colonists in America, who were mostly members of various Protestant religious sects. Subsequent immigrant populations had to adopt the language and cultural values of this population or risk isolation or exclusion. In this way, the cultural
ideals of the initial group of white Anglo-Saxon Protestant (WASP) colonists became
the dominant cultural force in America.

The constellation of cultural values that became known as the "Protestant ethic"
found its greatest expression among the various Puritan sects that formed the
dominant religious backgrounds of many of the early American colonists. German
sociologist Max Weber analyzed the principles of the Protestant ethic in his classic
work *The Protestant Ethic and the Spirit of Capitalism* (1905). The core of Weber's
argument is that the twin ethics of hard work and self-denial were associated with the
early development of capitalism. Hard work generated productivity, while self-denial
encouraged investment through savings. Capitalism, particularly early capitalism,
needed both a highly motivated labor force and investment "capital."

As part of the break with Catholicism, Protestantism emphasized an individual
rather than communal relationship with God. Puritans in particular eschewed Catholicism's communalism and the elaborate ritual system associated with it. Instead,
the emphasis was on a direct relationship with God through individual prayer and
reading of the Bible. The Protestant Reformation also shifted the traditional Catholic
view of work as "punishment" for "original sin" to the idea of work as a sacred call-
ing, a mission from God to subdue nature and gain control over it. People should
become instruments of God's will on Earth, and were called upon to transform the
world and remake it in God's image, which Weber called "world mastery."

The greatest expression of this ethic was in the Puritan sect of Calvinism. The
Calvinists believed in predestination, which meant that people did not earn salvation
but were "elected" to it by God. This belief created among the followers what Weber
called "salvation anxiety," which led individuals to attempt to ascertain whether they
were among the elect. Individuals came to believe that worldly success could be taken
as a sign of God's grace. So, driven by salvation anxiety, people worked very hard to
become successful so that they could demonstrate to themselves and others that they
were among the elect.

These Puritan values of individual "industry, frugality, and prudence" were reflected in early American moralistic novels (Weiss 1969) and were integrated into
the core of an emerging national culture (Cullen 2003; Samuel 2012). The best-
known of these was a popular series of 107 "rags-to-riches" novels by Horatio Alger
(1832–1899), the son of a Unitarian minister and a Harvard graduate who for a

short time also served in the ministry. Puritan themes were reinforced as well in a series of widely used early American primary school readers, written by William McGuffey, who was also a minister turned writer.

While perhaps useful for stimulating the early development of capital, the diligence/asceticism twin ethic was not as useful for sustaining its continued expansion. The problem is that the twin ethic contains within it an internal economic contradiction. With everyone working hard to succeed, it does not take long to produce more than enough goods to meet minimum standards of living. The asceticism part of the ethic, while good for savings, depresses the demand for goods. This hardwork/no-play combination eventually results in an imbalance between supply and demand. For supply and demand to be reasonably balanced, something has to give. People need either to produce less or to consume more.

Americans came to consume more, motivated in part by the growth of media, which promoted consumerism on a massive scale. This was most evident especially in the period of prosperity following World War I, commonly known as the Roaring Twenties. The inhibitions, frugality, and austerity associated with the ascetic "no-play" part of the Puritan ethic waned. Consumption was redefined, not as an evil act of self-indulgence, but as a just reward for hard work. The "hard-work" part of the ethic was retained but transformed. Americans no longer worked hard simply for the glory of God, but increasingly for self-enhancement. In this way, the *Protestant* ethic has lost most of its religious underpinnings and survives now in American culture simply as the "work ethic," the moral underpinnings of which have severely eroded (Wuthnow 1996). Secularized vestiges of the Puritan tradition persist in the American values of self-reliance, independence, and individual responsibility.

Political Origins

Politically, the American emphasis on individualism found its expression in revolution. In 1776, the Declaration of Independence proclaimed the sovereignty of a new nation and the inalienable right of its citizens to "life, liberty, and the pursuit of happiness." These were God-given individual rights that the state could not abridge. The spirit of *individual* freedom contained in this document became the blueprint for how the political system of the new nation would operate. The details of the new political blueprint were later incorporated into the Articles of Confederation, adopted in 1781, and expanded with the ratification of the US Constitution in 1788. In the spirit of the previous documents, the Constitution outlined a contract between the citizen and the state, emphasizing (especially in the Bill of Rights) the limits of state power over individual freedoms.

The colonists under British rule gradually became more and more resentful of the political and economic constraints imposed by the Crown. More than a century after the first permanent settlements, the colonists revolted. With the success of the American Revolution, a new government was established. The revolutionaries who laid out the plan for the new government had risked everything to gain political and economic freedom, and they were determined not to re-create the same tyranny they had fought so bitterly to defeat. The new government would have no monarch and no unilateral system of control. In the aftermath of battles with the Crown, the framers of the new government were leery of centralized systems of political control. A constitutional system of checks and balances was formed to diffuse power and to hold those who wielded power accountable, and a compromise plan—the federal system—was worked out to balance the need for national unity with the desire for localized control. "Freedom" was a key ingredient in this formulation, although it had different meanings for different individuals: freedom of religion for some, freedom to acquire wealth for others, freedom from tyranny for yet others.

Alexis de Tocqueville, in his much-celebrated *Democracy in America* ([1835] 1967), praised America for the early success of its emerging democracy. Key to that success, according to de Tocqueville, was the American emphasis on individualism and equality. By individualism, de Tocqueville meant "a mature and calm feeling, which disposes each member of the community to sever himself from the mass of his fellow creatures" ([1835] 1967, 118). By "equality," de Tocqueville meant the absence of aristocracy, which he also linked to individualism:

> Aristocracy has made a chain of all the members of the community, from the peasant to the king: democracy breaks that chain, and severs every link to it. As social conditions become more equal, the number of persons increases who, although they are neither rich enough nor powerful enough to exercise any great influence over their fellow creatures, have nevertheless acquired or retained sufficient education and fortune to satisfy their own wants. *They owe nothing to any man, they expect nothing from any man; they acquire the habit of always considering themselves as standing alone, and they are apt to imagine that their whole destiny is in their own hands.* (Emphasis added) ([1835] 1967, 120)

In short, de Tocqueville maintained that in America individuals are free to achieve, not by virtue of hereditary title but by their own individual effort and merit. Thus, the emerging ideal of the American Dream incorporated two meanings of freedom: both political freedom from tyranny, and economic freedom to achieve on one's own merits.

Economic Origins

Freedom from political tyranny, however, is not the same as "market freedom," although the two are often mistakenly viewed as inextricable. Free markets mean that prices, profits, and wages are determined by the "free flow" of market forces—the outcome of innumerable matches of supply and demand for goods and services unregulated by governments. In free-market societies, "the invisible hand of the market" operates: The sole determinant of investment—the sale and purchase of land, labor, and business—is individual calculation of costs and benefits intended to maximize profits. But free markets themselves do not guarantee democracy, civil liberties, or political freedom.

In one of the great coincidences of American history, America's economic blue-print for a free-market economy was laid out in the same year, 1776, as its political blueprint for governance was set forth in the Declaration of Independence. In that pivotal year, the Scottish economist Adam Smith published *An Inquiry into the Nature and Causes of the Wealth of Nations* ([1776] 1976), which was adopted in the United States as the informal bible of American free-market capitalism. It empha-sized rational *self*-interest, *individual* competition, *private* ownership, and *laissez-faire* principles. At the time of the publication of Smith's book, roughly three-fourths of the new nation's labor force was, in fact, self-employed, comprising mostly small farmers, merchants, and artisans. A large number of mostly small producers encour-aged market competition. Government regulation of business was minimal. Indeed, the economic blueprint seemed to fit.

In feudal economies, all subjects of the aristocracy primarily work for the aris-tocracy. Peasants did not own land and had little opportunity to move up in the system. With the decline of feudalism and the rise of market economies, free markets emerged. Individuals could own their *own* land, be their *own* bosses, and move up on the basis of their *own* efforts. In America, the absence of a feudal past, the abundance of land, and periodic regional as well as local labor shortages enhanced these oppor-tunities, thus grounding these notions in the formative stages of the development of America's national value system.

It is important to point out, however, that the individual rights and free-market blueprint in America never applied equally to everyone. From the very beginning, indentured servants, slaves, non-WASPs, women, and others were systematically excluded from both the protections of the Constitution and the opportunities of free-market capitalism. Despite these exclusions, the dominant cultural image of individual rights and the free market prevailed.

Cultural Origins

The "can-do" rugged individualism associated with the American Dream was further reinforced by the formative experience of the American Western frontier. The "pioneer spirit" of striking out on one's own and staking a claim was captured in American author Horace Greeley's clarion call to "Go West, young man." The absence of formal government on the frontier, including effective law enforcement, also un-doubtedly contributed to feelings of independence and self-reliance. Historian Freder-ick Jackson Turner, in his classic book *The Frontier in American History* (1947), argued that the frontier was central to the development of American individualism. Turner further linked the rugged individualism of the pioneer with the ideals of democracy: "Quite as deeply fixed in the pioneer's mind as the ideal of individuals was the ideal of democracy. He had a passionate hatred for aristocracy, monopoly and special privilege; he believed in simplicity, economy and the rule of the people" (1947, 37).

Contemporary historians have sharply criticized Turner's largely nostalgic and romantic view of the frontier. But it is precisely this idealized image of the American frontier that has filtered into the American consciousness, reinforced by countless novels, TV Westerns, and Hollywood feature films. The frontier is portrayed as a rough and dangerous place, but one with abundant opportunity. Those who were able and willing could tame the wilderness, overcome any obstacle, and realize the American Dream.

MERIT AND NONMERIT
EXPLANATIONS FOR INEQUALITY

The American ethos of rugged individualism extends to culturally dominant explanations of behavior, attitudes, and life circumstances. That is, Americans strongly tend to look first to the characteristics of individuals to explain what happens to them. At the same time, there is an uneasy awareness that we are not entirely in control of our own fates. We are also all part of a social order not of our making or choosing that nevertheless profoundly affects us.

This tension between internal (merit) and external (nonmerit) factors in accounting for what happens to us is reflected in rival theoretical explanations for inequality in the social sciences. In sociology, these positions are represented by the functional and conflict theories of inequality. According to the functional theory, all societies make some provision or social arrangement for acquiring and distributing the resources necessary for the mutual survival of their members. As a result of these collective efforts, there are tasks that must be done in society as a whole, and individuals must be available to do them. According to this theory, some tasks are more important than others, and some individuals are more competent than others. In order to ensure that the most competent individuals fill the most important and demanding tasks in society, an incentive system of unequal rewards evolves. This unequal system of rewards is seen as necessary to entice the most capable individuals to take on the burden of, and responsibility for, performing these demanding tasks, and to develop the skills necessary to do so. Those who perform these most demanding and exclusive tasks both deserve and receive the most rewards. Or, to summarize the theory in more colloquial terms, those who put the most into the system, get the most out of it.

Conflict theories of inequality take very different views. According to these theories, the essential cause of inequality is conflict over surplus. Surplus refers to whatever is left over in the society as a whole after its members' minimum survival needs are met. Conflict over surplus produces winners and losers. Ever since societies have produced surplus, some have managed to get more of it than others. Winners may initially get more of the surplus because they are the shrewdest or most enterprising, or because they are the most devious, the most unscrupulous, or the most ruthless. Once "winners" accumulate more surplus than others by whatever means, they can expend a portion of the accumulated surplus both to protect their existing surplus and to acquire additional surplus. In addition, winners develop ideologies—narratives of justification regarding the *right* to own. Finally, accumulated surplus is transferred intergenerationally through the process of inheritance, thereby tending to perpetuate existing inequalities across generations. To summarize conflict theories in more colloquial terms, them that has, gets.

These sociological perspectives and other versions of them in other disciplines have been debated at length (cf. Kerbo 2012, 83–148; McNamee and Miller 1998). It is not my purpose here to fully explicate these theories but instead to put the current discussion into theoretical context. Functional theories imply a system of meritocracy in which individuals get ahead based on their individual talents and abilities. Conflict theories, on the other hand, imply a system of inheritance in which people's life chances are largely determined by their starting point within an existing structure of inequality. Functional theorists focus on individual characteristics such as talent, ability, and hard work as the primary determinants of inequality. Conflict theorists focus on nonmerit factors such as inheritance, discrimination, and variation in opportunities as the primary determinants of inequality.

Merit and nonmerit factors are not mutually exclusive explanations for individual economic outcomes. Such outcomes have both individual and structural causes. Indeed, a major challenge of social science research is to sort out how these factors interact in ways that fully account for the kind and extent of inequality that does exist, and with what consequences. It is the contention of this book, however, that the dominant ideology of meritocracy has historically tended to overestimate the effects of merit on economic outcomes and to underestimate the effects of nonmerit factors.

DOWNSIZING THE AMERICAN DREAM

In important ways, the prospects for achieving the American Dream have expanded over time. In particular, since the nation's founding, a number of groups—including minorities, and especially women—have been afforded greater economic, political, and social opportunities. Progress on the expansion of opportunities to groups formerly discriminated against or excluded, however, has been slow and uneven. While there is ongoing discrimination and the effects of past discrimination continue into the present, the overall expansion of greater opportunity to a wider segment of American society is undeniable. From its humble beginnings as a British colony, America has emerged as the wealthiest and most powerful nation in the world. For most of its history and for many, but not all, of its citizens, succeeding generations have enjoyed higher standards of living and expanded opportunities.

Recently, however, the prospects for attaining the American Dream have been diminishing for a large segment of the American population. The American Dream implies not just a general hopefulness for the future and a formula for success, but also a sense of what the fulfillment of the dream would mean. Although specifics vary, several outcomes are generally associated with the fulfillment of the American Dream, including home ownership, improved life chances for the next generation, opportunities to get rich, and a secure and comfortable retirement. In each case, the chances of achieving these aspects of the American Dream have dimmed, especially for younger generations.

Home Ownership

In a US Census study, appropriately entitled *Tracking the American Dream*, F. John Devaney (1994) examined housing trends in the fifty-year period between 1940 and 1990. In terms of fulfillment of the dream, the results are mixed. Between 1890 and 1940, rates of home ownership remained at slightly less than one-half of the American population. In the post–World War II period, stimulated by postwar prosperity and veterans' loans as part of the GI Bill, rates of ownership increased dramatically, from 44 percent in 1940 to 62 percent in 1960. Subsidized by government highway funds that linked surrounding communities with central cities, this was also a period of rapid expansion of American suburbs. For many, the ranch house in the suburbs with the two-car garage and meticulously maintained lawn symbolized the fulfillment of the dream. Commuters in these bedroom communities, who worked in the urban areas and had access to their cultural amenities, felt shielded from the problems of central cities. For them, it was the best of both worlds.

Yet, economic success—which resulted in white flight to the suburbs in the post-war period—exacerbated the problems of central cities and, in many cases, increased the rates of segregation and racial tension. The tax base of urban areas eroded along with public services, including schools, police and fire protection, and sanitation. The fulfillment of the dream for some was, for others, a nightmare of inner-city crime, drugs, unemployment, poverty, and despair.

After 1960, average quarterly home-ownership rates remained stable, hovering around 63 to 64 percent until the mid-1990s, when rates began to steadily increase, reaching a peak at the height of the housing bubble in 2004 at 69 percent (US Census Bureau 2016a). Home-ownership rates began to fall in the aftermath of the mortgage crisis that precipitated the Great Recession of 2008, resulting in a general financial meltdown, record numbers of foreclosures and bankruptcies, as well as a series of bank failures leading to a massive $700 billion federal bailout. Many Americans lost their homes altogether, or were "underwater," owing more on their mortgages than the value of their homes as housing prices plummeted. Mortgages became harder to attain as banks required higher levels of creditworthiness to obtain new mortgages. By the end of 2016, the home-ownership rate had fallen to 64 percent (US Census Bureau 2016a). Clearly, the prospect of "home ownership" as a central marker of having achieved the American Dream has dimmed in the decade since the onset of the Great Recession.

Moreover, it is important to note that these rates of "home ownership" are based on the government's definition of "owner-occupied" housing, which combines both homes that are mortgaged and homes that are owned outright. Mortgaged "home-owners" don't really "own" their homes until they pay off their mortgages. Over the long run, the percentage of homes in America that are owned outright has sharply declined over time. In 1890, for instance, 72 percent of owner-occupied residents owned their own homes outright (Devaney 1994). In 2015, only slightly more than one-third (35 percent) of owner-occupied residents owned their homes outright (US Census Bureau 2015).

Better Opportunities for the Next Generation

Another aspect of the American Dream is the idea that each new generation will have a higher standard of living and better opportunities than the previous one. For a long period of time in American history—with some stalls and notable setbacks, such as the period of the Great Depression—this was largely the case. As America moved from a mostly agrarian to a mostly industrial economy, opportunities expanded along with generally high rates of growth—in the economy as a whole, and with overall increases in the general standard of living. This was especially the case in the post–World War II era of general prosperity, in which the baby boomer generation came of age. Yet a combination of deindustrialization, globalization, and technological automation, beginning in the 1970s and accelerating ever since, has reduced overall opportunity, especially for younger cohorts and those born closer to the bottom of the system.

A recent comprehensive study of cohort mobility (Chetty et al. 2016) showed that chances for adult children to have higher real incomes than their parents (adjusted for inflation) have drastically declined in the past sixty years. For those born in 1940, the chance to out-earn their parents was 92 percent, compared to 79 percent of those born in 1950, 62 percent born in 1960, 61 percent for those born in 1970, and only 50 percent for those born in 1980.

Another way this decline in the prospects of attaining this aspect of the American Dream has been manifested is a steep decline in the home-ownership rate for young adults. As previously noted, overall rates of home ownership have declined since the Great Recession, but rates of home ownership for adults under the age of thirty-five have fallen more sharply, from 42 percent in 2007 to 35 percent in 2015 (US Census Bureau 2016b). While fewer young adults are buying homes, more are living at home with parents (sometimes referred to as "boomerangs"). In 2014, 32 percent of eighteen- to thirty-four-year-olds were living in their parents' homes, compared to 20 percent of the corresponding age group in 1960 (Fry 2016).

Several factors have contributed to these trends, including increased age at first marriage and childbearing, growing student loan debt, weakening labor market, and more stringent mortgage-lending criteria. Although survey results show that young adults continue to desire to buy homes instead of renting or living with parents, their capacity to do so has greatly diminished (Yu et al. 2015). For many Millennials, the delay in buying a home means a delay in building equity in a home, which is typically a family's greatest financial asset and primary basis for building wealth (Yu et al. 2015).

Providing a college education for children has been another important aspect of the American Dream. An increasing proportion of Americans have been able to realize this part of the American Dream. In 1910, only 3 percent of Americans twenty-five or older had completed a bachelor's degree or higher; by 2015, this figure had risen to 32 percent (US Department of Education, 2017a). Although more Americans are entering and completing college than in prior years, the costs of college education have been increasing at a rate far greater than either increases in family income or the general cost of living. For the 2013–2014 academic year, the average annual cost for tuition, fees, room, and board was $18,110 at public four-year colleges, and $35,987 at private nonprofit and for-profit colleges (US Department of Education 2017b). Controlling for inflation, these costs have more than doubled over the past thirty years for both public and private institutions (US Department of Education 2017b). States have drastically reduced funds for state-sponsored higher education over this period, and as a result a greater burden for increasing college expenses has shifted to students and their families. Parents and students are increasingly unable to afford these growing costs. As a result, more students themselves are working, taking longer to graduate, and in general taking on heavy student debt loads to finance their own educations. According to the Institute for College Access and Success (2016), nearly seven out of ten graduating 2015 college seniors had some level of student debt upon graduation, with an average debt per student of $30,100.

With an increase in college costs and debt and a flooded labor market for new college graduates, the overall return on the investment is being called into question. To put it simply, the labor force is being flooded with new college graduates. The economy is producing fewer college-level jobs than there are new college graduates. The result has been an increase in both underemployment (e.g., college graduates waiting tables) and credential inflation (employers requiring higher levels of education for positions without a corresponding increase in the skill or knowledge demands of the positions themselves).

Chance to Get Rich

Having at least a chance to get rich holds great appeal for most Americans, and has historically been a key component of the American Dream. The appeal is keenly felt, as evidenced by the excitement generated by state lotteries offering jackpots that soar into the millions. During the dot-com boom for the 1990s, the Internet became the equivalent of a modern "gold rush" as entrepreneurs anxiously sought to stake their dot-com website claims—until the bubble burst in 2000, much like the catastrophic collapse of the housing bubble that led to the Great Recession of 2008. According to the results of a *New York Times* poll (2014), the proportion of Americans who believe that it is possible to "start out poor in this country, work hard, and become rich" declined from 80 percent in 2005 to 64 percent in 2014, reflecting a sharp decline in the overall confidence in this prospect.

Self-employment, which is examined in greater detail in chapter 6, is relevant here because most meteoric rises in personal wealth come not from wages or salaries but through entrepreneurial activity—starting and owning businesses. With the decline of family farms and businesses and the ascendance of corporations in the twentieth century, rates of self-employment plummeted. New business starts are notoriously risky. For most Americans, these factors have decreased rather than increased the likelihood of "rags-to-riches" scenarios.

Secure and Comfortable Retirement

A secure and comfortable retirement is, in many ways, the closing chapter of the American Dream. In modern America, a comfortable retirement is achieved through a combination of savings, investments, pensions, and Social Security. In earlier times, people rarely "retired." Those who lived on farms, for instance, relied on adult children to provide for them if they survived and were no longer able to work. Through much of the earlier history of the United States, life expectancy was short, savings were limited, pensions were rare, and Social Security was nonexistent.

With the rise of industrial America and union-negotiated contracts, pensions became more common. In 1933, as part of Franklin D. Roosevelt's New Deal initiatives, the federally sponsored Social Security system was established. Until the mid-1970s, poverty rates for those over sixty-five were substantially higher than for other age groups. Many retirees were faced with small and fixed incomes and the erosion of purchasing power as prices increased. The longer they lived, the poorer they became. In 1965, however, Congress passed Medicare, which provided guaranteed access to health care for Americans over sixty-five. This greatly reduced the individual costs of health care for this population. In addition, in the mid-1970s Social Security payments were automatically adjusted to the Consumer Price Index, eliminating a major source of "fixed incomes" for elderly. These benefits, combined with post–World War II economic prosperity, greatly improved the economic conditions for elderly Americans, who now have a rate of poverty significantly below the national average.

Nevertheless, the future of secure retirement is in serious jeopardy. The Social Security fund is in trouble. Unless taxes are raised or benefits or eligibility reduced, the Social Security system will eventually become insolvent. As the large postwar baby boomer cohort becomes increasingly eligible for benefits, current projections are that after 2020, the Treasury will use trust fund assets in excess of interest earnings until the trust fund reserves are depleted in 2034, after which the fund will be sufficient to pay only about three-fourths of the scheduled benefits through the end of the projection period in 2090 (US Social Security Administration 2016).

There are other ominous developments. More than half of American workers have no employer-sponsored pension plans, and that percentage is increasing over time (Center for Retirement Research 2016). Of workers with pension plans, an increasing proportion of those plans are "defined-contribution" benefits tied to mutual funds and other stock programs instead of "defined-benefits" paid as guarantees to workers. In 1983, 62 percent of those who had pension plans had "defined-benefit" plans, compared to only 17 percent by 2013 (Center for Retirement Research 2014). As a result, pensions are not as secure as they were in the past because of potential downturns in the market, and the possibility of businesses going bankrupt prior to workers' retirements.

For older Americans, assets in home equity had always been part of their "nest egg" for retirement, but this too is in jeopardy. Housing prices plummeted during the recession of 2008 and have not yet recovered to pre-recession levels. Although rates of owner-occupied housing among Americans sixty-five and older remained constant between 2001 and 2011, at around 80 percent, the proportion of those Americans in owner-occupied housing who were still paying mortgages increased from 22 percent to 30 percent, with the median amount still owed on mortgages over the same time period increasing by 82 percent (US Consumer Financial Protection Bureau 2014).

Personal savings are not sufficient for most Americans to offset these losses. By the end of 2016, the average personal savings rate for Americans was 5.5 percent of disposable personal income (US Department of Commerce 2017), up somewhat from Great Recession levels, but still low by historical standards for the United States, and low compared to most other advanced industrial societies. A recent Associated Press study based on Federal Reserve data estimated that 35 percent of Americans in their prime earning years have saved nothing in a retirement account, and had no access to a traditional pension; of those who had managed some savings, the typical amount for this group was only $73,200, or about fifteen months of median household income (Choe 2016).

The American population as a whole is "graying" as birth rates remain low and life expectancy continues to increase. Pressures on Social Security, Medicare, and Medicaid are accelerating as the front end of a large cohort of baby boomers turns sixty-five at the rate of over ten thousand a day. The costs of health care continue to increase at a rate much higher than the general increase in the cost of living. These facts are significant because the greatest proportion of health-care expenditure is for the elderly. It is not at all clear that the health needs of an increasingly aging population can be met in the coming years.

In some significant ways, then, the American Dream of home ownership, increasing prospects for the next generation, and a comfortable retirement has been downsized in recent years. Whatever the likelihood of attaining the American Dream in the future, however, one thing is certain—it will be more attainable for those closer to the top of the system than the bottom.

PLAN OF THE BOOK

In chapter 2, "On Being Made of the Right Stuff," I identify key individual traits usually associated with the meritocratic formula for success: innate talent, hard work, proper attitude, and playing by the rules. I then examine the relationship between these characteristics and where people end up in the system. If getting ahead were simply a matter of being individually made of the right stuff, it would be a relatively short and simple story to tell. However, there is much more to it than this, and the remainder of this book is devoted to telling that story.

Subsequent chapters identify key nonmerit structural barriers to mobility that neutralize or suppress the effects of individual merit. The most consequential determinant of where people end up in the economic pecking order of society is where they start in the first place. Inheritance and the "staggered start" are nonmerit factors discussed in chapter 3, "The Silver Spoon." The nonmerit advantages of being born wealthy are cumulative and substantial, including having a high childhood standard of living, friends and relatives in high places, cultural advantages, infusions of parental capital while parents are still alive, insulation against failure, better health and greater life expectancy, and inheritance of bulk estates when parents die. Growing up in a privileged family entails greater opportunities to acquire and develop individual competence as well, and having that competence recognized and rewarded. These advantages accrue not only to the wealthiest of Americans, but in varying degrees to all those born closer to the top of the system than the bottom.

In chapter 4, "It's Not What You Know But . . . ," two important nonmerit factors are discussed. While part of the American folklore of social placement, these factors are nevertheless typically underestimated in their effects: whom you know (social capital), and fitting in (cultural capital). *Social capital* refers to social resources: individual and family connections that mediate access to opportunity. *Cultural capital* refers to a set of cultural resources—bodies of often esoteric and specialized information and knowledge, including style, bearing, manner, and self-presentation skills—that are needed to travel and be fully accepted in high-powered social circles. These resources are acquired beginning in childhood and typically reinforced and extended throughout the life course. As with the ownership of wealth, the possession of social and cultural resources is not necessarily evidence of individual merit, but provides substantial yet often subtle nonmerit advantages, especially to the offspring of the rich and powerful.

In chapter 5, "Making the Grade," the complex relationship between education and the American Dream is examined by evaluating competing arguments concerning the relationship between education and social mobility. One view is that education serves as a mechanism that identifies and selects intelligent, talented, and motivated individuals, regardless of class background, and provides educational training in direct proportion to individual merit. The amounts and kinds of education achieved are taken as indicators of merit and used as criteria of eligibility for occupations and the material rewards attached to them. An alternate view is that the American educational system is highly tracked by social class, reflecting and re-creating existing inequalities in society across generations. In this way, education is both a merit and a nonmerit factor. That is, students "earn" educational credentials (merit), but access to education—and, especially, quality education—is unequally distributed by family background and social class (nonmerit).

Besides education, the other most historically significant pathway for upward social mobility in America has been through some form of entrepreneurial activity. Americans embrace the ideal of the "self-made person" who starts with little or nothing and grows a successful business. In chapter 6, "I Did It My Way," entrepreneurship and its central place in the American Dream is discussed. This chapter examines the rise of the giant corporations, the concomitant decline in self-employment, the numerous barriers to self-employment, and their implications for entrepreneurial activity. The growing concentration, collective assets, and associated economies of scale of the corporate giants tend to undercut competition from small companies and discourage new entrants. Americans cling to the historical legacy and language of free enterprise and the entrepreneurial spirit, even though it no longer accurately describes the circumstances of the vast majority of Americans who now work for somebody else.

Upon leaving school, most Americans enter the "rat race" of the labor market. In chapter 7, "The Luck Factor," I examine the relationship between the supply of people available to fill jobs (supply) and the kinds of jobs available to fill (demand). While individuals have some control over how skilled they are, they do not have control over what kinds of jobs are available, how many jobs are available, or how many others are seeking those jobs. Being in the right place at the right time also matters, not just for getting a good job, but for acquiring great wealth as well. Striking it rich—whether it be through inheritance, entrepreneurial ventures, investments, or even hitting the lottery—necessarily involves at least some degree of just plain dumb luck.

After launching a career as an adult of some sort, the next significant stage of the life course has historically most often been marriage. Chapter 8, "Marriage and Mobility," examines the impact of marriage on prospects for mobility. For the most part, people tend to marry people of similar social backgrounds. To the extent that the rich marry the rich and the poor marry the poor, economic, social, and cultural advantages or disadvantages are consolidated and passed on to future generations. In some cases, however, people can become upwardly mobile through marriage. Because men in general typically control access to wealth and power, this particular indirect pathway to mobility has historically been more available to women than men.

The effects of discrimination, which are typically encountered throughout the life cycle, are discussed in chapter 9, "An Unlevel Playing Field: Racism, Sexism, and Other Isms." Simply put, discrimination is the antithesis of merit. Where there is discrimination, there is no meritocracy, because discriminatory allocations of opportunity and rewards discount or ignore merit and instead replace it with nonmerit criteria. Although discrimination against racial minorities and women is the most visible and damaging, at least in terms of costs and numbers affected, other forms of discrimination also interfere with the pursuit of the American Dream, including heterosexism, ageism, ableism (discrimination against the disabled), religious bigotry, and "lookism" (preference for the attractive). While these forms of discrimination claim fewer overall victims than racism and sexism, it would be difficult to convince the victims of these forms of discrimination that their effects are any less real. Moreover, many are subject to multiple forms of discrimination. Discrimination, which is encountered throughout the life course, often trumps merit. The more forms of discrimination that one is subject to, the more effective the trump.

In the concluding section, chapter 10, "Growing Inequality in the Twenty-First Century: What Can Be Done," the implications of deindustrialization, globalization, automation, the long wage recession, and increasing economic inequality since the 1970s on the sustainability of the American Dream in the twenty-first century are discussed. Strategies that individual Americans have developed to cope with the problems created by these changes are examined, along with potential policy changes and reforms that might reduce inequality and make the American system as a whole more meritocratic.

REFERENCES

Adams, James Truslow. 1931. *The Epic of America*. New York: Blue Ribbon Books.

Carlin, George. 1997. *Brain Droppings*. New York: Hyperion.

Center for Retirement Research. 2014. "Workers with Pension Coverage by Type of Plan, 1983, 1992, 2001, and 2013." Boston College, Boston, Massachusetts. http://crr.bc.edu/wp-content/uploads/1012/01/figure-15.pdf (accessed January 16, 2017).

Chetty, Raj, David Grusky, Maximilian Hell, Nathaniel Hendren, Robert Manduca, and Jimmy Narang. 2016. "The Fading of the American Dream: Trends in Absolute Income Mobility Since 1940." Working Paper 22910. National Bureau of Economic Research, Cambridge, Massachusetts.

Choe, Stan. 2016. "Divided America: Easy Retirement Only for a Privileged Few." Associated Press: http://bigstory.ap.org/article/a0f8d3ab3aed48b2809f3081e2361336/divided-america-easy-retirement-only-privileged-few (accessed January 16, 2017).

Collero, Peter L. 2009. *The Myth of Individualism: How Social Forces Shape Our Lives*. Lanham, MD: Rowman and Littlefield.

Cullen, Jim. 2003. *The American Dream: A Short History of an Idea That Shaped a Nation*. New York: Oxford University Press.

de Tocqueville, Alexis. [1835] 1967. *Democracy in America*. New York: Schocken Books.

Devaney, F. John. 1994. *Tracking the American Dream: 50 Years of Housing History from the Census Bureau: 1940–1990*. Washington, DC: US Census Bureau.

Fry, Richard. 2016. "For the First Time in Modern Era, Living with Parents Edges Out Other Living Arrangements for 18- to 34-Year Olds." Washington, DC: Pew Research Center.

Hochschild, Jennifer. 1995. *Facing Up to the American Dream: Race, Class and the Soul of the Nation*. Princeton, NJ: Princeton University Press.

Institute for College Access and Success. 2016. "Student Debt and the Class of 2015: 11th Annual Report," http://ticas.org/sites/default/files/pub_files/classof2015.pdf (accessed January 17, 2017).

Jefferson, Thomas. 1813. "Letter to John Adams on Aristocracy, October 28, 1813." In *The Adams–Jefferson Letters: The Complete Correspondence between Thomas Jefferson and Abigail and John Adams*, ed. Lester J. Cappon, 388. Chapel Hill: University of North Carolina Press for the Institute of Early American History and Culture, Williamsburg, Virginia, 1959.

Kerbo, Harold R. 2012. *Social Stratification and Inequality: Class Conflict in Historical, Comparative, and Global Perspective,* 8th ed. New York: McGraw-Hill.

Longoria, Richard T. 2009. *Meritocracy and Americans' Views on Distributive Justice.* Lanham, MD: Lexington Books.

McCall, Leslie. 2013. *The Undeserving Rich: American Beliefs about Inequality, Opportunity, Redistribution.* New York: Cambridge University Press.

McNamee, Stephen J., and Robert K. Miller, Jr. 1998. "Inheritance and Stratification." In *Inheritance and Wealth in America,* ed. Robert K. Miller, Jr., and Stephen J. McNamee, 193–213. New York: Plenum Press.

New York Times Poll. 2014. December 4–7, 2014. https://s3.amazonaws.com/s3.documentcloud.org/documents/1377502/poll-finds-a-more-bleak-view-of-american-dream.pdf (accessed January 16, 2017).

Samuel, Lawrence. 2012. *The American Dream: A Cultural History.* Syracuse, NY: Syracuse University Press.

Smith, Adam. [1776] 1976. *An Inquiry into the Nature and Causes of the Wealth of Nations,* ed. R. H. Campbell and A. S. Skinner. Oxford: Clarendon Press.

Turner, Frederick Jackson. 1947. *The Frontier in American History.* New York: Henry Holt.

US Census Bureau. 2015. Fact Finder. "Mortgage Status: Owner-Occupied Housing Units: 2011–2015, American Community 5-Year Estimates." Author's calculation for 2015. https://factfinder.census.gov/faces/tableservices/jsf/pages/productview.xhtml?pid=ACS_15_5YR_B25081&prodType=table (accessed January 16, 2017).

———. 2016a. "Housing Vacancies and Homeownership," Historical Tables, Table 14, "Quarterly Homeownership Rates for the U.S. and Regions 1964 to Present." https://www.census.gov/housing/hvs/data/histtabs.html (accessed January 16, 2017).

———. 2016b. "Housing Vacancies and Homeownership," Historical Tables. Author's calculations from Table 12. "Annual Estimates of the Housing Inventory by Age of Householder 1982 to Present." https://www.census.gov/housing/hvs/data/histtabs.html (accessed January 16, 2017).

US Consumer Financial Protection Bureau. 2014. "Snapshot of Older Consumers and Mortgage Debt." http://files.consumerfinance.gov/f/201405_cfpb_snapshot_older-consumers-mortgage-debt.pdf (accessed January 16, 2017).

US Department of Commerce. 2017. 2016 Bureau of Economic Analysis. "Personal Income and Outlays." https://www.bea.gov/newsreleases/national/pi/pinewsrelease.htm (accessed January 2017).

US Department of Education. 2017a. National Center for Educational Statistics. Table 104.10, "Rates of High School Completion and Bachelor's Degree Attainment among Persons Age 25 and Over, By Race/Ethnicity and Sex: Selected Years." https://nces.ed.gov/programs/digest/d14/tables/dt14_104.10.asp (accessed January 16, 2017).

———. 2017b. "Tuition Costs of Colleges and Universities." https://nces.ed.gov/fastfacts/display.asp?id=76 (accessed January 16, 2017).

US Social Security Administration. 2016. *A Summary of the 2016 Annual Reports.* https://www.ssa.gov/oact/trsum/ (accessed January 17, 2017).

Weber, Max. [1904–1905] 2002. *The Protestant Ethic and the Spirit of Capitalism,* trans. Stephen Kahlberg. Los Angeles: Roxbury Publishing.

Weiss, Richard. 1969. *The American Myth of Success: From Horatio Alger to Norman Vincent Peale.* New York: Basic Books.

Wuthnow, Robert. 1996. *Poor Richard's Principle: Recovering the American Dream through the Moral Dimensions of Work, Business, and Money.* Princeton, NJ: Princeton University Press.
Young, Michael. 1961. *The Rise of the Meritocracy, 1870–2033: An Essay on Education and Equality.* Baltimore: Penguin Books.
Yu, Yilan, Carrie Johnson, Susanne Bartholomae, Barbara O'Neil, and Michael S. Gutter. 2015. "Homeownership among Millennials: The Deferred American Dream?" *Family and Consumer Sciences Research Journal* 44(2):201–12.

2

On Being Made of the Right Stuff

The Case for Merit

The rich feel full of merit.

—Mason Cooley, US aphorist

In 1959, seven astronauts were chosen for NASA's Mercury space program. These seven men, selected from an initial pool of thousands of military pilots,[1] were considered the best and the brightest, the strongest and the bravest. In short, they were made of the "right stuff."[2] Getting ahead in America is widely seen in these terms. The popular perception in America is that those who are made of the right stuff are the cream of the crop that rises to the top, whereas the dregs fall to the bottom.

Although there are variations on the theme of meritocracy, I have identified four key ingredients in the American formula for being made of the right stuff: talent, the right attitude, hard work, and moral character. Each of these will be reviewed in terms of its impact on getting ahead.

INNATE TALENTS AND ABILITIES

Innate individual talent, natural ability, or some variant are among the most important factors that Americans attribute to the importance of getting ahead (McCall 2013). The central issue here is not whether innate capacity of all sorts helps some people get ahead. It clearly does. The issue is how much difference does it make, for how many people, and under what circumstances? This is a complex issue, and it is difficult to know precisely what mix of innate endowments and environmental influences has an effect on life outcomes. Most social scientists, neuroscientists, and geneticists now conclude that trying to isolate the effects of "nature" from "nurture" in predicting the probabilities of life outcomes is a wild goose chase; rather than one or the other, what matters is combinations of both, and how those factors interact in complex ways (cf. Conley and Fletcher 2017). It is clear, however, that innate capacity alone accounts for nothing. Our innate biological capacity as human beings is analogous to the "hardware" of a computer. A computer can have tremendous capacity for processing and analyzing information as indicated by the amount of memory available and the processing speed. Nurture or learning for human beings is similar to "software" or programming in computers. Computing capacity alone does nothing without either the input of information to process or programming that tells the computer what to do with that information.

Among innate capacities for getting ahead, the most prominent capacity that is usually discussed is raw intelligence or cognitive ability. IQ tests, the standard measure of intellectual capacity, have a long and controversial history. One of the problems in measuring raw intellectual capacity is that it is unmeasurable at birth. By the time a reliable IQ test can be administered (usually around age four or so), individuals have already been subject to a myriad of environmental influences. Indeed, we know that the first environment of human beings—in utero—can profoundly affect IQ. It is possible, for instance, that a fetus would have the raw biological capacity of a genius but that conditions in utero—such as maternal malnutrition or fetal alcohol syndrome—could result in a child born with severe mental retardation. Even identical twins with the same genes can be alternately affected by one twin in utero taking more nutrients from the mother than the other (Conley and Fletcher 2017, 164). Or a newborn could be born with a potentially high IQ only to be rendered inoperative because of early exposure to lead poisoning, known to cause brain damage and hamper future cognitive development, much less the effects of countless other environmental influences prior to an age of reliable testability for IQ. So one of the major controversial aspects of IQ tests, then, is "hereditability," or the extent to which IQ is strictly genetic. While estimates vary, the general consensus is that IQ tests by young childhood are on average estimated to be only two-thirds genetic and one-third environmental (Conley and Fletcher 2017).

The hereditability controversy was reignited with the 1994 publication of Richard Herrnstein and Charles Murray's *The Bell Curve: Intelligence and Class Structure in American Life*. Herrnstein and Murray asserted that intelligence is largely genetically inherited and that it largely determines socioeconomic success. Herrnstein and Murray argued that the distribution of intelligence in the general population takes the form of a symmetrical bell curve, or what statisticians refer to as a normal distribution. In normal distributions, the most common score is the average, with most cases bunched closely around it. Variation around the middle is symmetrical in either direction (below and above the average), with most cases close to the average, and the number of cases dropping off rapidly the farther away from the average, becoming rare at either end of the distribution.

Herrnstein and Murray further argued that barriers to upward mobility on the basis of natural talent have largely been eliminated, and that a new "cognitive elite" is emerging in America. They contended that as colleges and universities have opened opportunities to a broader economic spectrum of students, educational attainment is increasingly based on academic performance and less on the inheritance of wealth and privilege. Moreover, with new technological demands, there is an increasing premium in society on intellectual prowess.

The publication of *The Bell Curve* was met with a barrage of criticism (cf. Fischer et al. 1996; Bowles et al. 2005). The upshot of the many criticisms of *The Bell Curve* is that as a result of faulty assumptions and measurement error, Herrnstein and Murray greatly overestimated the influence of innate intelligence (nature) and greatly underestimated the influence of environmental factors (nurture). Most recently, rigorous reanalysis by Dalton Conley and Jason Fletcher (2017) found no empirical support for the three main assertions in *The Bell Curve*: that the effect of genetic endowment on economic outcomes is increasing over time; that through intermarriage, the "cognitive elite" are passing on enhanced genetic endowments to their children compared to the children of the noncognitive elite; and that because of higher birthrates among the noncognitive elites, there is a decline in cognitive capacity in the population as a whole.

Other research shows that IQ is only modestly correlated with income (.30) and negligibly correlated with wealth (.16) (Zagorsky 2007). That is, the vast amount of variance in what you earn (income) and especially what you own (wealth) is most likely due to something else. Furthermore, it stands to reason that IQ would be more associated with income than wealth. IQ is likely to have at least some bearing on the capacity to do certain kinds of more complicated tasks for which some individuals would receive higher compensation than others. Wealth acquisition, however, is more about owning than doing (for instance, it does not take superior intellect to inherit the family fortune). Most people know intuitively that the question "If you're so smart, then why aren't you rich?" is not really a question at all, but a rhetorical comment implying that there is much more to monetary "success" than intelligence, whatever that means and however it might be measured.

IQ is likely to make the most difference at the extremes, especially at the lower end of the scale. It is unlikely that those with severe mental disabilities, for instance, could become neurosurgeons. And it probably helps to have a lot of inherent capacity to perform high-level and intellectually demanding tasks, although other factors might determine who makes the most of what capacities they have. It is not required to be the "smartest" to perform most high-level tasks, but rather to be "smart enough," and a fairly high proportion of the population is likely to have sufficient mental capacity to perform most tasks.

Beyond the issue of whether generalized raw intellectual capacity can be measured precisely or what minimal thresholds of capacity might be required, other dimensions of what most people would consider "smart" could vary independently. One might distinguish, for instance, "street smarts," "people smarts," or "book smarts" from raw intellectual capacity alone. Individuals with these various kinds of "smarts," who may or may not score high on standardized IQ tests, would nevertheless be perceived by others as clever, shrewd, or knowledgeable in ways that may have an economic advantage.

Besides raw intellectual capacity, other presumably innate talents and abilities are also popularly perceived as part of the merit formula. These include, but are not limited to, athletic and artistic abilities. These traits are often associated with meteoric social mobility. The view that such talent can propel someone from rags to riches is not entirely without foundation. When people think of who is really rich in America, professional athletes and artists (e.g., actors, singers, writers), who command huge salaries for their services, often come to mind first. Although star entertainers and athletes earn huge annual incomes for their services, such as singer Taylor Swift ($170 million), radio personality Howard Stern ($85 million), singer Madonna ($76.5 million), basketball player LeBron James ($77 million), basketball player Kevin Durant ($56 million), and actor Matt Damon ($55 million) (*Forbes* 2017a), the really big money in America comes not from working for a living at all but from owning income-producing property. Among the one hundred highest-paid celebrities in America who are athletes or entertainers, none is among the wealthiest four hundred Americans. It is instructive that while there are no star athletes among the richest four hundred Americans, more than a dozen on the list are owners of professional sports teams. And while there are no actors included in the list of the wealthiest four hundred Americans, there are two movie producers, George Lucas and Steven Spielberg, who own their own production companies (*Forbes* 2017b).

Although not typically among the four hundred wealthiest of all Americans, celebrity athletes and entertainers are well known to the general public. Several come from modest or even poor social backgrounds. The phenomenal success of these celebrities tends to reinforce the public perception that in America, you can go as far as your talents and abilities can take you.

One could argue that "superstar" athletes, for instance, are truly talented and have extraordinary physical qualities not available to the average person (e.g., size, speed, agility, hand–eye coordination). Raw talent alone, however, is not enough. Talent has to be cultivated through recruitment and opportunities for training. Potential talent can go unnoticed, particularly in the absence of opportunities to develop and exhibit it. Training may be expensive and not easily available to people of modest means, particularly in such sports as golf, tennis, swimming, and figure skating.

Sociologist William Chambliss (1989), who studied the world of champion Olympic swimmers, suggests that the concept of inherent talent in and of itself is essentially useless because inherent talent as a cause cannot be separated from its effects. That is, talent cannot be used to distinguish success and failure because one does not "know" it is there until success occurs. Chambliss argues that the thresholds for natural ability needed for athletic success (minimum physical strength, coordination, heart/lung capacity, and the like) are remarkably low. Many of the key factors to success in the swimming world are unrelated to raw talent, like living in warm climates, having wealthy and supportive parents, and the availability of expert coaching. Where milliseconds often separate "winners" and "losers," Chambliss points out that what distinguishes champions from mere contenders is not inherent physical superiority but more mundane considerations, such as technique and training.

Historically, the conspicuous lack of people of color in these individual middle- and upper-middle-class sports is telling. Team sports such as baseball, basketball, and football have generally been more accessible (at least recently), and this is reflected in the racial and socioeconomic makeup of the athletes in these professional sports. Overall, there is a strong relationship between type of sport and the race and class of origin of the professionals within it, which strongly suggests that differential recruit- ment and opportunity are at work rather than athletic prowess alone (Buffington 2015; Coakley 2017). In this regard, it is also noteworthy that athletics as a means of upward social mobility, regardless of talent level, is more available to males than females, since there are more paid professional opportunities in men's sports. Even in sports in which both men and women compete, until quite recently prize money has been much greater for men.

The notion of raw artistic talent as a means of upward social mobility is even more suspect. Although "talented" Hollywood actors make millions, it is not clear that the potential pool of "talent" is small. It is unknown how many potential Meryl Streeps or Matt Damons are out there, but chances are great that there are more of them than there are potential Steffi Grafs or Kobe Bryants. While there may be millions in the general population who could become movie stars (if "discovered," with the "right" breaks, the "right" acting coaches, the "right" roles, the "right" looks, and so forth), there is probably a much smaller potential pool of individuals who can dunk a basketball from the foul line. This is indicated, for instance, by the high number of crossovers from sports to acting (or broadcasting) but not the other way around.

Beyond the performing arts, untapped creative potential extends to the potential for scientific innovation as well. As with other extraordinary "talents," these too have to be nurtured even to be noticed much less developed to an elite level. In a recent comprehensive study of individuals filing US patents, Alex Bell and his as- sociates (2017) found large disparities in innovation rates by socioeconomic class, race, and gender. They note, for instance, that if women, minorities, and children from low-income families were to invent at the same rate as white men who grew up in high-income families, the rate of innovation in America would quadruple. The study refers to children from these disadvantaged groups with high scientific and mathematical aptitude and low rates of innovation as "lost Einsteins."

Unlike celebrity athletes and entertainers, scientific inventors are typically not well known to the general public. The presumed link between raw talent and celeb- rity athletes and artists in particular tends to reinforce the meritocracy myth. The presumption is that if *some* celebrities with these talents came from humble origins, then *anyone* who had those potential talents could do the same. However, it does not follow that if *only* those with talent rise to the level of celebrity athlete or artist, then *all* those with talent will become celebrity athletes or artists. Indeed, the actual probabilities of social ascent through athletics or the arts are extremely remote. The illusion of potential success in glamour areas such as sports and entertainment ends up being a "mobility trap" for many youthful aspirants who end up investing time and effort in the long-shot pursuit of fame and fortune at the expense of more realistic avenues of social mobility (Wiley 1967).

In short, in the meritocratic formula for success, it is clear that innate capacity alone accounts for nothing. Innate talents and abilities do not just spontaneously produce life outcomes. Minimum biological capacity for success in most human endeavors is probably modest. Beyond minimum thresholds (e.g., smart enough, coordinated enough, and so on), additional increments of capacity probably have negligible economic return for most people. Moreover, there is undoubtedly substantially more inherent potential capacity among individuals in any society than is ever identified, cultivated, or realized.

HAVING THE RIGHT ATTITUDE

Beyond innate talents and cognitive skills, various attitudes and behavioral traits are often presumed to be associated with economic success. In more familiar terms, these attitudes and traits are summarized by the phrase "having the right attitude." Having the right attitude is associated with qualities like ambition, energy, motivation, and trustworthiness. It may also involve subtler traits like good judgment, a sense of personal responsibility, willingness to defer gratification, persistence in the face of adversity, willingness to take risks, getting along with others, assertiveness, independence, emotional control, and the like. Conversely, a lack of proper attitudes, as evidenced by laziness, shiftlessness, indolence, lack of self-discipline, unreliability, disruptiveness, and so on, is associated with the failure to achieve.

It would seem that these represent two sides of the same coin. However, which side is emphasized makes a big difference in estimating the effects of attitudes and values on life outcomes. Most of the research linking attitudes with mobility has focused not so much on how the "right" attitudes help one get ahead, but on how the "wrong" attitudes keep one from getting ahead. This implies that, in effect, one could have the "right" attitudes but not get ahead anyway. Having the "wrong" attitudes, however, would prevent one from getting ahead, and may even be responsible for one's falling further behind.

One of the early attempts to link attitudes to prospects for attainment is the "culture-of-poverty" theory. This theory was developed initially in the 1960s by anthropologist Oscar Lewis (1959, 1966), who conducted ethnographic studies of Mexican families living in poverty. This general perspective was later applied mainly to African Americans in the United States (Banfield 1970). For proponents of culture-of-poverty theory, the cause of poverty in these settings is not rooted in inherent individual biological deficiencies but in the "culture" of the poor. The "subculture" of poverty in the groups Lewis studied was said to be fatalistic, hedonistic, and impulsive. There was a high incidence of early initiation into sexual activity, consensual unions, and familial disruption. Lewis interpreted this subculture of poverty as pathological and self-perpetuating. Poor people hang around with other poor people, as these values are reinforced in interaction within the group. Children are socialized into antiwork, antischool, antimarriage, and antiauthority values that are passed on from one generation to the next in what becomes a "vicious cycle of poverty."

One of the central issues in the culture-of-poverty debate is whether poverty creates deviant attitudes or whether deviant attitudes create poverty. For Lewis, it is both. Lack of opportunity creates conditions that favor the development of these values, which—while adaptive to a life of poverty—are maladaptive to prospects for upward mobility. Lewis argued that the poor become so ingrained with a lifestyle of poverty that they reject opportunities to move ahead even when opportunities to do so become available. To this extent, poverty is a freely chosen lifestyle. However, the "blame" is not on individuals but on the group to which individuals belong, and the group itself is seen as resistant to change.

Culture-of-poverty theory has been sharply criticized on several grounds. It rests on the twin assumptions that 1) the poor have attitudes or values different from the nonpoor; and 2) these attitudes or values are responsible for the condition of poverty itself. Critics (Coward, Feagin, and Williams 1974; Della Fave 1974; Gould 1999; Rodman 1963; Valentine 1968; Ryan 1971; Greenbaum 2015) have attacked both of these key assumptions. According to critics of the theory, the poor do not have values significantly different from those of the nonpoor. Rather, the poor, like everyone else, adjust their perceptions of reality to accommodate the reality of their situation, resulting in what Hyman Rodman refers to as "the lower-class value stretch." It is one thing, for instance, to say that the poor have a "present-time orientation" because they are hedonistic thrill seekers who live for the moment. However, it is another thing altogether to say that, regardless of one's personal value system, one is forced to focus on the present if one is not sure where one's next meal might come from. The middle and upper classes have the luxury of being able to plan ahead and defer gratification (for instance, going to college instead of accepting a low-paid service job) precisely because their present is secure. Similarly, the poor may have more modest ambitions than the wealthy not because they are unmotivated, but because they make a realistic assessment of limited life chances. In this formulation, exhibited behaviors and perceptions associated with a "culture of poverty" reflect the *effects* of poverty, not the causes.

The idea of a situational view of poverty is consistent with psychologist Abraham Maslow's well-known "hierarchy-of-needs" theory. According to Maslow (1970), humans have a hierarchical order of needs that begins at the fundamental levels of food, clothing, and shelter and advances to "higher-order" needs for independence and "self-actualization." Maslow points out that one cannot attend to higher-order needs if the lower-order needs are not satisfied. In other words, poverty keeps people stuck at lower-order needs, regardless of their desire for higher-order fulfillment.

In addition to a presumption of a "culture of poverty," some commentators have suggested at the other end of the continuum that there is something akin to a "culture of wealth" (Samuel 2009). Two prominent examples of this line of research include Thomas Stanley's *The Millionaire Mind* (2000) and Jim Taylor, Doug Harrison, and Stephen Kraus's *The New Elite: Inside the Minds of the Truly Wealthy* (2009). In both cases, the authors survey wealthy individuals to assess their attitudes and values, suggesting there is a "mind-set" of wealth, presumed to include such traits as "working harder than most people" and "being honest with people." In both of these studies, however, there are no control groups; that is, there is no statistical comparison between the wealthy and the non-wealthy, so we don't know how unique the mind-set of the so-called self-made millionaire respondents really is, or if these attitudes are more prominent among the wealthy than anyone else. In addition, the surveys in both studies were conducted among people who were already wealthy, so we don't know if these attitudes were responsible for the acquisition of wealth, or whether wealthy people retrospectively simply attributed their success to attitudes their culture tells them are its source.

Along similar lines, Charles Murray, coauthor of *The Bell Curve*, published a subsequent book, *Coming Apart: The State of White America, 1960–2010* (2012). Consciously staying away from the controversial claims of innate racial differences in average intelligence alleged in *The Bell Curve*, Murray in this newer book depicts a growing gap between a "new upper class" and a "new lower class" among white Americans. He suggests that the growing economic inequality between these groups can be accounted for by a combination of differences in intellectual capacity and "virtues." The new upper class is part of the "cognitive elite" previously identified in *The Bell Curve* who are increasingly being sorted out by "the college sorting machine." With an increasing "market value for brain," the less capable and less competent lower class falls behind both in terms of first academic and then economic achievement. Murray asserts that these patterns are reinforced by acute differences in culture between the two groups. Both groups, he argues, are declining in the "founding virtues" that made America great and constitute the basis for "American exceptionalism," but the decline is much faster for the new lower class than for the new upper class.

Similar to other flattering portrayals of the wealthy discussed above, Murray identifies four "founding virtues" that he claims are in greater preponderance among the new upper class: industriousness, honesty, marriage, and religiosity. What is again conflated, however, is cause and effect. Are these "virtues" a cause or an effect of wealth? For instance, Murray measures "industriousness" by such indicators as hours worked, rates of employment, and rates of disability, which can obviously be a consequence of economic circumstance rather than a cause of it. Likewise, Murray measures "honesty" by rates of arrests and incarceration, which are widely known to be higher for the poor than the rich—not because the rich are more "honest," but because the types of criminality engaged in by the lower class are much more likely to result in arrest and incarceration than the types of criminality engaged in by the upper class (Reiman 2013). Likewise, marriage rates are higher for the wealthy than for the poor—not because the poor do not value marriage, but because economic deprivations make the prospects of finding suitable marriage partners slimmer for the poor than the affluent (Wilson 2012). On religiosity, Murray finds more convergence between the new upper class and the new lower class on indicators such as belief in God and attendance at religious services, as well as toward greater degrees of secularization and less religiosity, but, again, those trends are more pronounced for the new lower class than the new upper class.

All of these portrayals of what Murray describes as "the new elite" have in common an ideology of economic success that historian Richard Huber (1971) refers to as the "mind-power ethic." According to this ethic, success is a case of mind over matter. Presumably, success can be acquired through sheer willpower. The mind-power ethic is a major theme running throughout American success self-help books of the twentieth century (Dunkleman 2000). Fueled by a tradition of Protestant individualism, which was later secularized, and reflected in an American fascination with psychology, the mind-power ethic peaked with the publication of Norman Vincent Peale's *The Power of Positive Thinking* (1952) and his success formula of "prayerize, picturize, and actualize." This ethic speaks especially to the notion that determination and persistence in the face of whatever obstacles may exist are the true secret of success. In this formulation, individuals are not responsible for where they start out in life, but they are responsible for where they end up. In other words, according to these formulations, wealth or poverty is ultimately a matter of "attitude" broadly defined.

Beyond the culture-of-poverty theories and, more recently, culture-of-wealth theories, there has been surprisingly little systematic research into the effects of attitudes and behavioral traits on who gets ahead in America. The results of what research has been done are mixed at best (see Farkas 2003 for a systematic review). The lack of research findings in this area is at least partly due to the difficulty in clearly separating out the effects of all the possible "causes" of who gets ahead (and conversely, who falls behind). In this regard, "panel studies" that survey the same individuals in "waves," beginning at young ages while still in school, and then subsequent waves as they move into the labor force, are superior to both "cross-sectional" surveys in which respondents are interviewed at a given time, and surveys in which only poor or only wealthy people are interviewed.

In one of the few studies using panel studies, for instance, Matthew Hall and George Farkas (2011) find that expressed degrees of self-reported self-esteem, locus of control (belief that one has control one's own fate), and higher educational aspirations among adolescents are associated with subsequent higher career wages as adults. However, the wage return in terms of subsequent wages associated with these characteristics varies by race and gender, with white males having the highest return, and nonwhites and women having the lowest—or even, in some cases (e.g., black women), negative—returns. This result strongly suggests that discrimination may blunt or negate the potential effects of attitudes on career wages.

Other research suggests that what might matter for getting ahead is not a particular attitude or set of attitudes so much as a *match* of attitudes or orientations in particular arenas of endeavor (Jencks et al. 1979). For instance, the kind of "mind-set" that might make for a successful accountant might be very different than the kind of "mind-set" that might make for a successful artist.

It is not clear, then, what specific attitudes are individually determinative of economic success as opposed to being merely associated with it or a consequence of it. It is also not clear which particular attitudes are associated with success in particular tasks, occupations, or professions. Furthermore, it is not clear how to measure these attitudes or to distinguish their effects from other related factors, such as family background. Much of what passes as the right attitude, for instance, is likely to be at least partially the result of differential access to preferred forms of cultural capital (see chapter 4). Such intangibles as comportment, demeanor, and presentation of self to others (interpreted by others as "attitude") may be more a reflection of upbringing than uniquely personal or individual attitudes. These traits may be seen as desirable by people in positions of authority even if such traits may not actually affect job performance.

WORKING HARD OR HARDLY WORKING

In the formula for getting ahead, hard work typically ranks by far as the most prominent factor for most Americans (McCall 2013, 151). It is difficult to disentangle the effects of attitudes such as motivation, industriousness, ambition, and so on from actual hard work. Attitudes alone, however, are likely not as important as actual behavior.

Americans nod their heads knowingly and approvingly whenever the importance of hard work is mentioned in association with the likelihood of success. But what does working hard really mean? Does it refer to the number of hours worked? Does it refer to the level of exertion expended in the conduct of work? How are these factors related to concrete measures of economic success—that is, wealth and income?

As Barbara Ehrenreich (2001) discovered when she spent a year doing menial jobs in America in a participant observation study, often the hardest-working Americans are those who get paid the least. It is the waitress with sore feet at the end of the day after several miles of trudging between the kitchen and dining area, taking orders, pouring drinks, and carrying dishes and heavy trays of food. It is the lowest-paid member of the construction crew with aching muscles and a sore back after a day of toting heavy loads of construction materials on the work site. It is the secretary with carpal tunnel syndrome who works her fingers to the bone typing departmental reports. It is the janitor who moonlights as a housepainter and works over sixty hours a week because neither job pays enough to make ends meet. Individuals such as these represent the backbone of the American *working* class. Additional "hard" work of this kind, however, is unlikely to result in any significant wealth or upward social mobility.

Conversely, those with high-paying jobs may not be working any "harder" than those with less-well-paying jobs in the same employing organizations. In most jobs in America, compensation is more directly related to levels of responsibility and authority than it is to number of hours worked or intensity of effort exerted (Kalleberg 2011). Further, those who have the most may actually expend the least amount of effort. The really big money in America, as shown in the following chapter, does not come from working for a living at all, but from ownership of property—especially the kind of property that produces additional wealth, such as stocks and bonds, real estate, business assets, and so on. Indeed, those who live off *unearned* income from investments may not need to work at all. If one is wealthy enough, it is possible to hire small armies of accountants, lawyers, and brokers to manage one's holdings and still be among the wealthiest of all Americans.

Still, one wonders how one would actually know how hard people work. If we consider the obvious measure of hours worked, the data show that Americans already work more than workers in most other developed countries. Americans, for instance, on average work 19 percent more hours a year than Europeans, or about 265 hours more a year (Bick et al. 2016). Americans also retire later and have fewer and shorter vacations than Europeans. In addition, Americans are increasingly subject to employer "wage theft" through "off the clock" overtime and other unpaid work (Cooper and Kroeger 2017), aided by the long reach of employers into the private sphere of their workers through new digital technologies such as cell phones.

Moreover, working "hard" in terms of working long hours can have dire detrimental consequences for workers, employing organizations, and the general public (Carter 2015; Derickson 2013; Schor 2008). Data show, for instance, that alertness, effectiveness, and productivity can decline with excessive hours worked, which is why, for instance, there are safety restrictions on how many consecutive hours or total hours per day that pilots, medical doctors, truck drivers, and others can work (Derickson 2013).

But do more hours worked translate into greater occupational or economic success? In *Outliers: The Story of Success*, Malcolm Gladwell (2008) refers to the "10,000 hour rule," citing studies that show that it takes a minimum of about ten thousand hours of practice to develop world-class expertise in most areas of human endeavor. Gladwell was making the point that talent alone does not spontaneously produce results. That is, any capacity that individuals have must not only be initially identified and provided an opportunity to flourish, but also honed through hours of application and practice to reach elite levels. That does not mean, however, that ten thousand hours of application in doing different things produces equivalent results. Most people spend considerably more than ten thousand hours in the work that they do in a lifetime, but they are not all equally successful. Spending ten thousand hours working as a waitress or mastering the yo-yo is unlikely to have as much economic benefit, for instance, as ten thousand hours working as a neurosurgeon.

Since there is a biological limit on how much any one person can "work," and most Americans appear in general to work hard, there is simply not enough variation in hours worked or intensity of effort to account for the substantial and growing extent of income and wealth inequality. Those at the very top of the system, for instance, do not and cannot possibly work billions of times more than average Americans. Yet as previously noted, when respondents are asked to state the reason(s) for their success, they almost always answer, "hard work," or some variant. People claim that they deserve their success because they work hard. Yet deservedness is not equivalent to hard work; and, as has been repeatedly shown, many people who work hard are not especially economically successful, and many who are economically "successful" do not work especially hard (or at all). Clearly, hard work alone is neither a necessary nor a sufficient condition for receiving the most compensation for whatever it is that people do. Hard work matters, but in terms of compensation, what people do matters far more than how "hard" they do it. When people cite hard work as a factor in getting ahead, they really mean hard work in combination with other factors, especially opportunity and acquired skills, both of which are more related to social background than individual capacities.

MORAL CHARACTER

In addition to persistence in the face of adversity, another frequent theme in the American cultural folklore of meritocracy is that being made of the right stuff includes moral character and integrity. Moral fiber and character have been a constant theme in American self-help success books (Dunkleman 2000; Starker 2002; McGee 2005). The early advice manuals, in particular, echoed the twin pillars of the Protestant ethic: diligence and asceticism. In addition to working hard, the "truly" successful person had honor and dignity. People should pursue wealth not for the purposes of self-gratification or personal indulgence but for the glory of God and to help others. In this formulation, success is taken as evidence of God's grace; successful people saw themselves as moral people. There was always some tension, however, between materialism and idealism in the pursuit of wealth.

While honesty and integrity are certainly worthy goals in their own right, in the final analysis, do they help or hinder in the making of money? There is little direct evidence suggesting that these virtues help or hinder the prospects for social mobility. On the one hand, we have numerous testimonials of wealthy individuals who claim such virtues. One of the few studies on the effect of integrity on success comes from *Who Gets Ahead* (Jencks et al. 1979, 154). Among the many noncognitive factors that they examined was integrity, as measured by teachers' accounts of students' personalities longitudinally related to later mobility. They reported that, controlling for other factors, integrity produced a small *inverse* but statistically significant effect. That is, everything else being equal, integrity was associated with less upward mobility.

The overall effect of integrity is likely to suppress rather than enhance upward mobility. This is because not cheating, not stealing, and not choosing to get ahead at the expense of others restricts prospects for social mobility and the accumulation of wealth. Wealth can be achieved by honest or dishonest means. The logic of this argument is that those who limit themselves to strictly honest means to get ahead have fewer opportunities to do so than those who do not limit themselves in this way. Direct evidence for the wealth-enhancing character of ruthless and unethical behavior comes from the history of industrial capitalism. Many of the wealthy industrialists of the last century earned notorious reputations as "robber barons" for their relentless and cutthroat pursuit of wealth and power. The indirect evidence for the wealth-enhancing character of unethical behavior comes from the substantial extent of white-collar crime in America (Balleisen 2017; Barak 2017; Rosoff et al. 2013). Assuming that the amount of exposed white-collar crime represents only the tip of the iceberg of unscrupulousness, it is reasonable to conclude that making money in America is often accomplished through less than impeccably honest or ethical means.

It is difficult to estimate the full extent of white-collar crime in America. This type of crime has become more sophisticated and includes a variety of financial crimes, such as securities and commodities fraud, health-care fraud, financial institution fraud, embezzlement and employee theft, identity theft and Internet fraud, mortgage fraud, insurance fraud, check fraud, marketing fraud, and money laundering. Because much of this type of crime is hidden in financial complexities and goes undetected, it is difficult to determine its exact cost. Nevertheless, the total cost to society of these kinds of financial crime is staggering. The total annual financial cost of this type of crime in the United States has been estimated to be well over $1 trillion annually, which does not include intangible loss, such as the psychological impact of victimization (Cohen 2016).

It is more difficult to detect white-collar crime since enforcement efforts of the criminal-justice system are directed toward crimes committed by the poor rather than the rich (Messner and Rosenfeld 2007; Reiman and Leighton 2017; Rosoff et al. 2013), and people are often unaware that they have been victimized. When white-collar crimes are exposed, the sums procured in their commission are often shocking—often totaling in the millions, and sometimes even in the billions, of dollars. The Ponzi scheme stock fraud perpetrated by Bernard Madoff totaling $65 billion is one particularly glaring example. Other examples include the notorious and illegal stock manipulations of Ivan Boesky (deal stocks), Michael Milken (junk bonds), and Charles Keating (the savings-and-loan scandal); and corporate wrongdoing, including ethics scandals at Enron, WorldCom, Arthur Andersen, Volkswagen, and many others.

Suffice it to say, at least some of the wealth of financiers, executives, and professionals has been gained through often illegal or less than ethical means. This is in addition to untold wealth realized from more-conventional organized crime, including drug trafficking, prostitution and sex trafficking, bribery, counterfeiting, racketeering, extortion, gambling, and the like. In an ideal world, the virtuous succeed and the corrupt fail. But in the real world, too often this is not the case.

A NOTE ON HUMAN CAPITAL

Human capital factors are often included in the "merit" formula for success. Human capital refers to whatever *acquired* skills, knowledge, or experience workers possess that they can exchange for income in open markets. Clearly, having acquired capacity is not the same as being inherently made of the right stuff, because opportunities to acquire skills and experience are independent of the inherent capacity to do things. In human capital theory, wage laborers can "invest" in themselves through the accumulation of education and training, thus increasing their skills and presumably their productive capacities. But, as with investments in other forms of economic capital, investments in human capital require resources and entail an element of risk. Capacities to do things represent the "supply" side of the labor market; the specific capacities employers actually need represent the "demand" side of the labor market. The biggest returns on human capital investments are those in which the capacities acquired are both scarce and in high demand. It is possible, however, to invest in the "wrong" capacities. This can occur, for instance, when individuals are trained for jobs that become obsolete, sometimes even before the training period is complete. Or too many individuals may invest in acquiring the same skills, glutting the market and reducing return on investment. In both cases, one can be very meritorious but also very unemployed. Although we explore the supply effects of human capital in greater detail in chapter 5 and the demand side of the equation in greater detail in chapter 7, the point here is that this type of merit alone does not guarantee success.

THE MYTH OF THE MOST QUALIFIED

Defenders of meritocracy (and critics of affirmative action) often proclaim that the issue of who should get what is simple and straightforward: just hire the *most* qualified person for the job. However, even ignoring the fact that the big money in America comes from economic investments and not from jobs for which people are hired, this is not as simple and straightforward as many presume.

If merit were the sole cause of achievement, for instance, one would wonder why the vast amount of meritocratic talent is found in white males, who clearly dominate leadership positions in key institutions in society. Even setting discrimination and differential access to opportunity aside, how, in fact, would one recognize the *most* qualified applicant for every position in America?

Consider a somewhat extended example from my own profession. In addition to my own experience in the academic labor market, I have been on scores of faculty hiring committees in my own department, and, in my former roles as an associate dean and dean, I have also conducted scores of interviews of job candidates for other departments, representing over thirty academic disciplines.

I need to make two caveats. Hiring in academia is somewhat unusual compared to other sectors of the economy in that it is, for the most part, highly collegial; that is, the decision to hire is a collective one, typically made jointly by the existing members of the faculty in a given department, subject to approval at higher levels. This joint decision-making process reduces the chance of capriciously hiring any one person based on the singular decision of the "boss." Another unique quality of academic hiring is that faculty positions involve national searches; that is, job openings are advertised nationally (and internationally), casting the widest possible net. All of this is intended to increase the chances of hiring the best person for the job.

Although the intent is to hire the best person for the job, as anyone who has ever participated in the process knows, the problem comes in figuring out what is "best" and who that "best" person might be. The first qualification for the job is to have a PhD from an academically accredited institution in the discipline in which the faculty member will teach and do research. So far, so good. For a typical faculty position in our department, we might receive around one hundred applications. Among these, almost all of the applicants have a PhD in the appropriate field or are in the process of completing one. That is, only a handful of the applicants can quickly be eliminated as unqualified on that basis. It should be noted, however, that automatically eliminating those without the PhD might itself be a "merit mistake," since every academic field of study has at least a few cases of famous scholars who were giants in their fields of study but who never earned a PhD.[3]

After screening candidates for meeting the minimum paper qualifications, the hiring committee then carefully reviews the remaining applications, which consist of a letter of application, an academic résumé, called a "vita," and three letters of recommendation. Together, these materials represent a "paper presentation of self" of the applicant to the committee. After serving on a few of these committees, one realizes very quickly that holding experience, ability, and qualifications constant, some individuals are simply better than others at presenting their case on paper. Presentation of a case on paper and actual ability to do a job are two different things. More on this later. Based on these paper presentations of self, the hiring committee will develop a short list of maybe ten individuals for closer review. The short list is generated based on all reasonable indicators of merit: teaching record and experience, research record and potential, and "goodness of fit" with the needs of the department. With respect to the latter quality, it should be noted that we often have applicants who are truly outstanding but do not fit the advertised position; that is, they may appear to be the *most* talented or meritorious people in their respective pools overall, but they do not have areas of specialization for the position as advertised (e.g., an applicant is a great demographer, but we are really looking for a gerontologist). Further, as with most academic hires at most universities, we are most often looking to fill entry-level positions at the assistant professor level. This means that we will not usually consider the candidate who is literally the "best" in our pool if such a candidate is, for instance, a senior full professor with a proven track record, because such a candidate would be too expensive for the institution to hire. In this sense, we are not looking for the *most* meritorious professor we can find; we are looking for the most meritorious *new* assistant professor we can afford, in a specific area we need to fill.

In developing the short list, there are typically differences of opinion among members of the search committee. We try to reach a consensus, but perfect agreement rarely occurs. Majority sentiment prevails, but lack of consensus is itself an indicator of the difficulty of determining what "best" represents. We make a collective best guess as to who the ten best applicants in the pool might be. In developing an initial short list, the committee may well have overlooked the candidate who was, in fact, the best in the pool in terms of how that person ultimately could have done the job, but presented her- or himself poorly on paper. We will never know. One could argue that how one presents oneself on paper is an indicator of merit. However, we also know that many candidates, especially more recently minted PhDs, are better coached than others, and paper presentation of self is often more a reflection of the good advice of senior mentors than of candidate skills. We now have ten or so short-listed candidates but still only one position. The next step is to select three from among the top ten for on-campus interviews.

Perhaps we would do a better job of screening for raw talent if we interviewed more candidates. But resources are limited—both the money kind that is required to pay for on-campus interviews, and the time kind related to faculty who must also do all the other things faculty are supposed to do. Often, the short-listed candidates seem indistinguishable in terms of merit. All appear excellent, and looking for distinctions can become an exercise in splitting hairs. Frequently, there is another twist to the hiring drama. A dilemma that frequently unfolds is related to the amount of experience a candidate has. Since we most often hire at the assistant professor level, this means that most of the applicants are new or relatively new PhDs. Relatively new PhDs present a comparison problem. If candidates are already assistant professors at other institutions, they have more teaching experience and typically more extensive research track records than brand-new PhDs—but that does not necessarily make them "better" or more "meritorious." It is strictly a judgment call for a committee to decide whether potential exceeds track record in comparing new and almost-new PhDs—a source of more than one fierce debate in hiring committees I have been on.

Another potential hiring dilemma concerns "internal" candidates—candidates who are already associated with, or employed by, the university in some other capacity, such as part-time instructor or temporary lecturer. In some cases, the internal candidate may be applying for a particular permanent position that they currently occupy on a temporary basis. If strictly merit criteria apply, then internal candidates should be evaluated in the same manner as all other candidates without any preferential consideration. In practice, however, internal candidates often have a distinct advantage apart from strictly merit considerations. They are known by the hiring agents, and often friendships and emotional ties have already been formed. The internal candidate may be "qualified" and "doing a good job" but not necessarily the *most* qualified among all candidates who have applied, some of whom may be not just "good" but "outstanding." Social accountability also comes into play here. It is much easier to send a stranger a letter of rejection than to tell someone in the office next door that he or she did not get the job (and is thus out of his or her current job). The emotional burden of all this may weigh heavily on the decision-making process. To the extent that this is the case, strictly merit considerations are compromised.

It is an "open secret" in higher education that in some cases internal faculty candidates are essentially "wired in." That is, the application process is only a formality needed to satisfy human resource department requirements for public advertisement. One way institutions can "game" the system in this way is to write a job ad for a position that matches the particular internal candidate that the institution has in mind to such a degree of specificity of background, skills, experience, and specialties that only that particular internal candidate would likely match the advertised position. Qualified external candidates may apply in good faith, not realizing that a decision has essentially already been rendered. In other cases, competitive searches are suspended and candidates are merely presented to departments for up or down consideration.

The issue of "trailing partners" presents another potential hiring dilemma. With the postponement of age of first marriage, increasing higher educational attainment for women, and the growing proportion of women in the professoriate, there is an increasing prospect of academic couples simultaneously seeking positions at the same university. The problem is compounded if the couples are in the same discipline and have the same areas of specialty. Typically, only one position is available in an academic department at any one time. It is also unlikely that each partner will be identically "meritorious" in all respects, and that both will emerge from a strictly meritocratic review process as more meritorious than all other applicants combined. At the same time, universities are increasingly sensitive to this very human dilemma and are anxious to develop "family-friendly hiring practices."

One way some universities have responded to this potential dilemma is to allow couples to "share" a single position. Another way is for universities to try to find or create a suitable position for a partner. In short, there may be very human, legitimate, and practical reasons to make accommodations under these circumstances (for instance, you lose the most qualified candidate you want unless you can find suitable employment for a partner who may also be as qualified but for whom you have no existing position). At the same time, it should be recognized that such accommodations represent hiring decisions on criteria other than strictly merit considerations alone.

Finally, in an ironic twist, some candidates may be less aggressively pursued if they are viewed as "overly qualified." Here, the hiring agents may predict that a particularly outstanding applicant will likely receive more lucrative or attractive job offers elsewhere. The hiring committee might anticipate that it could not possibly match offers from other high-profile institutions likely interested in such candidates, and thus deem pursuing them to be a waste of time and other resources, which would risk losing more viable candidates for the position under consideration. Sometimes this emerges as a sentiment (or post hoc justification) in which the hiring officials speculate that the "overly qualified" person would end up "not being happy here."

Still other potentially nonmerit factors may come into play in the hiring drama. Do we know any of the people who are writing letters of recommendation for the candidates? Here the social network among the professoriate comes into play. New PhDs are typically not well known, but their professors and references might be. We may give more weight to candidates who are students of professors we know personally or who have "big names" writing for them. Everything else being equal or indistinguishable, the familiarity or prestige of the references might become a factor, as might the prestige of the institution where the candidates were trained. Here, some candidates may benefit from a "halo" effect of the glow of the institution from which they received their training, even though this in itself does not necessarily measure the merit of an individual.

Some of the most heated debates in hiring, however, have more to do with the faculty on the hiring committees than the candidates themselves. Hiring can become a political battle over which faction or coalition will prevail. Factions might develop over methodological, theoretical, or substantive differences within the hiring committee. Everything else being equal (and frequently even when it is not), faculty members will try to hire someone like themselves. Individual faculty may also be interested in promoting the power of their own faction or in hiring someone who might be a personal asset to them, even if that person is not the most "meritorious" in the pool.

When the dust of these debates clears, normally three candidates are brought to campus for an extended interview, usually lasting two or three full days each. During this time, candidates have one-on-one interviews with faculty and administrators and typically teach a class and give a research presentation. There are also a number of opportunities for informal interaction at dinners, receptions, and community tours. I have been amazed over the years at how frequently the top three on paper do not end up being ranked in the same order after on-campus interviews, reflecting the differences alluded to above between real and paper presentations of self. Another intangible screening factor is how well the candidates are "liked." Here, social skills may be more important than technical expertise or paper qualifications. How people present themselves in a job interview, however, may not predict how well they will actually perform on the job. Everything else being equal (and sometimes not so equal), at this final stage of the hiring process the candidate who "gets along" best with the most influential members of the committee will typically triumph over others.

In the end, a job offer is made to one person. Although the hiring committee, the department, and administrators may congratulate themselves for having selected the "best" person in the pool, the reality is that there is, in fact, no way to determine that with certainty. Do we routinely hire highly qualified candidates who are very meritorious? Absolutely. Have we always hired the *most* meritorious person for the job? Probably not, but we will never know for sure. The point of this extended example is to show that even within the professoriate, a profession in which academic qualifications and individual merit are highly extolled, there is no assurance that the "best" ultimately prevails. The hiring process is likely to be even more slippery and uncertain for real estate agents, store clerks, janitors, and a host of other jobs for which the merit criteria may be less agreed upon and more difficult to measure, and for which the screening processes are far less rigorous. When it comes to hiring the "best" or "most qualified," there are many slips betwixt the cup and the lip.

SUMMARY

This chapter has explored the meritocratic formula for getting ahead in America: being talented, having the right attitude, working hard, and having high moral standards. With the exception of high moral standards, all of them have some bearing on getting ahead in America. That is, individual capacity, certain attitudes, and hard work all probably do help people get ahead. High moral standards, however, may actually have the opposite effect by reducing the options available to get ahead. While being made of the "right stuff" in general helps people to get ahead, the reality is that these qualities exist in far greater quantity in the general population than is ever actually realized. Moreover, many individual traits often have social origins, and the effects of these traits are often much less than is presumed. By themselves, these traits are not typically enough to make the difference. It is not innate capacity alone, or hard work alone, or the proper frame of mind alone, that makes a difference. Rather, it is the *combination* of opportunity and these other factors that makes a difference.

The presumption that people know merit when they see it is also called into question. How do we really know who is the most meritorious? Recall that it is a cardinal principle in meritocracy that the "most" qualified or "best" person should be hired for the job. An example from the process for hiring professors illustrates that it is often difficult or impossible to know who the best is.

Subsequent chapters examine various nonmerit factors that affect where people end up in the system, beginning with the effects of inheritance or where one starts out in the first place.

REFERENCES

Ackmann, Martha. 2003. *The Mercury 13: The Untold Story of Thirteen American Women and the Dream of Space Flight.* New York: Random House.

Balleisen, Edward J. 2017. *Fraud: An American History from Barnum to Madoff.* Princeton, NJ: Princeton University Press.

Banfield, Edward C. 1970. *The Unheavenly City: The Nature and Future of Our Urban Crisis.* Boston: Little, Brown.

Barak, Gregg. 2017. *Unchecked Corporate Power: Why the Crimes of Multinational Corporations Are Routinized Away and What We Can Do about It.* New York: Routledge.

Bell, Alex, Raj Chetty, Xavier Jaravel, Neviana Petkova, and John Van Reenen. 2017. "Who Becomes an Inventor in America? The Importance of Exposure to Innovation." Equality of Opportunity Project. http://www.equality-of-opportunity.org/assets/documents/inventors_paper.pdf (accessed January 2, 2018).

Bick, Alexander, Bettina Bruggemann, and Nicola Fuchs-Schundeln. 2016. "Hours Worked in Europe and the US: New Data, New Answers." Working Paper, Arizona State University, McMaster University, and Goethe University.

Bowles, Samuel, Herbert Gintis, and Melissa Osborne Groves. 2005. "Introduction." In *Unequal Chances: Family Background and Economic Success,* ed. Samuel Bowles, Herbert Gintis, and Melissa Osborne Groves, 1–22. New York: Sage.

Buffington, Daniel. 2015. " 'Blacks Are Naturally Good Athletes': The Myth of a Biological Basis for Race." In Stephanie M. McClare and Cherise A. Harris, ed., *Getting Real about Race: Hoodies, Mascots, Model Minorities and Other Conversations,* 39–49. Thousand Oaks, CA: Sage Publications.

Carter, Christine. 2015. *The Sweet Spot: How to Find Your Groove at Home and Work*. New York: Ballantine Books.

Chambliss, William. 1989. "The Mundanity of Excellence." *Sociological Theory* 7:70–86.

Coakley, Jay. 2017. *Sports in Society: Issues and Controversies*. 12th ed. Boston: McGraw-Hill.

Cohen, Mark D. 2016. "The Costs of White Collar Crime." In *Handbook of White Collar Crime*, ed. Shanna R. Van Slyke, Michael L. Bensen, and Francis Cullen, 78–98. New York: Oxford University Press.

Conley, Dalton, and Jason Fletcher. 2017. *The Genome Factor: What the Social Genomics Revolution Reveals about Ourselves, Our History and the Future*. Princeton, NJ: Princeton University Press.

Cooper, David, and Teresa Kroeger. 2017. "Employers Steal Billions from Workers' Paychecks Every Year." Washington, DC: Economic Policy Institute, www.epi.org/files/pdf/125116. pdf (accessed September 25, 2017).

Coward, Barbara E., Joe R. Feagin, and Allen J. Williams Jr. 1974. "The Culture of Poverty Debate: Some Additional Data." *Social Problems* 21:621–34.

Della Fave, L. Richard. 1974. "The Culture of Poverty Revisited: A Strategy for Research." *Social Problems* 21:609–21.

Derickson, Alan. 2013. *Dangerously Sleepy: Overworked Americans and the Cult of Manly Wakefulness*. Philadelphia: University of Pennsylvania Press.

Dunkleman, Allen J. 2000. "Our American Ideology of Success." Unpublished senior research project, University of North Carolina at Wilmington.

Ehrenreich, Barbara. 2001. *Nickel and Dimed: On (Not) Getting By in America*. New York: Metropolitan Books.

Farkas, George. 2003. "Cognitive Skills and Noncognitive Traits and Behaviors in Stratification Processes." In *Annual Review of Sociology*, Vol. 29, ed. Karen S. Cook and John Hagan, 541–62. Palo Alto, CA: Annual Reviews.

Fischer, Claude S., Michael Hout, Martin Sanchez Jaankowski, Samuel R. Lucas, Ann Swidler, and Kim Voss. 1996. *Inequality by Design: Cracking the Bell Curve Myth*. Princeton, NJ: Princeton University Press.

Forbes. 2017a. "The World's Highest Paid Celebrities (2016)." www.forbes.com/celebrities/list/#tab:overall (accessed February 15, 2017).

———. 2017b. "Forbes Richest People in America List (2016)." www.forbes.com/forbes-400/list/ (accessed February 15, 2017).

Gladwell, Malcolm. 2008. *Outliers: The Story of Success*. New York: Little, Brown.

Gould, Mark. 1999. "Race and Theory: Culture, Poverty, and Adaptation to Discrimination in Wilson and Ogbu." *Sociological Theory* 17:171–200.

Greenbaum, Susan D. 2015. *Blaming the Poor: The Long Shadow of the Moynihan Report on Cruel Images about Poverty*. New Brunswick, NJ: Rutgers University Press.

Hall, Matthew, and George Farkas. 2011. "Adolescent Cognitive Skills, Attitudinal/Behavioral Traits and Career Wages. *Social Forces* 89(4):1261–85.

Herrnstein, Richard, and Charles Murray. 1994. *The Bell Curve: Intelligence and Class Structure in American Life*. New York: Free Press.

Huber, Richard. 1971. *The American Idea of Success*. New York: McGraw-Hill.

Jencks, Christopher, Susan Bartlett, Mary Corcoran, James Crouse, David Eaglesfield, Gregory Jackson, and Kent McClelland. 1979. *Who Gets Ahead? The Determinants of Economic Success in America*. New York: Basic Books.

Kalleberg, Arene. 2011. *Good Jobs, Bad Jobs: The Rise of Polarized and Precarious Employment Systems in the United States, 1970s to 2000s.* New York: Sage.

Lewis, Oscar. 1959. *Five Families: Mexican Case Studies in the Culture of Poverty.* New York: Basic Books.

———. 1966. *La Vida: A Puerto Rican Family in the Culture of Poverty.* New York: Random House.

Maslow, Abraham. 1970. *Motivation and Personality.* 2nd ed. New York: Harper & Row.

McCall, Leslie. 2013. *The Undeserving Rich: American Beliefs about Inequality, Opportunity, and Redistribution.* New York: Cambridge University Press.

McGee, Micki. 2005. *Self-Help, Inc.: Makeover Culture in American Life.* New York: Oxford University Press.

Messner, Steven F., and Richard Rosenfeld. 2007. *Crime and the American Dream.* Belmont, CA: Thomson Higher Education.

Murray, Charles. 2012. *Coming Apart: The State of White America, 1960–2010.* New York: Crown Forum.

Peale, Norman Vincent. 1952. *The Power of Positive Thinking.* New York: Prentice Hall.

Reiman, Jeffrey, and Paul Leighton. 2017. *The Rich Get Richer and the Poor Get Prison: Ideology, Class, and Criminal Justice.* 11th ed. New York: Routledge.

Rodman, Hyman. 1963. "The Lower Class Value Stretch." *Social Forces* 42:205–15.

Rosoff, Stephen M., Henry N. Pontell, and Robert Tillman. 2013. *Profit without Honor: White Collar Crime and the Looting of America.* 6th ed. New York: Pearson.

Ryan, William. 1971. *Blaming the Victim.* New York: Vintage Books.

Samuel, Larry. 2009. *Rich: The Rise and Fall of the American Wealth Culture.* New York: American Management Association.

Schor, Juliet. 2008. *The Overworked American: The Unexpected Decline of Leisure.* New York: Basic Books.

Stanley, Thomas. 2000. *The Millionaire Mind.* Kansas City, MO: Andrews McMeel Publishing.

Starker, Steven. 2002. *Oracle at the Supermarket: The American Preoccupation with Self-Help Books.* Edison, NJ: Transaction Publishers.

Taylor, Jim, Doug Harrison, and Stephen Kraus. 2009. *The New Elite: Inside the Minds of the Truly Wealthy.* New York: American Management Association.

Valentine, Charles. 1968. *Culture and Poverty.* Chicago: University of Chicago Press.

Wiley, Norbert. 1967. "The Ethnic Mobility Trap and Stratification Theory." *Social Problems* 15:147–59.

Wilson, William Julius. 2012. *The Truly Disadvantaged: The Inner City, the Underclass, and Public Policy.* Chicago: University of Chicago Press.

Wolfe, Thomas. 1979. *The Right Stuff.* New York: Farrar, Straus and Giroux.

Zagorsky, Jay L. 2007. "Do You Have to Be Smart to Be Rich: The Impact of IQ on Wealth, Income and Financial Distress." *Intelligence* 35(5):489–501.

3

The Silver Spoon

Inheritance and the Staggered Start

To heir is human.

—Jeffrey P. Rosenfeld, *Legacy of Aging*

A common metaphor for the competition to get ahead in life is the foot race. The imagery is that the fastest runner—presumably the most meritorious—will be the one to break the tape at the finish line. But in terms of economic competition, the race is rigged. If we think of money as a measure of who gets how much of what there is to get, the race to get ahead does not start anew with each generation. Instead, it is more like a relay race in which we inherit a starting point from our parents. The baton is passed, and for a while, both parents and children run together. When the exchange is complete, the children are on their own as they position themselves for the next exchange to the next generation. Although each new runner may gain or lose ground in the competition, each new runner inherits an initial starting point in the race.

In this intergenerational relay race, children born to wealthy parents start at or near the finish line, while children born into poverty start behind everyone else. Those who are born close to the finish line need no merit to get ahead. They already are ahead. The poorest of the poor, however, need to traverse the entire distance to get to the finish line on the basis of merit alone. In this sense, meritocracy applies strictly only to the poorest of the poor; everyone else has at least some advantage of inheritance over others that places them ahead at the start of the race.

In comparing the effects of inheritance and individual merit on life outcomes, the effects of inheritance come first, *followed by* the effects of individual merit—not the other way around. Figure 3.1 depicts the intergenerational relay race to get ahead. The solid lines represent the effects of inheritance on economic outcomes.

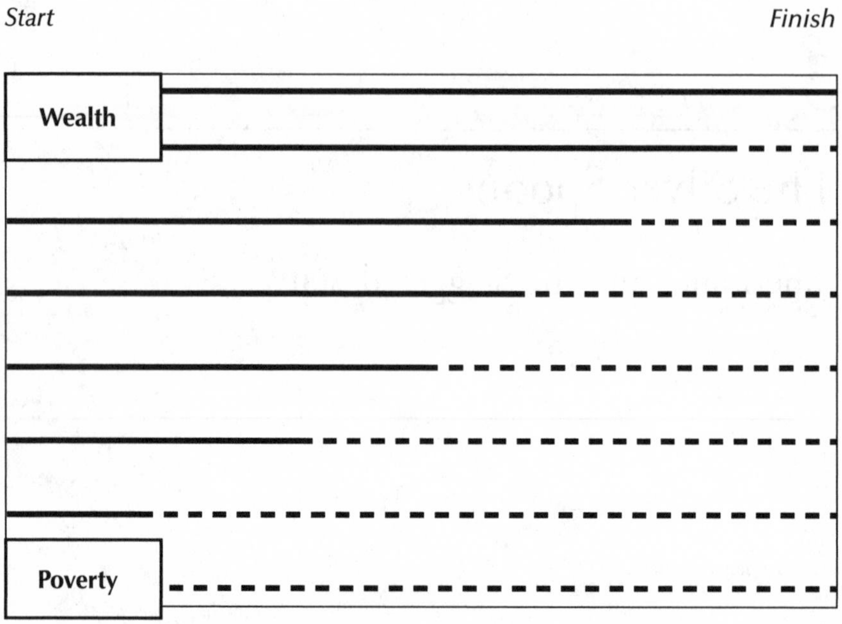

Start   *Finish*

Solid lines = Effects of inheritance
Dotted lines = Potential effects of merit

Figure 3.1. The Intergenerational Race to Get Ahead

The dotted lines represent the potential effects of merit. The "distance" each person needs to reach the finish line on the basis of merit depends on how far from the finish line each person starts the race in the first place.

It is important to point out that equivalent amounts of merit do not lead to equivalent end results. If each dash represents one "unit" of merit, a person born poor who advances one unit on the basis of individual merit over a lifetime ends up at the end of her life one unit ahead of where she started, but still at or close to poverty. A person who begins life one unit short of the top can ascend to the top based on an equivalent one unit of merit. Each person is equally meritorious, but his or her end position in the race to get ahead is very different.

Heirs to large fortunes in the world start life at or near the finish line. Barring the unlikely possibility of parental disinheritance, there is virtually no realistic scenario in which they end up destitute—regardless of the extent of their innate talent or individual motivation. Their future is financially secure. They will grow up having the best of everything and having every opportunity money can buy.

Most parents want the best for their children. Except in relatively rare cases of child abuse or neglect, most parents try to do everything possible to secure their children's futures. Indeed, the parental desire to provide advantages for children may even have biological origins. Under the "inclusive fitness-maximizing" theory of selection, for instance, beneficiaries are favored in inheritance according to their biological relatedness and reproductive value. Unsurprisingly, research shows that benefactors are much more likely to bequeath estates to surviving spouses and children than to unrelated individuals or institutions (Schwartz 1996; Willenbacher 2003). Moreover, most parents relish any opportunity to boast about their children's accomplishments. Parents are typically highly motivated to invest in their children's future in order to realize vicarious prestige through the successes of their children, which may, in turn, be seen as a validation of their own genetic endowments or child-rearing skills. Finally, in a form of what might be called "reverse inheritance," parents may be motivated to invest in children to secure their own futures in the event that they become unable to take care of themselves.

Regardless of the source of parental motivation, the point is that most parents clearly wish to secure their children's futures. The key difference among parents is not in parental motivation to pass on advantages to the next generation, but in the capacity to do so, with some parents having more resources than others. Affluent parents spend more on their children than the less affluent, and this tendency appears to be increasing over time (Moynihan, Smeeding, and Rainwater 2004; Kornrich and Furstenberg 2013; Kornrich 2016). Moreover, much of the spending on children by affluent adult parents appears to be geared specifically to educational programs, enrichment programs, extracurricular activities, and other experiences designed specifically to enhance their children's competitiveness and future life chances (Duncan and Murnane 2011; Lareau 2011; Smeeding et al. 2011; Friedman 2013). To the extent that parents are actually successful in passing on advantages to their children, existing inequalities are reproduced across generations, and meritocracy does not operate as the basis for who ends up with what. Despite the pervasive ideology of meritocracy, the reality in America, as elsewhere, is inheritance first and merit second.

INCOME AND WEALTH INEQUALITY

In considering how parents pass on advantages to children in the race to get ahead, researchers have usually looked at occupational mobility—that is, at how the occupations of parents affect the occupations of children. The results of this research show that parental occupation has strong effects on children's occupational prospects. Some of this effect is mediated through education, meaning, the prestige of parental occupation increases the educational attainment of children, which in turn increases the prestige of the occupations they attain. Looking at occupational prestige alone, however, underestimates the full extent of inequality in society and overestimates the amount of movement within the system.

A fuller appreciation of what is at stake requires examination of the kind and extent of economic inequality within the system—who gets how much of what there is to get. Economic inequality includes inequalities of both income and wealth. *Income* is typically defined as the total flow of financial resources from all sources (e.g., wages and salaries, interest on savings and dividends, pensions, and government transfer payments such as Social Security, welfare payments, and other government payments) in a given period, usually annually. *Wealth* refers not to what people earn but to what they own. Wealth is usually measured as net worth, which includes the total value of all assets owned (such as real estate, trusts, stocks, bonds, business equity, homes, automobiles, banking deposits, insurance policies, and the like) minus the total value of all liabilities (e.g., loans, mortgages, credit card and other forms of debt). For purposes of illustration, income and wealth inequalities are usually represented by dividing the population into quintiles and showing how much of what there is to get goes to each fifth, from the richest fifth of the population down to the poorest fifth. These proportions are illustrated in table 3.1.

In terms of income, in 2015 the richest 20 percent of households received a 51.1 percent share of all before-tax income, compared to only 3.1 percent received by the bottom 20 percent.

When wealth is considered, the disparities are much greater. In 2013, the richest 20 percent of American households accounted for 81.1 percent of total net household worth. The bottom 20 percent of American households combined accounted for –2 percent net worth. Net worth can be negative, since it is possible to owe more than you own.

Even among the richest of Americans, income and wealth are very unequally distributed and highly concentrated among a very small segment of the American population. In 2015, for instance, the top 1 percent of American households received 22 percent of all available income (Saez 2016). The minimum threshold of annual income received that is needed to be included in the top 1 percent of household income in 2015 was $443,000 (Saez 2016). With regard to wealth, the top 1 percent of the wealthiest households in 2012 held 41.8 percent of total net worth, with a minimum threshold of $3.9 million net worth needed to be included among the richest 1 percent (Saez and Zucman 2016). Wealth is especially concentrated at the very top of the system, with a mere .01 percent of American households alone owning 22 percent of all net worth (Saez and Zucman 2016). This amount

Table 3.1.   Share of Total Available Household Income and Total Net Worth, by Income Group

Income Group	Share of Income, 2015 (%)[a]	Share of Net Worth, 2013 (%)[b]
Top Fifth	51.1	81.1
Fourth Fifth	23.2	12.8
Third Fifth	14.3	5.7
Second Fifth	8.2	1.2
Bottom Fifth	3.1	–.2

[a] US Census (2016).
[b] US Congressional Budget Office (2016).

of wealth held is significant not only for the amount of wealth held that sets this group distinctly apart from the rest of American society, but for the source of that wealth. In 2013, the top 1 percent of households owned a staggering 62.6 percent of all business equity, 54.7 percent of all financial securities, 49.5 percent of all trusts, 49.8 percent of all stocks and mutual funds, and 33.7 percent of all nonhome real estate (Wolff 2014).

Because of these holdings, income shares at the very top of the system are derived primarily from returns to investment capital rather than wages and salaries from jobs. In 2014, the top 1 percent of income earners derived over half of their annual income from investment capital; for the top .01 percent of income earners, more than two-thirds of income was derived from investment capital (Piketty, Saez, and Zucman 2016). Because of the high level of concentration of wealth within the richest 1 percent, as well as the primary source of that wealth in income-generating forms of capital investment, the wealthiest 1 percent of Americans are often referred to as "the ownership class," with the richest 1 percent threshold used as a proxy for inclusion in the American "upper class."

Another indication of income inequality is revealed by a comparison of pay for the chief executive officers of major corporations with that of rank-and-file employees. For the largest 350 corporations, and with some year-to-year fluctuation, CEO pay as a ratio of average worker pay increased from 20 to 1 in 1965 to 276 to 1 by 2015 (Mishel and Schieder 2016), with much of the compensation package for CEOs coming in the form of stock options. Since CEO compensation is increasingly in the form of stock options, the ratio to worker pay in recent years is sensitive to changes in the market, but always substantially higher than in previous decades.

In short, the degree of economic inequality in the United States is substantial by any measure. In fact, the United States now has significantly greater income and wealth inequality than other industrial countries (Zucman 2016). Moreover, the extent of economic inequality is increasing. The share of average pre-tax income adjusted for inflation that went to the top 1 percent doubled from 10.7 percent in 1980 to 20.2 percent in 2014, while the share of income going to the bottom 50 percent declined from 19.9 percent to 12 percent (Piketty et al. 2016). In 1980, the top 1 percent of adults on average received twenty-seven times more income than the bottom 50 percent of adults; by 2014, the top 1 percent received eighty-one times more (Piketty et al. 2016). The share of wealth going to the wealthiest 1 percent has increased even more dramatically, from 25 percent in 1986 to 42 percent in 2012, with most of the rise of the top 1 percent accounted for by an increased share in just the top 0.1 percent, whose share of total wealth held more than doubled, from 10 percent in the late 1980s to 22 percent in 2012 (Saez and Zucman 2016).

The overall conclusions drawn from these data are that 1) income and wealth in America are highly concentrated at the very top of the system; 2) the really big money in America comes not from wages and salaries but from returns on capital investments; 3) the levels of income and wealth inequality in America are higher than other advanced industrial societies; and 4) the degree of income and wealth inequality is increasing over time.

It is instructive to point out that the level of economic inequality in America is greatly underestimated by the American public. A Duke University study, for instance, showed that Americans estimate that the richest 20 percent of Americans account for 59 percent of the total wealth available, compared to the actual 84 percent (Norton and Ariely 2011). Moreover, in the same survey, Americans indicated that ideally, the richest 20 percent *should* own 32 percent of the total wealth, or about 50 percent less than they actually hold.

Consideration of wealth as opposed to just income in assessing the total amount of economic inequality in society is critical for several reasons. First, the really big money in America comes not from wages and salaries but from owning property, particularly the kind that produces more wealth. If it "takes money to make money," those with capital to invest have a distinct advantage over those whose only source of income is wages. Apart from equity in owner-occupied housing, assets that most Americans hold are the kind that tend to *depreciate* in value over time: cars, furniture, appliances, clothes, and other personal belongings. Many of these items end up in used-car lots, garage sales, and flea markets, selling at prices much lower than their original cost. The rich, however, have a high proportion of their holdings in the kinds of wealth that *appreciate* in value over time. Second, wealth is especially critical with respect to inheritance. When people inherit an estate, they inherit accumulated assets—not incomes from wages and salaries. Inheritance of estates, in turn, is an important nonmerit mechanism for the transmission of privilege across generations. In strictly merit terms, inheritance is a form of getting something for nothing.

INTERGENERATIONAL MOBILITY

Defenders of meritocracy sometimes argue that the *extent* of economic inequality is not a problem as long as there is ample *opportunity* for social mobility based on individual merit. Overwhelming evidence, however, shows that a substantial amount of economic advantage is passed on across generations from parents to children (Ermisch, Jantti, and Smeeding 2012; Smeeding, Erikson, and Jantti 2011; Urahn et al. 2012). The mechanisms by which parental privilege is transferred to children are varied, ranging from direct advantages, such as inheritance of material resources, to indirect advantages, such as increased capacity and opportunity for cognitive and physical development, better educational preparedness and opportunities, access to influential social networks, and access and exposure to prestigious cultural resources.

One way to measure the extent of intergenerational mobility is the correlation between parent and child incomes. Correlations can range from a low of zero to a high of one. If we had a pure merit system and assumed random transfer of genetic endowments across generations, we would expect a correlation of parent and adult child incomes to approach zero. On the other hand, in a strict caste system in which children inherit entirely the social position of parents and in which no mobility occurs, we would expect a correlation to approach one. The correlation between parents' and adult children's incomes in the United States is actually about 0.50 (Stiglitz 2012; Mitnik and Grusky 2015), a correlation midway between these extremes, suggesting that about half of the adult income is tied to family background.

Moreover, the prospect for intergenerational income mobility appears to be sharply decreasing over time. As noted in chapter 1, one of the major indicators of the realization of the American Dream is that each generation would have better opportunities and a rising standard of living than the generation preceding it. In a comprehensive recent study of absolute income mobility in America, Stanford sociologist Rai Chetty and his associates (2017) found that the percent of American children who subsequently as adults out-earn their parents has steadily declined in the last half century. The study compared household incomes of adult children at age thirty with their parents' household incomes at age thirty, controlling for inflation, taxes and transfers, and household size. Whereas 92 percent of Americans born in 1940 subsequently out-earned their parents at equivalent ages, only 50 percent of Americans born in 1984 subsequently out-earned their parents at equivalent ages, with progressive declines for cohorts born between 1940 and 1984. Chetty and his associates primarily attribute this sharp drop to a decline in rates of growth in the economy as a whole over that time span, and greater degrees of inequality in the distribution of that growth.

While annual income mobility is important to consider, the prospects for attaining wealth and accumulating assets over a lifetime are even more critical to the promise of fulfillment of the American Dream. Table 3.2 shows the extent of intergenerational wealth transfers from parents to children as reported as part of a comprehensive study, *Pursuing the American Dream: Economic Mobility across Generations*, conducted by the Pew Research Center (2012). These data show a great deal of "stickiness" between generations, especially in the top and bottom of the system. For instance, 41 percent of children born to parents in the lowest wealth quintile of the population remain in the lowest wealth quintile as adults, while, correspondingly,

Table 3.2.   Intergenerational Wealth Transmission from Parents to Children

Child's Wealth Quintile	Parents' Wealth Quintile				
	Lowest (%)	Second (%)	Middle (%)	Fourth (%)	Top (%)
Lowest	41	27	15	11	7
Second	25	30	17	17	11
Middle	17	19	26	23	16
Fourth	10	14	24	27	25
Top	8	10	17	23	41
Total	100	100	100	100	100

Source: Pew Research Center (2012).

41 percent of those born to parents in the top wealth quintile remain there as adults. Most movement that does take place between generations occurs as "short-distance" mobility between adjacent quintiles. For instance, of children born into the poorest quintile, only 8 percent move into the highest wealth quintile as adults, while 66 percent either stay in the quintile they started in or make it as far as the middle quintile. Likewise, of those born in the top quintile, only 7 percent fall to the bottom quintile, while 66 percent either stay in the quintile they started in, or do not fall further than the middle quintile.

Americans tend to not only *underestimate* the extent of economic inequality that actually exists, as previously noted, but they also tend to *overestimate* the extent of economic mobility that actually exists (Kraus and Tan 2015; Kraus 2015). In one national study, Kraus and Tan (2015) found, for instance, that Americans substantially overestimated the percentage of Americans 1) who move from the bottom quintile of income to the top quintile; 2) who move from the top 1 percent of income to the bottom quintile of income; 3) who move from the bottom quintile by working one thousand extra hours; and 4) who attend the top one hundred colleges and universities who are from the bottom quintile of income. In this study, Kraus and Tan found that Americans overestimated the extent of economic mobility along these dimensions by an average of nearly 19 percentage points. The authors attributed these overestimations to lack of knowledge of actual rates of mobility, and the need to satisfy a sense that they live in a society that is fair and merit-based.

The increasing degree of concentration of wealth at the top of the system and the high stability of wealth over time is also significant for the prospects of wealth mobility in the future. The rapidly accumulating concentration of wealth at the very top of the system will not simply evaporate between generations. Most of this wealth will be passed on to succeeding generations. Instead of the American Dream of equal opportunity for all, we are witnessing what some observers suggest is the unfolding of an entrenched economic aristocracy of dynastic wealth in America (Grusky and Kricheli-Katz 2012; Freeland 2012; Piketty 2014).

Despite the overwhelming evidence of wealth stability over time, much is made of the investment "risks" that capitalists must endure to justify returns on such investments. To some extent, this is true. Most investments involve some measure of risk. The superwealthy, however, protect themselves as much as possible from the vicissitudes of "market forces"—most have professionally managed, diversified investment portfolios. As a result, established wealth has great staying power. In short, what is good for America is, in general, good for the ownership class. The risk endured, therefore, is minimal. Instead of losing vast fortunes overnight, the more common scenario for the super-rich is for the *amount* of their wealth to fluctuate with the ups and downs in the stock market as a whole. And, given the very high levels of aggregate and corporate wealth concentration in the economy, the only realistic scenario in which the ownership class goes under is one in which America as a whole goes under.

THE CUMULATIVE ADVANTAGES
OF WEALTH INHERITANCE

Inheritance is more than bulk estates bequeathed to descendants; more broadly defined, it refers to the total impact of initial social-class placement at birth on future life outcomes. Therefore, it is not just the superwealthy who are in a position to pass advantages on to children. Advantages are passed on, in varying degrees, to all of those from relatively privileged backgrounds. Even minor initial advantages may accumulate during the life course. In this way, existing inequalities are reinforced and extended across generations. Specifically, the cumulative advantages of wealth inheritance include those discussed below.

Childhood Quality of Life

Children of the privileged enjoy a high standard of living and quality of life regardless of their individual merit or lack of it. For the privileged, this not only includes high-quality food, clothing, and shelter, but also extends to luxuries such as travel, vacations, summer camps, private lessons, and a host of other enrichments and indulgences that wealthy parents and even middle-class parents bestow on their children. These advantages do not just reflect a higher standard during childhood, but have important long-term consequences for future life chances. Children raised in privileged settings are much more likely to have better and more rapid physical, cognitive, emotional, and social development, better school readiness, and higher academic achievement.

Conversely, children raised in poverty have higher risks for basically everything that is bad that can happen to them as adults later in life—dropping out of school, becoming victims of crime and violence, having more physical and mental health problems, having lower economic prospects, and having greater likelihood of familial disruption. The more severe these deprivations and the earlier they occur, the greater the negative consequences (Duncan and Murnane 2011; Smeeding, Erikson, and Jantti 2011; Alexander et al. 2014).

In short, the effects of early childhood development have a "long reach" into later life. It is important to emphasize that children of privilege do not "earn" a privileged childhood lifestyle; they inherit it, and benefit from it long before their parents are deceased.

Knowing Which Fork to Use

Cultural capital refers to what one needs to know in order to function as a member of the various groups to which one belongs. (The issue of cultural capital is examined more fully in chapter 4.) All groups have norms, values, beliefs, ways of life, and codes of conduct that identify the group and define its boundaries. The culture of the group separates insiders from outsiders. Knowing and abiding by these cultural

codes of conduct is necessary to maintain one's status as a member in good standing within the group. By growing up in privilege, children of the elite are socialized
into elite ways of life. This kind of cultural capital has commonly been referred to
as "breeding," "refinement," "social graces," "savoir faire," or simply "class" (meaning
upper-class). Although less pronounced and rigid than in the past, these distinctions
persist into the present. In addition to cultivated tastes in art and music ("highbrow"
culture), cultural capital includes, but is not limited to, interpersonal styles and
demeanor, manners and etiquette, and vocabulary. Those from more humble backgrounds who aspire to become elites must acquire the cultural cachet to be accepted
in elite circles, and this is no easy task. Those born to it, however, have the advantage
of acquiring it "naturally" through inheritance, a kind of social osmosis that takes
place through childhood socialization (Lareau 2011).

Having Friends in High Places

Everybody knows somebody else. *Social capital* refers to the "value" of whom you
know. (The importance of social capital on life outcomes is discussed more fully in
chapter 4.) For the most part, privileged people know other privileged people, and
poor people know other poor people. In general, affluent individuals have more
close friends, broader social networks, and a wider range of informal mentors than
the less affluent (Putnam 2015). Another nonmerit advantage inherited by children
of the wealthy is a network of connections to people of power and influence, or
what sociologist Thomas Shapiro (2017) refers to as a "web of wealth." These are
not connections that children of the rich shrewdly foster or cultivate on their own.
The children of the wealthy travel in high-powered social circles; these connections
provide access to power, information, and other resources. The difference between
rich and poor is not in knowing people; it is in knowing people in positions of power
and influence who can do things for you.

Early Withdrawals on the Family Estate

Children of the privileged do not have to wait until their parents die to inherit assets from them. Inter vivos transfers of funds and "gifts" from parents to
children can be substantial, and in many cases represent a greater proportion of
intergenerational transfers than lump-sum estates at death. Parents provide inter
vivos transfers to children to advance their children's current and future economic
interests, especially at critical junctures or milestones of the life cycle (Shapiro 2017;
Zissimopoulos and Smith 2011). These transfers continue beyond early childhood,
and include milestone events for adult children such as going to college, getting
married, buying a house, and having their own children, or at crisis events such as
income shocks related to job loss, divorce, or medical crisis. At each event, there
may be a substantial infusion of parental capital—in essence, an early withdrawal
on the parental estate.

As sociologist Thomas Shapiro (2017) points out, these inter vivos transfers are often "transformative" in terms of the impact on the quality and trajectory of the recipients' lives. The amounts transferred are highly skewed. One study of parents over the age of fifty (Zissimopoulos and Smith 2011), for instance, showed that in the United States over a sixteen-year period, the bottom 50 percent of parental households gave an average of only $500 to their adult children, but parents in the top 1 percent gave an average of $137,641 per child to their adult children. Moreover, households that give substantially to children give more as a percentage of their total income and wealth than other households, further reflecting the differential capacity of parents to transfer advantages across generations. For those with great wealth, inter vivos gifts to children also provide a means of legally avoiding or reducing estate taxes. In this way, parents can "spend down" their estates during their lives to avoid estate and inheritance taxes upon their deaths.

One of the most common current forms of inter vivos gifts is payment for children's education. (I address education more fully in chapter 5.) A few generations ago, children may have inherited the family farm or the family business. With the rise of the modern corporation and the decline of family farms and businesses, inheritance increasingly takes on more fungible or liquid forms, including cash transfers. Indeed, for many middle-class Americans, education has replaced tangible assets as the primary form by which advantage is passed on between generations. Also, with rising overall life expectancy, there is a longer period of time during the lives of parents and children in which inter vivos gifts can take place.

What Goes Up Doesn't Usually Come Down

If America were truly a meritocracy, we would expect fairly equal amounts of both upward and downward mobility. Until very recently, and for most of American history, however, there have been much higher rates of upward than downward mobility. There are two key reasons for this. First, most mobility that people have experienced in America in the past century, particularly occupational mobility, was due to industrial expansion and the rise of the general standard of living in society as a whole. Sociologists refer to this type of mobility as "structural mobility," which has more to do with changes in the organization of society than with the merit of discrete individuals. (I discuss the effects of social structure on life outcomes in more detail in chapter 7.)

A second reason why upward mobility is more prevalent than downward mobility is that parents and extended family networks insulate children from downward mobility. That is, parents frequently "bail out," or "rescue," their adult children in the event of life crises such as sickness, unemployment, divorce, or other setbacks that might otherwise propel adult children into a downward spiral. In addition to these external circumstances, parents also rescue children from their own failures and weaknesses, including self-destructive behaviors. Parental rescue as a form of inter vivos transfer is not a generally acknowledged or well-studied benefit of inheritance.

Indirect evidence of parental rescue may be found in the recent increase in the number of "boomerang" children—adult children who leave home only to return later to live with their parents. Richard Fry (2016) of the Pew Research Center reports that in 2014, 32 percent of all young adults, ages eighteen to thirty-four, were living with their parents compared to 20 percent in 1960. The reasons for adult children returning to live at home are usually financial: adult children may be between jobs, between marriages, or without other viable means of self-support.

If America operated as a "true" merit system, people would advance solely on the basis of merit and fail when they lacked merit. In many cases, however, family resources prevent, or at least reduce, "skidding" among adult children. As Robert Putnam (2015) puts it, when personal mistakes or other misfortunes occur among children of the privileged, the "air bags" of familial resources are deployed. This is not the case among the children of the poor. To relate a personal example, when I left home as an adult, my parents of modest means took me aside and told me that no matter how bad things became for me out there in the world, if I could manage to get to a phone (before the era of cell phones, access to phones in an emergency was not always readily available), they would send me money to come home. This was my familial safety net against homelessness and destitution. Fortunately, I never needed to take my parents up on their offer, but neither did I forget it. Without always being articulated, the point is that this informal familial insurance against downward mobility is available, in varying degrees, to all except the poorest of the poor, who simply have no resources to provide.

Live Long and Prosper

From womb to tomb, the more affluent one is, the less the risk of injury, illness, and death (Budrys 2017; Chetty et al. 2016; Cockerham 2016; National Center for Health Statistics 2016). Among the many nonmerit advantages inherited by those from privileged backgrounds is higher life expectancy at birth, and a greater chance of better health throughout life. For instance, American men born in the top 10 percent of income have a life expectancy that is 5 years greater than men born in the bottom 10 percent (Bosworth et al. 2016). The gaps are even larger between the richest and poorest 1 percent, with the richest 1 percent of men living on average 14.6 years longer than the poorest 1 percent (Chetty et al. 2016).

There are several reasons for the strong and persistent relationship between socioeconomic status and health. Beginning with fetal development and extending through childhood, increasing evidence points to the impact of early childhood on adult health. Prenatal deprivations, more common among the poor, for instance, are associated with later life conditions such as retardation, coronary heart disease, stroke, diabetes, and hypertension. Poverty in early childhood is also associated with increased risk of adult diseases. This may be due in part to higher stress levels among the poor and less control over that stress. Cumulative wear and tear on the body over time occurs under conditions of repeated high stress.

Another reason for the health-wealth connection is that the rich have greater access to quality health care. Even with the recent passage of the Patient Protection and Affordable Care Act in 2010 (more commonly referred to as Obamacare), access to quality health care in America is still largely predicated on the ability to pay. Under these conditions, prevention and intervention are more widely available to the more affluent. Finally, not only does lack of income lead to poor health, but poor health leads to reduced earnings. That is, if someone is sick or injured, he or she may not be able to work or may have limited earning power.

Overall, the less-affluent are at a health disadvantage due to higher exposure to a variety of unhealthy living conditions. The less-affluent, for instance, are also likely to have nutritional deprivations and, ironically, are also more likely to be obese. Obesity is related to poor nutrition linked to diets that are high in low-cost sugar and carbohydrates and low in high-cost fruits, vegetables, and other sources of protein. The less-affluent are also more likely to be exposed to physical risks associated with crowding, poor sanitation, and living in closer proximity to chemical and biological sources of pollution (Brulle and Pellow 2006; Budrys 2017).

Part of the exposure to health hazards is occupational. According to the US Department of Labor (2016), those in the following occupations (listed in order of decreasing risk) have the greatest likelihood of being killed on the job: logging workers, fishers, airplane pilots and flight engineers, roofers, refuse and recyclable material collectors, structural iron and steelworkers, truck and delivery drivers, farmers, electrical power-line workers, and landscaping and groundskeeping workers. With the exception of airline pilots and flight engineers, all the jobs listed are working-class jobs. Since a person's occupation is strongly affected by family background, the prospects for generally higher occupational health risks are in this sense at least indirectly inherited. Finally, although homicides constitute only a small proportion of all causes of death, it is worth noting that the less-affluent are at higher risk for being victims of violent crime, including homicide.

Some additional risk factors are related to individual behaviors, especially smoking, drinking, and drug abuse—all of which are more common among the less-affluent (Budrys 2017). These behaviors are also associated with higher psychological as well as physical stress. Indeed, the less-affluent are not just at greater risk for physical ailments; research has shown that the less-affluent experience higher levels of stress, and are at significantly higher risk for mental illness as well (Cockerham 2017).

Despite the adage that "money can't buy happiness," social science research has consistently shown that happiness and subjective well-being tend to be related to the amount of income and wealth people possess (Cieslik 2017; Frey and Stutzer 2002; Easterlin 2010; Layard 2005; Wilkinson and Pickett 2009). This relationship is complicated, however, in part because several factors other than economic status affect perceived levels of happiness and well-being, including health, social relationships, and job satisfaction, which are themselves also related to economic status. Overall, research shows that people living in wealthier (and more democratic) countries tend to be happier. In general, poor people are less happy than others, although increments that exceed average amounts of income tend not be related to additional levels of happiness. A fair assessment of the relationship between money and happiness is that although money may not *guarantee* a long, happy, and healthy life, it most likely aids and abets it.

You Can't Take It with You

Whatever assets one has accumulated in life that remain at death represent a bulk estate. "Inheritance" is usually thought to refer to bequests of such estates. Because wealth itself is highly skewed, so are bequests from estates. Beyond personal belongings and items of perhaps sentimental value, most Americans at death have little or nothing to bequeath. There is no central accounting of small estates, so reliable estimates on the total number and size of estates bequeathed are difficult to come by. Only about 20 percent of all households reported having received a bequest (Wolff 2015, 3). And, as we have seen, even among the top wealth decile, wealth is highly skewed, so that "average" is likely highly skewed to a relatively small portion of very wealthy family fortunes receiving much larger sums. The wealthiest 20 percent of all Americans received 84 percent of all wealth transfers; the wealthiest 1 percent alone received 35 percent of all wealth transfers (Wolff 2015, 4). Economist and wealth researcher Edward Wolff (2015, 233) estimates that over a lifetime, about one-third of total American household wealth derives from inter vivos transfers; another one-third from bulk inheritance; and the remaining one-third from savings. In short, although few are likely to inherit great sums, bequests from estates are nevertheless a major mechanism for the transfer of wealth and privilege across generations (McNamee and Miller 1989, 1998; Miller, Rosenfeld, and McNamee 2003).

Some may argue that those who receive inheritances often deplete them in short order through spending sprees or unwise investments, and that the playing field levels naturally through merit or lack of it. Although this may occur in isolated cases, it is not the general pattern—at least among the superwealthy. Although taking risks may be an appropriate strategy for acquiring wealth, it is not a common one for maintaining wealth. Once secured, the common strategy for protecting wealth is to play it safe—to diversify holdings and make safe investments. The superwealthy often have teams of accountants, brokers, financial planners, and lawyers to "manage" portfolios for precisely this purpose. One of the common ways to prevent the quick spending down of inheritances is for benefactors to set up "bleeding trusts" or "spendthrift trusts," which provide interest income to beneficiaries without digging into the principal fund. Despite such efforts to protect wealth, estates may, in some families, be gradually diminished over generations through subdivision among descendants. The rate at which this occurs, however, is likely to be slow, especially given the combination among the wealthy of low birthrates and high rates of marriage within the same class. Even in the event of reckless spending, poor financial management, or subdivision among multiple heirs, the fact remains that those who inherit wealth benefit from it, and from opportunities that such wealth provides, for as long as it lasts, regardless of how personally meritorious they may or may not be.

WHAT IS IT LIKE TO BE RICH?

In his 1926 short story "The Rich Boy," F. Scott Fitzgerald wrote, "Let me tell you about the very rich. They are different from you and me." By the very rich, I mean the 1 percent or so of Americans who own over 40 percent of all the net worth in America. Most of the very rich either inherited their wealth outright, or converted modest wealth and privilege into larger fortunes. How different are they? By the sheer volume and type of capital owned, this group is set apart from other Americans. This group is further distinguished by common lifestyles, shared relationships, and a privileged position in society that produce a consciousness of kind (Domhoff 2014). In short, they are a class set apart in both economic and social terms.

Sociologist Lisa Keister (2014) has created a demographic profile of the wealthiest 1 percent of Americans. Compared to all households, the wealthiest 1 percent as measured by net worth are much more likely to be white (93 percent for the top 1 percent, compared to 67 percent for the bottom 90 percent of net worth holders), older (average age of the top 1 percent is sixty, compared to fifty for the bottom 90 percent of net worth holders), and male (98 percent of the top 1 percent of net worth holders, compared to 71 percent of the bottom 90 percent of net worth holders). Moreover, the top 1 percent of wealth holders are much more likely to be highly educated (with 86 percent having at least a college degree, compared to 27 percent of the bottom 90 percent of net worth holders with at least college degrees), and much more likely to have managerial or professional occupations (72 percent of the top 1 percent of net worth holders, compared to 24 percent of the bottom 90 percent of net worth holders).

Besides being almost exclusively white, the inner circle of the upper class has historically been predominantly Protestant and of Anglo-Saxon heritage. The acronym *WASP* (for white Anglo-Saxon Protestant) was first coined by sociologist E. Digby Baltzell, himself a member of the upper class, to describe its social composition. Although the upper class is gradually becoming less exclusively Protestant, especially with more recent and considerable upward mobility of Jews and Catholics with European backgrounds, there is still a strong association of the inner circle of upper-class status with those from particular establishment Protestant denominational backgrounds. Research has shown, for instance, that Episcopalians, Presbyterians, Unitarians, and Congregationalists continue to occupy the highest socioeconomic strata in America, while those from evangelical and fundamentalist Protestant denominations continue to occupy the lowest, just as they did in the colonial period nearly 250 years ago (Pyle and Davidson 2014). Beyond these demographic characteristics, how else are the rich different from most other Americans?

Exclusivity

An important defining characteristic of the upper class is that it is exclusive. Wealth in America is highly concentrated. Money alone, however, does not grant full admission into the highest of elite circles. Full acceptance requires the cultural capital and cachet that only "old money" brings. And "old money" means inherited money. The exclusiveness of old money is exemplified by the *Social Register*, a list of prominent upper-class families first compiled in 1887. The list has been used by members of the upper class both to recognize distinction and as a guide for issuing invitations to upper-class social events. For years separate volumes of the *Social Register* were published in different cities throughout the United States. But since the Malcolm Forbes family took over the publication in 1976, the *Social Register* has been consolidated into one national book. To be listed, a potential member must have five letters of nomination submitted by those already on the list, and not be "blackballed" by any current members.

There is great continuity across generations among the names included in these volumes. One study (Broad 1996), for instance, shows that of the eighty-seven prominent founders of family fortunes listed in the 1940 *Social Register*, 92 percent had descendants listed in the 1977 volume. The percentage of descendants of these prominent families included in the 1995 volume, fifty-five years later, dipped only slightly, to 87 percent. Highlighting connections to the past, almost half of those listed in 1995 attached Roman numerals to their surnames, such as II, III, IV, V, VI, and so on. Another common practice among upper-class families is to use maternal surnames as first names or middle names. The use of these "recombinant" names highlights connections to prominent families on both sides, as well as patterns of intraclass marriage. Almost 50 percent of those listed in 1995 had such recombinant names. Most social clubs of the upper class also show connections to the past—if only because they have been in existence for a long time and their membership shows intergenerational continuity (Domhoff 2014; Kendall 2008; Sherwood 2010).

It is not mere coincidence that the upper class has great reverence for the past. In a highly meritocratic culture, it is an ongoing challenge for those who inherit great wealth to justify their claim to it. The past, therefore, is a source of the justification of wealth for the upper class and a claim to status.

The children of the wealthy in America are not immune to the ideology of meritocracy that pervades the culture as a whole. Reconciling unearned inheritance of wealth in a culture that extols meritocracy poses a unique challenge for those who were born into wealth and privilege (Sherman 2017; Aldrich 1988; Forbes 2010; Schervish et al. 1994). As one inheritor of an oil fortune put it, "The feelings of guilt put me through much agony. For a long, long, long time, it gave me low self-esteem: who am I to deserve all of this good fortune?" (Schervish et al. 1994, 118). Unlike the children of European aristocrats who felt entitled to privilege as a matter of birthright, American inheritors of great wealth are victims of an ideology that, through no fault of their own, essentially invalidates them.

Isolation

In addition to exclusivity, the upper class in America is relatively anonymous and hidden from the public view. A second defining characteristic of the upper class in America is that it is isolated. The upper class is separated from the mainstream of society in a world of privacy: remote private residences, private schools, private clubs, private parties, and private resorts. With the exception of service staff, throughout their lives, upper-class individuals interact mostly with people like themselves. The geography of the upper class shows a distinct pattern of isolation, intentionally maintained and reinforced through land-use strategies that include incorporation, zoning, and restrictive land covenants (Higley 1995; Ganong and Shoag 2015). Houses and mansions are tucked away in exclusive communities. Individual residences within these communities, often with long and meandering driveways, are typically set back from the public roads that connect them with the larger world. Once approached, the residences are fortresses of security, complete with bridges, fences, gates, guard dogs, and sophisticated electronic surveillance. Children raised within these confines are isolated as well, separated from the outside world by a series of private nannies, private tutors, private preparatory boarding schools, and private elite Ivy League colleges. Even travel within the upper class is often isolated—in private planes and limos, and on private yachts. And even when resorting to more commercial forms of transportation, there is always the more isolated and pampered option of traveling "first class."

The upper-class tendency to isolate itself geographically from the rest of society has been emulated by the upper-middle classes. The overall trend in the past several decades has been toward increasing socioeconomic residential segregation in American society as a whole (Massey et al. 2009; Fry and Taylor 2012; Bischoff and Reardon 2014). The creation of white-flight suburbs in the post–World War II era began a trend that has now extended to the rising popularity of "gated" communities (Blakely and Snyder 1997; May 2017). Once restricted to the superwealthy and some retirement villages, gated communities are now for the merely privileged. One reason for this self-imposed isolation is security. Those who have more also have more to lose. Keeping potential criminals out, however, also has the effect of keeping the rich in.

Class Endogamy

One consequence of social and geographic isolation is high rates of class endogamy, or marriage within one's own social class. (Marriage and mobility is examined in greater detail in chapter 8.) Americans in general tend to marry roughly within their own social class (Carbone and Cahn 2014; Cherlin 2009, 2014; Gonalons-Pons and Schwartz 2017; Elmelech 2008; Mare 2016; Greenwood et al. 2014). Given the high level of geographic and social isolation of the upper class, upper-class endogamy is likely to be especially high. Traditional upper-class social institutions such as the debutante ball, at which young upper-class women are first "presented" to "society," certainly increase these probabilities. As sociologist Digby Baltzell put it, "The debutante ritual is a *rite de passage* which functions to introduce the post-adolescent into the upper-class adult world, and to insure upper-class endogamy as a normative pattern of behavior, in order to keep important functional class positions within the upper class" (1992, 60). Other upper-class institutions include elite boarding prep schools, elite social clubs, and elite summer resorts, all of which provide settings and organized activities that bring upper-class individuals together. Combining upper-class and upper-middle-class familial assets through marriage and then transferring those assets to children born into these families, in turn, increases existing levels of economic inequality and further solidifies nonmerit economic advantage across generations.

Distinctive Lifestyle

In the late nineteenth century, America entered the Gilded Age, so named for its opulent and even ostentatious displays of great wealth. During the Gilded Age the rich competed with one another to flaunt their wealth. During this time, some of the great mansions were built, including George Vanderbilt's Biltmore Estate in Asheville, North Carolina, a 175,000-square-foot, 250-room, Renaissance-style chateau completed in 1895, and still the largest private house ever built in America (Frank 1999, 14). In some ways, America's wealthy of this period were insecure about their status and were envious of the more established European aristocracy. As a result, the newfound industrial wealth in the United States patterned itself after everything old and European. With the Great Depression, such displays were no longer considered in good taste. In subsequent decades, more subdued forms of luxury were preferred. Nevertheless, a lifestyle organized around formal parties, exclusive resorts and clubs, and such upper-class leisure activities as golf, tennis, horseback riding, and yachting persisted.

Some segments of the upper class indulge themselves as patrons of the arts—theater, opera, orchestra, and other highbrow forms of cultural consumption. The wealthy have always been able to indulge in various forms of material conspicuous consumption, including luxury cars, boats, and homes. Evidence suggests that the wealthy are also increasingly spending less on conspicuous material acquisitions and more on less conspicuous, quality-of-life investments in education, health care, child care, and retirement, in ways that are likely to extend their existing social, cultural, and economic advantages over time and across generations (Currid-Halkett 2017). It should be noted, however, that the rich are not all alike in their consumption behavior. One of the advantages of being rich is that you can choose to display wealth ostentatiously, or crassly, or not at all. For the most part, however, the lifestyles of the wealthy set them apart as a distinct social class.

Political Power

In a substantial sense, the upper class in America is also a ruling class. Despite the ideology of democracy in which everyone has an equal say in deciding what happens, the reality is that those who have the most economic resources wield the most power. In *Gospels of Wealth: How the Rich Portray Their Lives*, sociologists Paul Schervish, Platon Coutsoukis, and Ethan Lewis describe the power of the wealthy to make things happen (and other things not happen) as "hyperagency."

To the extent that it is possible to convert wealth into political power, the upper class can exert influence on political outcomes far beyond their numbers alone. The specific mechanisms by which this influence is exerted are well documented (Bartels 2016; Page and Gilens 2017; Domhoff 2014; Gilens 2012; Hacker and Pierson 2010; Potter and Penniman 2017; Phillips 2003). Moreover, the influence of money in American politics appears to be increasing, especially since the 2010 *Citizens United* US Supreme Court decision, allowing organizational entities such as corporations to make unlimited contributions to political campaigns. Much of this money is so-called dark money (Mayer 2017) that comes from unnamed sources. To the extent that government policy is for sale to the highest bidder and sources of influence are not identified, America functions more in practice as a plutocracy than a democracy. Beyond direct forms of influence such as substantial campaign contributions and holding government positions, economic elites exert indirect, but no less important, forms of influence through the corporate community, a policy-planning network comprising foundations, think tanks, and lobbies, and the media—all of which are dominated by propertied interests. For all of the key measures of political power as identified by Domhoff (2014)—who decides policy, who wins in disputes, and who benefits from political outcomes—the interests of the wealthy usually prevail.

It should be pointed out, however, that the upper class is not a political monolith. That is, as with all groups, there are always internal differences of opinion. On the estate tax issue, for instance, several very prominent members of the upper class—including Bill Gates and Warren Buffett—have been outspoken critics of proposals to abolish estate taxes. Both maintain that it is entirely appropriate for the government to heavily tax recipients of large estates as a form of unearned income, and both plan to give the bulk of their accumulated fortunes to charitable causes rather than bequeath them to heirs. Similarly, there are other members of the upper class who advocate for more equitable distribution of societal resources, including groups such as Responsible Wealth, Wealth for the Common Good, Business for Shared Prosperity, and Patriotic Millionaires (Collins 2016, 218).

The power of the upper class, while considerable, falls short of complete control. Labor unions, civil rights groups, women's rights groups, consumer groups, environmental groups, and others chip away at the edges of the system of privilege on behalf of their constituencies. But in the final analysis, although these groups and the general public as a whole win some of the battles, propertied interests continue to win the class wars. As financier Warren Buffett noted in response to those who question the fairness of the system as "class warfare," "There's class warfare, all right, but it's my class, the rich class, that's making war, and we're winning" (*New York Times* 2006).

SUMMARY

The United States has high levels of both income inequality and wealth inequality. In terms of the distribution of income and wealth, America is clearly not a middle-class society. Income and especially wealth are not evenly distributed, with a relatively small number of well-off families at one end and a small number of poor families much worse off at the other. Instead, the overall picture is one in which the bulk of the available wealth is concentrated in a narrow range at the very top of the system. In short, the distribution of economic resources in society is not symmetrical and certainly not bell-shaped: The poor, who have the least, greatly outnumber the rich, who have the most. Moreover, in recent decades, by all measures, the rich are getting richer, and the gap between the very rich and everyone else has appreciably increased.

The greater the amount of economic inequality in society, the more difficult it is to move up within the system on the basis of individual merit alone. Indeed, the most important factor in terms of where people will end up in the economic pecking order of society is where they started in the first place. Economic inequality has tremendous inertial force across generations. Instead of a race to get ahead that begins anew with each generation, the race is in reality a relay race in which children inherit different starting points from parents. Inheritance—broadly defined as one's initial starting point in life based on parental position—includes a set of cumulative nonmerit advantages for all except the poorest of the poor. These include enhanced childhood standards of living, differential access to cultural capital, differential access to social networks of power and influence, infusion of parental capital while parents are still alive, insulation against downward mobility, greater health and life expectancy, and the inheritance of bulk estates when parents die.

At the top of the system are members of America's ownership class—roughly the 1 percent of the American population who own about one-third of all the available net worth. The upper class is set apart from other Americans not only by the amount and source of the wealth it holds, but also by an isolated, exclusive, distinctive, and self-perpetuating way of life that reduces opportunities for merit-based mobility within it.

The nonmerit advantages of inheritance begin at birth and typically extend throughout the life course. In the next chapter, I discuss the nonmerit advantages of social and cultural capital, the acquisition of which typically begins to accrue early in childhood for those born into more privileged familial backgrounds.

REFERENCES

Aldrich, Nelson W., Jr. 1988. *Old Money: The Mythology of America's Upper Class*. New York: Knopf.

Alexander, Karl, Doris Entwisle, and Linda Olson. 2014. *The Long Shadow: Family Background, Disadvantaged Urban Youth, and the Transition to Adulthood*. New York: Russell Sage Foundation.

Baltzell, E. Digby. 1992. *The Philadelphia Gentlemen: The Making of a National Upper Class*. New Brunswick, NJ: Transaction.

Bartels, Larry. 2016. *Unequal Democracy: The Political Economy of the New Gilded Age*. New York: Russell Sage Foundation.

Bischoff, Kendra, and Sean F. Reardon. 2014. "Residential Segregation by Income, 1970–2009." In *Diversity and Disparities: America Enters a New Century*, ed. John R. Logan, 228–33. New York: Russell Sage Foundation.

Blakely, Edward J., and Mary Gail Snyder. 1997. *Fortress America: Gated Communities in the United States*. Washington, DC: Brookings Institute.

Bosworth, Barry, Gary Burless, and Kan Zhang. 2016. "Later Retirement, Inequality in Old Age, and the Growing Gap in Longevity between Rich and Poor." Washington, DC: Brookings Institute. www.brookings.edu/wp-content/uploads/2016/02/BosworthBurtlessZhang_retirementinequalitylongevity_012815.pdf (accessed May 25, 2017).

Broad, David. 1996. "The Social Register: Directory of America's Upper Class." *Sociological Spectrum* 16:173–81.

Brulle, Robert J., and David N. Pellow. 2006. "Environmental Justice: Human Health and Environmental Inequalities." *Annual Review of Public Health* 27:102–24.

Budrys, Grace. 2017. *Unequal Health: How Inequality Contributes to Health or Illness*. 3rd ed. Lanham, MD: Rowman & Littlefield.

Carbone, June, and Naomi Cahn. 2014. *Marriage Markets: How Inequality Is Remaking the American Family*. New York: Oxford University Press.

Cherlin, Andrew J. 2009. *The Marriage-Go-Round: The State of Marriage and the Family in America Today*. New York: Vintage.

———. 2014. *Labor's Love Lost: The Rise and Fall of the Working Class Family in America*. New York: Russell Sage Foundation.

Cherlin, Andrew, Caitlin Cross-Barnet, Linda M. Burton, and Raymond Garrett-Peters. 2008. "Promises They Can Keep: Low-Income Women's Attitudes toward Motherhood, Marriage, and Divorce." *Journal of Marriage and Family* 70 (4):919–33.

Chetty, Raj, David Grusky, Maximilian Hell, Nathaniel Hendren, Robert Manduca, and Jimmy Narang. 2017. "The Fading of the American Dream: Trends in Absolute Income Mobility since 1940." *Science* 24 (April): 1–15.

Chetty, Raj, Michael Stepner, Sarah Abraham, Shelby Lin, Benjamin Scuderi, Nicholas Turner, Austin Bergeron, and David Cutler. 2016. "The Association between Income and Life Expectancy in the United States, 2001–2014." *Journal of the American Medical Association* 315(16):1750–66.

Cieslik, Mark. 2017. *The Happiness Riddle and the Quest for a Good Life*. London: Springer.

Cockerham, William. 2016. *Medical Sociology*. 13th ed. New York: Routledge.

———. 2017. *Sociology of Mental Disorder*. 10th ed. New York: Routledge.

Collins, Chuck. 2016. *Born on Third Base: A One-Percenter Makes the Case for Tracking Inequality, Bringing Wealth Home, and Committing to the Common Good.* White River Junction, VT: Chelsea Green Publishing.

Currid-Halkett, Elizabeth. 2017. *The Sum of Small Things: A Theory of the Aspirational Class.* Princeton, NJ: Princeton University Press.

Domhoff, G. William. 2014. *Who Rules America? The Triumph of the Corporate Rich.* New York: McGraw-Hill.

Duncan, Greg J., and Richard J. Murnane, eds. 2011. "Introduction: The American Dream, Then and Now." In *Whither Opportunity? Rising Inequality, Schools, and Children's Life Chances,* 3–23. New York: Sage.

Easterlin, Richard. 2010. *Happiness, Growth, and the Life Cycle.* Oxford: Oxford University Press.

Edin, Kathryn, and Maria Kefalas. 2005. *Promises I Can Keep: Why Poor Women Put Motherhood before Marriage.* Los Angeles: University of California Press.

Elmelech, Yuval. 2008. *Transmitting Inequality: Wealth and the American Family.* Lanham, MD: Rowman & Littlefield.

Ermisch, John, Markus Jantti, and Timothy Smeeding. 2012. *From Parents to Children: The Intergenerational Transmission of Advantage.* New York: Sage.

Forbes, John Hazard. 2010. *Old Money America: Aristocracy in the Age of Obama.* New York: iUniverse.

Frank, Robert H. 1999. *Luxury Fever: Why Money Fails to Satisfy in an Era of Excess.* New York: Free Press.

———. 2007. *Richistan: A Journey through the American Wealth Boom and the Lives of the New Rich.* New York: Crown.

Freeland, Chrystia. 2012. *Plutocrats: The Rise of the New Global Super-Rich and the Fall of Everyone Else.* New York: Penguin.

Frey, Bruno S., and Alois Stutzer. 2002. *Happiness and Economics: How the Economy and Institutions Affect Well-Being.* Princeton, NJ: Princeton University Press.

Friedman, Hilary Levey. 2013. *Playing to Win: Raising Children in a Competitive Culture.* Berkeley: University of California Press.

Fry, Richard. 2016. "For the First Time in Modern Era, Living with Parents Edges Out Other Living Arrangements for 18- to 34-Year-Olds." Washington, DC: Pew Research Center. www.pewsocialtrends.org/2016/05/24/for-first-time-in-modern-era-living-with-parents-edges-out-other-living-arrangements-for-18-to-34-year-olds/ (accessed May 25, 2017).

Fry, Richard, and Paul Taylor. 2012. "The Rise of Residential Segregation by Income." Washington, DC: Pew Research Center. www.pewsocialtrends.org/2012/08/01/the-rise-of-residential-segregation-by-income/ (accessed May 23, 2017).

Ganong, Peter, and Daniel Shoag. 2015. "Why Has Regional Income Convergence in the U.S. Declined?" Working Paper. Harvard University. https://scholar.harvard.edu/files/shoag/files/why_has_regional_income_convergence_in_the_us_declined_01.pdf (accessed May 23, 2017).

Gilens, Martin. 2012. *Affluence and Influence: Economic Inequality and Political Power in America.* Princeton, NJ: Princeton University Press.

Gonalons-Pons, Pilar, and Christine R. Schwartz. 2017. "Trends in Economic Homogamy: Sorting into Marriage or Changes in the Division of Paid Labor?" *Demography* 54(3): 985–1005.

Greenwood, Jeremy, Nezih Guner, Georgi Kocharkov, and Cezar Santos. 2014. "Marry Your Like: Assortative Mating and Income Inequality." *American Economic Review* 104(5):348–53.

Grusky, David B., and Tamar Kricheli-Katz, eds. 2012. *The New Gilded Age: The Critical Inequality Debates of Our Time.* Stanford, CA: Stanford University Press.

Hacker, Jacob S., and Paul Pierson. 2010. *Winner-Take-All Politics: How Washington Made the Rich Richer—and Turned Its Back on the Middle Class.* New York: Simon & Schuster.

Higley, Stephen R. 1995. *Privilege, Power and Place: The Geography of the American Upper Class.* Lanham, MD: Rowman & Littlefield.

Keister, Lisa A. 2014. 2011. *Faith and Money.* Cambridge: Cambridge University Press.

———. 2014. "The One Percent." *Annual Review of Sociology* 40:16.1–16.21.

Kendall, Diana. 2008. *Members Only: Elite Clubs and the Process of Exclusion.* Lanham, MD: Rowman & Littlefield.

Kornrich, Sabino. 2016. "Inequalities in Parental Spending on Young Children: 1972–2010." *AERA Open* 2(2): 1–12.

Kornrich, Sabino, and Frank Furstenberg. 2013. "Investing in Children: Changes in Parental Spending on Children, 1972–2007." *Demography* 50:1–23.

Kraus, Michael W. 2015. "Americans Still Overestimate Social Mobility: A Pre-Registered Self-Replication." *Frontiers in Psychology* 6 (November):1–5.

Kraus, Michael W., and Jacinth J. X. Tan. 2015. "Americans Overestimate Social Class Mobility." *Journal of Experimental Social Psychology* 58:101–11.

Lareau, Annette. 2011. *Unequal Childhoods: Class, Race, and Family Life.* 2nd ed. Berkeley: University of California Press.

Layard, Richard. 2005. *Happiness: Lessons from a New Science.* London: Allen Lane.

Mare, Robert D. 2016. "Educational Homogamy in Two Gilded Ages: Evidence from Intergenerational Social Mobility Data." *Annals* 663:117–39.

Massey, Douglas S., Jonathan Rothwell, and Thurston Domina. 2009. "The Changing Bases of Segregation in the United States." *Annals of the American Academy of Political and Social Science* 626:74–90.

May, Elaine Tyler. 2017. *Fortress America: How We Embraced Fear and Abandoned Democracy.* New York: Basic Books.

Mayer, Jane. 2017. *Dark Money: The Hidden History of the Billionaires behind the Rise of the Radical Right.* New York: Anchor Books.

McNamee, Stephen J., and Robert K. Miller, Jr. 1989. "Estate Inheritance: A Sociological Lacuna." *Sociological Inquiry* 38:7–29.

———. 1998. "Inheritance and Stratification." In *Inheritance and Wealth in America,* ed. Robert K. Miller, Jr., and Stephen J. McNamee, 193–213. New York: Plenum Press.

Miller, Robert K., Jr., Jeffrey Rosenfeld, and Stephen J. McNamee. 2003. "The Disposition of Property: Transfers between the Living and the Dead." In *Handbook of Death and Dying,* ed. Clifton D. Bryant, 917–25. Thousand Oaks, CA: Sage.

Mishel, Lawrence, and Jessica Shieder. 2016. "CEOs Make 276 Times More Than Typical Workers." Economic Policy Institute. Washington, DC. www.epi.org/publication/ceos-make-276-times-more-than-typical-workers/ (accessed September 27, 2017).

Mitnik, Pablo, and David Grusky. 2015. *Economic Mobility in the United States.* New York: Pew Charitable Trusts. www.pewtrusts.org/~/media/assets/2015/07/fsm-irs-report_artfinal.pdf (accessed May 25, 2017).

Moynihan, Daniel Patrick, Timothy M. Smeeding, and Lee Rainwater. 2004. *The Future of the Family.* New York: Sage.

National Center for Health Statistics. 2016. "Health, United States, 2015: With Special Feature on Racial and Ethnic Health Disparities." Hyattsville, MD: US Department of Health and Human Resources.

New York Times. 2006. As quoted in an interview reported in "In Class Warfare, Guess Which Class Is Winning," by Ben Stein, November 26, 2006. www.nytimes.com/2006/11/26/business/yourmoney/26every.html (accessed August 30, 2012).

Norton, Michael I., and Dan Ariely. 2011. "Building a Better America: One Wealth Quintile at a Time." *Perspectives on Psychological Science* 6(9):9–12.

Page, Benjamin, and Martin Gilens. 2017. *Democracy in America? What Has Gone Wrong and What We Can Do About It.* Chicago: University of Chicago Press.

Pew Research Center. 2012. "Pursuing the American Dream: Economic Mobility across Generations." Washington, DC: Pew Research Center. www.pewtrusts.org/-/media/legacy/uploadedfiles/wwwpewtrustsorg/reports/economic_mobility/pursuingamericandreampdf.pdf (accessed May 25, 2017).

Phillips, Kevin. 2003. *Wealth and Democracy: A Political History of the American Rich.* New York: Random House.

Piketty, Thomas. 2014. *Capital in the Twenty-First Century.* Cambridge, MA: Harvard University Press.

Piketty, Thomas, Emmanuel Saez, and Gabriel Zucman. 2016. "Distributional National Accounts: Method and Estimates for the United States." Working Paper 22945. Cambridge, MA: National Bureau of Economic Research.

Potter, Wendell, and Nick Penniman. 2017. *Nation on the Take: How Big Money Corrupts Democracy and What to Do About It.* New York: Bloomsbury Press.

Putnam, Robert D. 2015. *Our Kids: The American Dream in Crisis.* New York: Simon & Schuster.

Pyle, Ralph E., and James D. Davidson. 2014. "Social Reproduction and Religious Stratification." In *Religion and Inequality in America: Research and Theory on Religion's Role in Stratification,* ed. Lisa A. Keister and Darren E. Sherkat, 195–218. New York: Cambridge University Press.

Rosenfeld, Jeffrey P. 1980. *Legacy of Aging: Inheritance and Disinheritance in Social Perspective.* Norwood, NJ: ABLEX.

Saez, Emmanuel. 2016. "Striking It Rich; The Evolution of Top Incomes in the United States." https://eml.berkeley.edu/-saez/saez-UStopincomes-2013.pdf (accessed April 21, 2017).

Saez, Emmanuel, and Gabriel Zucman. 2016. "Wealth Inequality in the United States since 1913: Evidence from Capitalized Income Tax Data." *Quarterly Journal of Economics* 131 (2): 519–78.

Schervish, Paul G., Platon E. Coutsoukis, and Ethan Lewis. 1994. *Gospels of Wealth: How the Rich Portray Their Lives.* Westport, CT: Praeger.

Schwartz, T. P. 1996. "Durkheim's Prediction about the Declining Importance of the Family and Inheritance: Evidence from the Wills of Providence, 1775–1985." *Sociological Quarterly* 26:503–19.

Shapiro, Thomas M. 2017. *Toxic Inequality: How America's Wealth Gap Destroys Mobility, Deepens the Racial Divide, and Threatens Our Culture.* New York: Basic Books.

Sherman, Rachel. 2017. *Uneasy Street: The Anxieties of Affluence*. Princeton, NJ: Princeton University Press.

Sherwood, Jessica Holden. 2010. *Wealth, Whiteness, and the Matrix of Privilege: The View from the Country Club*. Lanham, MD: Rowman & Littlefield.

Smeeding, Timothy, Robert Erikson, and Markus Jantti, eds. 2011. *Persistence, Privilege and Parenting: The Comparative Study of Intergenerational Mobility*. New York: Sage.

Stiglitz, Joseph E. 2012. *The Price of Inequality: How Today's Divided Society Endangers Our Future*. New York: W. W. Norton.

Urahn, Susan K., Erin Currier, Diana Elliott, Lauren Wechsler, Denise Wilson, and Daniel Colbert. 2012. "Pursing the American Dream: Economic Mobility Across Generations." Pew Research Center, Washington, D.C. http://www.pewtrusts.org/~/media/legacy/up loadedfiles/pcs_assets/2012/pursuingamericandreampdf.pdf (accessed May 25, 2017).

US Congressional Budget Office. 2016. "Trends in Family Wealth, 1989–2013. www.cbo .gov/publication/51846 (accessed April 24, 2017).

US Department of Labor. 2016. "National Census of Fatal Occupational Injuries in 2015." Bureau of Labor Statistics. www.bls.gov/news.release/pdf/cfoi.pdf (accessed May 17, 2017).

Wilkinson, Richard, and Kate Pickett. 2009. *The Spirit Level: Why Greater Equality Makes Societies Stronger*. New York: Bloomsbury Press.

Willenbacher, Barbara. 2003. "Individualism and Traditionalism in Inheritance Law in Germany, France, England, and the United States." *Journal of Family History* 28 (1):208–25.

Wolff, Edward. 2014. "Household Wealth Trends in the United States, 1962–2013: What Happened over the Great Recession?" Working Paper 20733. Cambridge, MA: National Bureau of Economic Research. www.nber.org/papers/w20733 (accessed May 25, 2017).

———. 2015. *Inheriting Wealth in America: Future Boom or Bust?* Oxford: Oxford University Press.

Zissimopoulos, Julie M., and James P. Smith. 2011. "Unequal Giving: Monetary Gifts to Children across Countries and over Time." In *Persistence, Privilege and Parenting: The Comparative Study of Intergenerational Mobility*, ed. Timothy Smeeding, Robert Erikson, and Markus Jantti, 289–328. New York: Sage.

Zucman, Gabriel. 2016. "Wealth Inequality." In *Pathways: The Poverty and Inequality Report, 2016*, 39–44. Stanford Center on Poverty and Inequality. http://inequality.stanford. edu/sites/default/files/Pathways-SOTU-2016-Wealth-Inequality-3.pdf (accessed April 21, 2017).

Zweigenhaft, Richard L., and G. William Domhoff. 2006. *Diversity in the Power Elite: How It Happened, Why It Matters*. New York: Rowman & Littlefield.

4

It's Not What You Know But . . .

Social and Cultural Capital

It's not what you know but whom you know.

—Anonymous

Social capital refers essentially to "who" you know, which is another type of non-merit resource that individuals can exploit to advance their position in society. All individuals are embedded in networks of social relations; that is, everybody knows somebody. Social capital focuses attention on differential access to opportunities through social connections. Individual and family social connections mediate access to educational, occupational, and economic opportunity.

Cultural capital refers to knowledge of the norms, values, beliefs, and ways of life of the groups to which people belong. It is information, often esoteric, specialized, costly, and time-consuming to accumulate, that, like social capital, mediates access to opportunity. It is a factor in social mobility, because as people move into different segments of society, they need to acquire the cultural wherewithal to travel in different social circles. In essence, cultural capital is a set of cultural credentials that certify eligibility for membership in status-conferring social groups. To "fit in" and "look and know the part" is to possess cultural capital; to "stick out like a sore thumb" is to be without the cultural cachet necessary to blend in and be fully accepted into groups to which we belong or aspire to belong.

In this chapter these forms of capital and how they are related are discussed. The related phenomenon of social climbing—or deliberate attempts to enhance one's social standing by accumulating and conspicuously displaying particular forms of social or cultural capital—is also examined.

SOCIAL CAPITAL: "WHO" YOU KNOW

Anyone who has ever filled out a job application knows that whom you know matters. Almost all job applications have a space for "references." References not only provide testimony to an applicant's character and ability, but they also signal a connection to the applicant. Apart from the merit of the candidate, applicants whose references are well known, prestigious, or powerful have an advantage over applicants whose references are none of those things. In some cases, an employer's interest in a job candidate may reflect the merit of the applicant's references rather than that of the candidate. Particularly in the professions, but also in other jobs, mentor–protégé relationships are critical—not just for training but, when the time comes, for job placement as well. Good mentors go to bat for their protégés and often risk their own stock of prestige and credibility to do so. Whom you know may become especially important when the quality of candidates is unknown or indistinguishable, which for neophytes just starting out with little or no track record is often the case.

Another indication of the importance of social contacts is that increasingly, career advisors urge job seekers to devote time to establishing professional relationships. Universities encourage students to cultivate close professional relationships with their professors, advisors, and peers and to seek out internships with potential employers, not just as a way to gain practical experience, but also as a way to get an "inside track" for future employment. Students are also encouraged to use social media sites to further expand and utilize their social connections. For instance, LinkedIn, a social networking site specifically designed to connect people with similar career or professional interests, has exploded in growth since its founding in 2003, and now has more than 460 million registered members worldwide, including over 133 million in the United States (LinkedIn 2017).

One of the first systematic modern analyses of social capital was produced in the 1980s by the French sociologist Pierre Bourdieu (1986). Bourdieu focused attention on the benefits that accrue to individuals from their participation in groups, and deliberate attempts by individuals to foster social relations for the purpose of creating this resource. Strategies that produce valuable social capital are not directly an indication or reflection of individual merit, especially in cases in which investments are made by others (e.g., parents, friends, or mentors). James S. Coleman (1988), an American sociologist, has also contributed much to the understanding of social capital and the examination of its effects. Coleman emphasizes the point that social capital is not a characteristic of people, but is embedded in relations among people.

One reason that social capital is dependent on the larger social context in which it occurs is that neither of its critical components, resources or access, is distributed evenly. For resources such as "insider information" to be converted into social capital, individuals must perceive that some specific resource is present within their social field and have some form of social relationship that provides access to that resource. Individuals can thus be said to have social capital when resources are present and accessible.

a relatively restricted variety of information and influence. They tend to use local ties, strong ties, and family and kin ties. Since these ties are usually homogeneous in resources, this networking tendency reinforces poor social capital. People in higher socioeconomic groups tend to be embedded in resource-rich networks characterized by relative richness, not only in quantity but also in kind—resource heterogeneity (Lin 1982, 2000; Lin and Erickson 2008; Lin and Dumin 1986; Campbell et al. 1986).

Numerous studies have shown how social connections utilized by whites have kept racial minorities out, or severely constrained their chances for occupational placement (Parks-Yancy 2006; Stainback 2008; McDonald and Elder 2006; McDonald and Day 2010; McDonald et al. 2009; McDonald et al. 2016; Massey 2007). Ultimately, such informal networks reduce organizational efficiency, since applicants who are otherwise qualified for positions are never considered. The lack of social connections or truncated networks in areas of concentrated poverty, such as inner cities, contributes to occupational problems for their inhabitants (Wilson and Portes 1980; Wilson 1987, 1996; Massey 2007). This problem is compounded by the departure of middle-class families from black inner-city areas, which has depleted the social capital of the remaining population, and contributed to high levels of unemployment and welfare dependency (Wacquant and Wilson 1989; Wilson 1987, 1996).

Women, likewise, have also historically confronted restricted access to privileged social networks, sometimes derisively referred to as "the old boys network," which has contributed to a "glass ceiling" of limited (nonmerit) opportunities for occupational placement and advancement (McDonald 2011; McDonald et al. 2009; McDonald and Mair 2010; McDonald and Day 2010; Grugulis and Stoyanova 2012; Lutter 2015). The process of this restriction is often subtle and can come in many forms. Women in business settings, for instance, may be restricted from inner male sanctums such as the golf course, the racquetball court, the bar, the poker game, or other arenas of mostly male interaction in which insider information is shared and business deals are often cut outside of "official" work environments. Women, especially professional women, are also systematically disadvantaged with respect to senior mentors—as previously mentioned, a critical social capital resource, especially for those just starting out. Although women are now entering professions such as medicine, law, and the professoriate at rates that are close to parity with men, those who occupy the senior positions in the professions (judges, senior partners, full professors, chief surgeons, etc.) are overwhelmingly men, in part because so few women entered those professions a mere generation ago. Senior professional men are often reluctant to take on younger professional female protégés, and younger professional females are likewise reluctant to cultivate ties with senior professional men. Younger professional women especially are at a systematic (nonmerit) disadvantage when it comes to accessing valuable information that could be imparted to them by those in their professions with the most experience, and in accessing the most critical professional resources, such as sponsorship for assignments, positions, promotions, and the like.

One of the consequences of restricted access to privileged social capital for some groups more than others is that over time, privileged groups tend to replicate their own social and demographic profile. If new positions are filled directly through contacts or where social connectedness is critical (such as through referrals or letters of reference), then the effective pool of eligibles for consideration is likely to be disproportionately drawn from the same social profile as those already occupying such positions. That is, the pools will likely replicate the same social milieu of those doing the hiring, since people tend to associate with people like themselves, which tends to further reinforce and extend existing inequalities. Unwitting or unintentional exclusion of some—which comes from the well-known tendency of individuals to associate primarily with people like themselves, as opposed to intentional discrimination—has been termed implicit bias. That the resulting discrimination was unintended, however, would be of small comfort to someone who has been passed over for consideration of job placement or promotion because of such implicit bias.

Since access to social networks is so critical for job placement, and since such access has historically been an effective basis for exclusion (both intended and unintended), most public institutions now require that job openings for any permanent position must be publicly advertised. Moreover, in those job announcements, there is often an explicit EOC (Equal Opportunity Employer) statement expressly encouraging previously excluded groups, such as women and minorities, to apply. Such efforts to reduce the nonmeritocratic effects of social capital, however, are still the exception rather than the rule, since most employment occurs in private settings where such efforts are typically not required or implemented.

Nepotism

The most blatant form of advantage through social capital is nepotism, often defined as the undue preference for close kin or friends where open merit-based competition should prevail. The beneficiaries of nepotism possess social capital—parents, siblings, other close kin, and friends—that is activated on their behalf, and is quite independent of their individual merit or qualifications. In *In Praise of Nepotism: A Natural History* (2003), Adam Bellow (son of famous author and Nobel laureate Saul Bellow) argues that nepotism has a biological basis (enhancing chances for survival by maximizing inclusive fitness). According to Bellow, nepotism is based on the "natural" preference for close kin, and is found in one form or another in all human societies. He emphasizes that America is no exception. Despite its meritocratic ideology, nepotism is as American as apple pie, has been endemic throughout its history, and is actually resurgent in a new form that he calls the "new nepotism." Bellow documents the pervasiveness of nepotism in America from colonial times to the present, correctly pointing out that many exemplars of the "self-made man" were in fact beneficiaries of significant nepotism.

For the privileged, nepotism provides considerable advantage and is an important means by which privilege is transferred from one generation to the next, enabling the formation of dynasties of wealth and power. For the privileged, nepotism takes the form of essentially unearned access to high appointive or elective office, as well as to high-income and high-authority occupations. Nepotism operates in all social classes, but potential benefits decline as one moves down the social-class ladder. Thus, members of the working class are also recipients of nepotism, but its payoffs are less valuable simply because the working class tends to have lower social capital. Nepotism in the working class tends to be limited to access to apprenticeships, unions, or the more "desirable" working-class occupations.

One of Bellow's least-compelling arguments is that the "new nepotism" in America is compatible with principles of merit. Bellow contends that although one might initially secure a position through nepotism, today the recipient must continually display merit to keep the position, often working harder to demonstrate competence, and hence, worthiness. The problem with this line of reasoning is that although nepotism and meritocracy can coexist in a social system, they ultimately represent zero-sum principles of distribution. That is, the more nepotism operates, the less merit operates, and no nuanced argument can escape this fundamental contradiction. The initial advantage of placement, for instance, is a crucial one that summarily denies others access to opportunity regardless of their level of merit. Further, contrary to Bellow's argument, there is precious little evidence that the beneficiaries of nepotism display self-consciousness about the nonmerit basis of their opportunity or express feelings of "unworthiness." Instead, they are effectively socialized to expect to receive and to manage differential opportunity. They tend to "get the benefit of the doubt" and operate in what might be called a "climate of positive expectations" that produces self-fulfilling prophecies that legitimate the nepotism.

Despite Bellow's endorsement of the supposed advantages of nepotism, most public as well as some private employers expressly forbid hiring relatives, or at least highly circumscribe the conditions under which this can occur. Even when the hiring of relatives is permitted, the usual rule is that anyone in the employing organization who is related to any job prospect must recuse themselves from the decision to hire. Antinepotism rules also usually forbid relatives in the same employing organization from having any supervisory or evaluative role over someone with whom they are related on the grounds that such activity would create a "conflict of interest," or even "the appearance of a conflict of interest."

CULTURAL CAPITAL: FITTING IN

The importance of something is sometimes most dramatically revealed by its absence. The lack of cultural capital, for instance, has been the gist of several classic comic moments on film. The musical comedy *My Fair Lady* is about the efforts—on a bet—of a stuffy professor played by Rex Harrison to coach a young London Cockney girl played by Audrey Hepburn to "pass" as a British socialite. A similar theme is at work in the popular American film *Pretty Woman*, in which a wealthy businessman played by Richard Gere befriends a prostitute played by Julia Roberts, who, with some crash-course coaching from the manager of the Beverly Hills Wilshire Hotel, attempts, with limited success, to "pass" as his dignified and refined escort. In one particularly revealing restaurant scene, Julia Roberts's character begins to eat the salad at the beginning of the dinner, only to be told that the salad comes at the end of the meal. Her exasperated response, "But that is the fork I knew!" exposes her lack of cultural capital. The lack of cultural capital is especially sharply drawn in the 1960s TV show *The Beverly Hillbillies*. In this situation comedy, a family of Tennessee hillbillies becomes instant millionaires. Although the hillbillies were portrayed as having enormous sums of economic capital, they were without upper-class cultural capital, and wildly out of place among the rich and famous in Beverly Hills. These are, of course, exaggerated and fictionalized accounts, but they serve to illustrate what sociologists refer to as "cultural capital" (Lewin 2005).

Social inequality is not just about wealth and power, but about culture as well. Claims that one group's culture ranks higher in social standing than another's can be based on almost anything—tastes in music, leisure, food, fashion—in short, anything that creates invidious status distinctions (Steinhauer 2005; Weber 1968; Veblen 1953). What is required is a claim of superiority and getting others to accede to it. Bourdieu (1986) has explored this dimension of inequality at length. For Bourdieu, cultural capital is cultural property, or, more specifically, the possession of knowledge and artifacts associated with groups. The source of cultural capital is located in, and transmitted through, what Bourdieu calls habitus—the whole panoply of practices, dispositions, and tastes that organizes an individual's participation within the culture of a group.

Acquiring Cultural Capital

The process of acquiring culture requires an investment of time and effort. Knowledge of a group's way of life cannot be transmitted instantaneously by gift or bequest, purchase, or exchange. It is acquired over time through the process of socialization. In this sense, it is a form of hereditary transmission that is heavily disguised. Indeed, the transmission of cultural capital through socialization is the most valuable hidden form of hereditary transmission of privilege (Kendall 2002, 2008). Because the social conditions of its transmission and acquisition are more disguised than those of economic capital, it is likely to be unrecognized as a form of inherited capital, and is instead claimed as individual competence. That is, the possession of cultural capital is generally claimed as "evidence" of individual merit, while its fundamental dependence on differential opportunities for its inheritance goes unrecognized. Cultural capital, therefore, receives proportionately greater weight in the justification of privilege (presumed merit) because more direct and visible forms of transmission (e.g., inheritance of economic capital) tend to be more strongly censored and controlled (e.g., getting something for nothing). Like other forms of capital, its value is based on the fact that not everyone possesses it. The logic of scarcity secures material and symbolic advantages for those who possess it. That is, any given cultural competence derives a scarcity value from its position in the distribution of cultural capital and yields profits of distinction for its owner (e.g., being able to read in a world of illiterates).

Research suggests that parents may influence children's cultural capital in three ways: Children may acquire cultural skills "frictionlessly" by living in a home where parents possess considerable prestigious cultural capital; they may acquire it effort-lessly in their friends' homes, whether or not their own parents are so oriented; or parents may invest strategically in cultural goods to improve their children's life chances (Mohr and DiMaggio 1995, 179). Middle-class or even working-class par-ents, for instance, may consciously invest in exposing their children to prestigious forms of cultural capital beyond their own level of cultural capital, and often even beyond their own economic means to do so, through study-abroad experiences, en-richment camps, music lessons, and the like. What is more, young adults may seek out cultural capital to escape their socioeconomic origins or to reject that which their family has provided. As opposed to the frictionless means of absorbing the culture one was initially socialized into, acquiring prestigious social or cultural capital from the outside is a much more daunting and difficult task.

Sociologist Annette Lareau (2000, 2003) convincingly demonstrates the numer-ous ways in which family–school connections operate to increase the relative suc-cesses of public school children. In a process that Lareau describes as "concerted cultivation," social and cultural advantages are passed on to children from privileged families not in an unwitting or unconscious way, but in a deliberate and strategic manner specifically intended to advance their children's futures.

Lareau shows how middle- and working-class families have different sets of "cul-tural repertoires" about how children should be raised, and act as cauldrons in which children are socialized to develop different social and cultural capacities that produce subsequent differences in opportunity. Specifically, the mothers of middle-class and more-privileged children more effectively deploy social and cultural capital for the benefit of their children than do the mothers of working-class and less-privileged children. For example, compared to the mothers of less-privileged children, middle-class mothers are more educated and more likely to read to their children, tutor them, and help them with their homework. They are much more likely to regulate their children's extracurricular time and plan activities that help them to build their own cultural capital: sports teams (soccer moms); lessons of all kinds (music, dance, cotillion); summer camps of all kinds, including sports camps; play dates; and the like. Middle-class moms are more likely to live in the same neighborhoods as their children's teachers, and thus to know them "out of class," possibly as friends or members of the same clubs. They often have teachers in their own extended families. They are more likely to have become friends with their children's classmates' parents, and can thus use these friendships for information about the effective deployment of social and cultural capital. In short, they have the advantages of knowing "the right thing to do" or "what works" with their children's teachers.

Meanwhile, the mothers of working-class and poorer children have few of these advantages. Being less educated themselves, the moms are less likely to read to their children. They feel less confident in interactions with teachers. More generally, their habitus suggests that the teachers are the experts—that it is the teachers' responsibility to teach the children—and thus these mothers are less likely to intervene. There is clearly less connection between families and schools, and the mothers allow their "children to be children." Outside school, the children are expected to entertain themselves and play with neighborhood friends in their own independent and unregulated activities. In general, the working-class habitus seems to produce less social and cultural capital, and the moms tend to use it in clumsy ways that teachers sometimes define as inappropriate and annoying. These and many other differences help to explain why the students of middle-class and more-privileged families "do better" in schools and reap the credential rewards.

Cultural capital can also be objectified in material artifacts. Bourdieu (1986), for instance, argues that cultural capital can be certified in the form of academic qualifications and serve as a testimony of cultural competence for its bearer. This objectification, he says, is what makes the difference between the capital of the self-educated person, which may be called into question at any time, and the cultural capital academically sanctioned by legally guaranteed qualifications, formally independent of the person of their bearer. With the academic qualification, a certificate of cultural competence confers on its holder a conventional, constant, legally guaranteed value with respect to culture. By conferring institutional recognition on the cultural capital possessed, the academic qualification also makes it possible to compare qualification holders and even to exchange them (by substituting one for another in succession). Furthermore, it makes it possible to establish conversion rates between cultural capital and economic capital by guaranteeing the monetary value of a given academic capital (e.g., the "going" starting salary for an MBA from the Wharton School of Business). This is important because what is being selected out is not practical knowledge necessary to do the job (which could be self-taught or acquired on the job), but the degree itself as a form of cultural capital. Degrees signify cultural capital and become filters for eligibility; in this sense, the lack of a degree creates an artificial barrier to mobility otherwise predicated on skill, ability, experience, or knowledge acquired through alternate means.

Cultural Capital and Jobs

In a highly acclaimed book, *Pedigree: How Elite Students Get Elite Jobs* (2015), sociologist Lauren Rivera examined the recruitment process at elite universities for entry-level positions in the highly sought-after and prestigious "holy trinity" of top law, investment banking, and consulting firms. While a graduate student at Harvard University, Rivera over a two-year period conducted in-depth interviews with 120 campus recruiters for these firms. Through a "personal contact" she was also brought on as an unpaid intern in the recruiting department of one of those firms. In this role, she also attended and helped plan several recruiting events. Instead of just documenting the tendency of students from elite schools ending in elite positions, this study is unique in examining the largely behind-the-scenes process in which graduates of elite universities are recruited and hired by elite firms in these fields. Rivera shows that employers not only sought out candidates who were competent, but also similar to themselves in terms of common leisure pursuits, experiences, and self-presentational styles. Cultural matching along these lines factored prominently into hiring decisions and often outweighed concerns about absolute productivity.

Competence counts in terms of minimum thresholds, but may not be as important as cultural considerations. Indeed, more than half of the hiring agents in the study reported that fitting in was the most important criterion for consideration at the job interview stage, taking precedence over factors such as analytical thinking ability and communication skills. Rivera identified three ways through which cultural similarities affect candidate selection in the interview process. First, employers actively sought out candidates that "fit in" to the prevailing culture of the employing firm as indicated by the interests and activities of those already employed in the firm. Second, employers felt better able to understand and evaluate the background and experiences of candidates who had similar social backgrounds and experiences as they had. Third, similarities of experiences with particular candidates generated excitement on the part of evaluators who would then fight for those candidates in deliberations regarding final selection. In short, cultural criteria not only affect hiring outcomes in these elite professional settings, but often trump strictly merit factors.

Old Money and New Money

Research on the upper class consistently demonstrates the importance of cultural capital in distinguishing "old money" from "new money" (Fabrikant 2005; Johnston 2005; Scott and Leonhardt 2005; Frank 2007; Kerbo 2012). One institution that serves as a site for upper-class production, deployment, and intergenerational transmission of social and cultural capital is the upper-class social club. Sociologist Diana Kendall in *Members Only: Elite Clubs and the Process of Exclusion* (2008) and sociologist Jessica Holden Sherwood in *Wealth, Whiteness and the Matrix of Privilege: The View from the Country Club* (2010) convincingly document numerous ways that the upper class uses exclusive clubs to maintain upper-class advantage. First, the clubs serve as private domains for the conducting of business—on the golf course and at private parties, dinners, and other social affairs. Second, the clubs serve as sites for making connections by providing occupational and political networks. Third, these clubs have numerous functions at which politicians and upper-class members meet and share insider information about political policy and strategy and at which members provide politicians with money and support, which William Domhoff (2009) has described well as a "policy-making process." Finally, these clubs provide resources for launching the next generation. For example, these clubs serve as sites for parties, organized activities for children, debutante balls, and the exchange of information about elite preparatory schools, colleges, and universities.

Clearly, cultural capital reproduction routinely occurs not just in formal settings such as schools but in informal settings such as social clubs and exclusive upper-class resorts. Even within the same class categories, however, the circumstances and settings in which cultural capital is transferred may vary. Muriel Egerton (1997), for instance, has shown that household cultural climate varies according to parents' level of formal education and the employment situation of the father. In those families in which the father is employed in an occupation for which cultural capital is recognized as important for success (e.g., one of the professions), there is investment in cultural resources in the home, and such investment leads to children's acquisition of cultural capital. Thus, occupational groups dependent for their authority on cultural rather than economic capital invest more in legitimate culture in their homes and transmit cultural capital more effectively to their children, and occupational effects are evident beyond the impact of family income and parents' education.

The reproduction of cultural capital has occurred with enough frequency to have generated commonplace stereotypes of subcultural differences among occupational groups, status groups, and social classes. Even within social classes, subcultural differences are manifest. For example, within the upper class, the *upper*-upper class, with its "old money" (dynastic wealth) and its cultural capital displayed as refined manners, styles, and tastes (Fabrikant 2005), is contrasted with the *lower*-upper class, the nouveau riche, whose members may possess as much or even more economic capital but are "betrayed" by lack of cultural capital, as indicated by deficiencies in savoir faire, unrefined manners, lack of style, and pedestrian tastes (Fabrikant 2005; Steinhauer 2005; Frank 2007).

SOCIAL CLIMBING

Social climbing and snobbery have long been stock material for novelists and are part of the American folklore of social ranking and mobility (Buckley 2005; McGrath 2005). The very existence of these terms reflects a cultural recognition of unequally ranked socioeconomic groups or social classes and individual efforts to move upwardly through them. In general discourse, the terms *social climber* and *snob* tend to be used interchangeably. Both snobs and social climbers engage in activities that exclude and usurp. Essentially, social climbing may be defined as strategies and activities used to achieve upward social mobility that come to be defined negatively because they are seen as violating accepted rules for the acquisition and use of social and cultural capital. To the extent that efforts for upward social mobility involve the inappropriate deployment of social and cultural capital, they run the risk of negative labeling as social climbing.

Social climbers, within the limits set by their economic capital, systematically cultivate social capital, then attempt to deploy it in the pursuit of upward social mobility. They cultivate social relationships and engage in those social activities that provide access to members of the group to which they seek membership. Such activities include the conscious construction of social networks that have a status appreciably higher than that of the networks of nonclimber peers. Climbers try to carefully select organizational memberships (the "right" clubs, churches, charities, boards, and the like), develop social relations, and cultivate friendships among members of the target group. They use numerous strategies, including "name dropping," segregating audiences when deemed necessary (Mills 1951; Goffman 1951, 1959, 1967), and refusing to associate with members of lower-ranked groups. They may even use their children as sources of social contacts or as symbols of attainment. The placement of children in exclusive preparatory schools and the selection of their children's friends and activities are means of translating economic capital into social capital.

Social climbers hope that if they associate with people of higher status, some of the higher status will "rub off" on them. Those who associate with social climbers, however, risk having their own status lowered by such associations. In this regard, Vance Packard, in his influential book *The Status Seekers* (1959), made a useful distinction between status lending and status declassing. Climbers may attach themselves to status lenders, individuals who voluntarily confer their status by association with lower-status individuals and organizations. Status declassing, however, reflects efforts by higher-status individuals to take on characteristics of the lower-status individuals with whom they are interacting. Higher-status individuals may "declass," as by professing a "we're just plain folks" perspective, if it is deemed socially useful for them to do so.

Social climbers also attempt to develop and use cultural capital in the pursuit of upward social mobility. But one impediment to social climbing lies in the very nature of cultural capital. Components of cultural capital can usually be acquired only through extended and informal socialization within the group. While it is possible for the climber to acquire cultural capital formally, as through education or systematic training, such formal acquisition is economically costly and typically results in a tense, subtly imperfect mastery that is always marked by the conditions of its acquisition (e.g., Julia Roberts's character in *Pretty Woman* not knowing which fork to use). The resulting uneasy, practiced, unnatural, or even stilted displays are easily detected by members of the target group, and thus betray the climber as a poseur—as not truly "one of us" (Buckley 2005; Fabrikant 2005).

Status competition within groups may lead to changes in what status pacesetters define as prestigious. This is most evident in the fickle nature of what is considered currently "fashionable" within elite circles. The constantly changing nature of status symbols suggests the source of yet another impediment to social climbing. Self-assured and long-established members of any group come to feel that adherence to its own standard canons is beneath them. Their status is so secure that to indulge in those observances would only lower them. They can best announce and display their unassailability by changing the canons. They have adopted an apparently non-invidious way of life for the quintessentially invidious purpose of showing that they are above taking part in a game played by "lessers." Such changes in cultural capital increase the difficulty of its acquisition and penetration of the target group by climbers: It is more difficult to hit a moving cultural target than a stationary one.

Social climbing elicits negative reactions for a variety of reasons. For some, the evidence of single-minded, obsessive preoccupation with status or the transparent, crudely instrumental efforts to deploy social and cultural capital are simply annoying (Buckley 2005; Fabrikant 2005). What is more, the actions of social climbers can make individuals acutely aware of their own cultural and social capital deficiencies. The American Dream encourages individuals to maintain or, if possible, improve their social positions by acquiring social, cultural, and economic capital and using them to their advantage. But such activity is governed by generally understood and accepted rules, and the social climber's actions challenge or violate them. Violating the rules is sufficient basis for negative labeling and exclusion. "Not knowing" the rules is no excuse, because knowing and adhering to the rules is a nonsubstitutable criterion of eligibility.

Further, the instrumental acquisition and deployment of social and cultural capital as a strategic means for the achievement of upward social mobility violates meritocratic notions. According to meritocratic ideology, individual merit is the only legitimate basis for mobility. Hence, the purposeful use of social and cultural capital as a means of social mobility is suspect to the extent that it is not the product of individual merit or that it is viewed as being a substitute for individual merit.

From another perspective, the actions of social climbers challenge the legitimacy of group ranking and the unequal distribution of social and cultural capital, and they lay bare class-based resentments and hostilities. Rejection and exclusion of the climber by the target group constitutes an exercise of power. In fact, the climber's own group may experience a threat to its status and attempt to impose sanctions on the climber because, at least by implication, the climber's actions constitute a negative evaluation of that group, and therefore a threat to its status claims and solidarity.

In sum, the actions of social climbers run counter to the individualistic and meritocratic components of the American Dream and the normative structure that underlies it. Climbing behavior also calls attention to inequalities among groups in the distribution of various forms of capital. Social climbers highlight the social and cultural insecurities of those with whom they interact. For all these reasons, the actions of social climbers tend to be viewed, especially by those of higher status, as fraudulent and shameful.

From this, we can conclude several things. First, the possession of cultural capital is related to social-class background, but the correlation is difficult to measure. The privileged do tend to have more cultural capital than those of lower socioeconomic status, but many cases do not fit this pattern, and there are differences among individuals in their ability to effectively deploy what cultural capital they possess. Second, while the possession of cultural capital may be viewed as evidence of individual merit, it is in fact acquired in ways that can hardly be attributable to individual effort or merit as conventionally defined. That is, much cultural capital is the result of familial socialization—cultural capital is often "frictionlessly" and effortlessly inherited. In this sense, the acquisition of cultural capital is best conceptualized as a process of differential cultural inheritance, not one of differential achievement. Third, strategies of mobility and reproduction are constrained, but not wholly determined, by social class. Thus, cultural resources enter into individual and familial strategies for advancement in a variety of ways. For some, investment in cultural capital is a conscious and purposeful effort or strategy, either for one's own mobility or for that of one's children (Lareau 2000, 2003). Fourth, cultural capital contributes directly to the acquisition of education. Educational credentials (cultural capital in its institutionalized form) then become criteria for access to occupational opportunity (eligibility requirements for hiring and promotion). Below I offer a brief example of the importance and advantages of social and cultural capital in the case of President Donald Trump.

THE CASE OF DONALD J. TRUMP

Donald J. Trump was born into wealth and privilege (D'Antonio 2016; Johnston 2016; Kranish and Fisher 2016). His paternal grandfather, Friedrich Trump, immigrated to the United States from Germany in 1885, and became a successful and wealthy restaurant and boardinghouse owner. Like many European immigrants of that era, Friedrich anglicized his surname by changing it first to "Trumph" and then to "Trump." Donald Trump's father, Fred Trump, extended the family business into real estate investments, focusing primarily in the rapidly expanding borough of Queens in New York City. Donald Trump's father amassed a considerable fortune building low- and middle-income housing in and around the borough of Queens.

Donald Trump's mother, Mary Anne MacLeod, emigrated from Scotland to New York, where she met Trump's father. Donald and his two sisters and two brothers grew up in relative luxury in a twenty-three-room mansion in Jamaica Estates in Queens (D'Antonio 2016; Kranish and Fisher 2016). Like his siblings, Donald attended private schools. He attended the elite Kew-Forest School through the seventh grade. Because of his reputed rebellious nature, his parents decided to then send him to the New York Military Academy, a private boarding school where Donald completed high school. Even as a young man and while still in school, Donald often accompanied his father in his real estate business dealings (D'Antonio 2016). This pattern continued for Donald while he attended Fordham University in New York, and after his transfer to the private Ivy League University of Pennsylvania, where he enrolled in a unique real estate degree program in the prestigious Wharton School of Business.

Upon graduation from the University of Pennsylvania, Donald entered the family business, working closely with his father full-time, and eventually branching out to pursue his own business ventures. Donald subsequently expanded his business empire to Atlantic City casinos, sporting events, golf courses and resorts, beauty pageants, an airline, and the private, for-profit "Trump University" school of real estate and other ventures. Trump further branded and licensed the Trump name with several products and services. Many of these business ventures failed, ending in bankruptcy proceedings, although Donald himself never declared personal bankruptcy. In addition to these business ventures, Donald Trump launched a media career including a radio program, cameo appearances in several films and television series, and as executive producer and host of the reality TV show *The Apprentice*. Donald Trump was listed by *Forbes* (2016) as the 156th wealthiest American, with an estimated total net worth of $3.7 billion. Trump, who had never previously held any political office at any level, or worked in government in any capacity, was elected in 2016 as the forty-fifth president of the United States.

Donald Trump has benefited enormously from the inheritance of economic, social, and cultural capital, apart from whatever innate talents he might possess. Not only did he grow up in an environment of privilege, but he also used investment capital from his father to launch his own business ventures, expanding his father's real estate empire in largely federally subsidized housing in Queens to luxury housing in upscale Manhattan. Equally critical was the social capital inherited in terms of established personal contacts with bankers, government officials, architects, contractors, union representatives, and others associated with the building and real estate industry. Throughout his adult life, Donald Trump traveled in elite social circles, befriending many prominent business executives, politicians, and celebrities. He has been married three times, twice to high-profile fashion models, and once to an actress / beauty pageant contestant.

In many ways, Donald Trump is "bicultural," equally comfortable in the working-class areas of Queens and the more upscale social scene among New York's elite society. This cultural fluency allows him to relate well to people in these different cultural settings, a significant asset to him in both his economic and political careers.

Donald Trump's nonmerit advantages of inheritance have extended to his five children as well. All of his children were raised in privilege and attended elite private prep schools. Three of his four adult children (Donald Jr., Ivanka, and Tiffany) also graduated from their father's Ivy League alma mater, the University of Pennsylvania. Son Eric graduated from Georgetown University. His two oldest sons, Donald Trump Jr. and Eric, entered the family business and became executive vice presidents. At the time that their father was inaugurated as president, the two brothers (aged forty and thirty-two, respectively) assumed operational control of Trump's multibillion-dollar business empire as its trustees.

Donald Trump's daughter Ivanka (aged thirty-five at the time her father became president), was also an executive vice president in her father's company. In addition to working in the family business, Ivanka worked as a fashion model and also formed a partnership with a diamond vendor and created Ivanka Trump Fine Jewelry. The company markets fine jewelry as well as her own line of apparel, including clothes, handbags, shoes, and accessories. Shortly after her father's election as president she became an informal advisor to the president, occupying an office in the West Wing of the White House. Her husband, Jared Kushner, at the age of thirty-six, was named by Donald Trump as senior advisor to the President of the United States. Kushner, son of a wealthy real estate developer, also grew up in privilege. He graduated from Harvard University and New York University Law School. Prior to his appointment as senior advisor, he was CEO of Kushner Companies.

Tiffany Trump (aged twenty-three at the time her father assumed the presidency) has worked as a model and as an intern at *Vogue* magazine. Donald Trump's youngest son, Barron (aged ten at the time his father became president), attended the private Columbia Grammar and Preparatory School in New York City.

In and of itself, family wealth and connections and an elite cultural upbringing do not diminish or demean the individual accomplishments of those born into great wealth and privilege. Such individual accomplishments and subsequent high-level appointments, however, must be understood within the larger social context of differing advantages in which they occur. Clearly, the effects of inheritance and nepotism are evident in the case of this familial dynasty. Donald Trump was able to expand the business he inherited from his father and has passed on advantages of privilege and familial connections to his children. Whatever individual talents members of the Trump family may possess, they most certainly did not achieve their positions or success entirely on their own. We do not know, for instance, how many individuals similarly situated with such initial advantages could have been as success-ful, and we never will know. Certainly through no fault of their own, but equally through no merit of their own, sons and daughters of the rich and powerful inherit, along with the family name, disproportionate access to substantial and influential forms of economic, social, and cultural capital.

SUMMARY

This chapter has reviewed the evidence on the importance of "whom you know" (social capital) and "fitting in" (cultural capital) for getting—and staying—ahead in America. Social and cultural capital are ultimately resources. As with the possession of wealth, the possession of social and cultural resources is not necessarily evidence of individual merit. Wealth can be converted into social and cultural capital, providing distinct nonmerit advantages that can be transferred to the children of the rich and powerful. We have explored the related phenomenon of social climbing. Conscious construction and use of social networks, conspicuous and invidious consumption, name dropping, and "showy" displays of highbrow culture are some of the tech-niques employed by social climbers in their attempts to attain higher status. Instead of gaining the prestige and rank that they desire, however, social climbers are often viewed as snobs within their own groups and as impostors by those in the groups to which they aspire to gain membership.

Beyond where one starts out in life at birth and initial exposure to sources of social and cultural capital, the next major institutional influence on where children will likely end up in the system is their experience with formal education and the schools they attend. The next chapter explores the effects of education on getting ahead in America.

REFERENCES

Bellow, Adam. 2003. *In Praise of Nepotism: A Natural History*. New York: Doubleday.

Bourdieu, Pierre. 1986. "The Forms of Capital." In *Handbook of Theory and Research for the Sociology of Education*, ed. John G. Richardson, 241–58. New York: Greenwood Press.

Buckley, Christopher. 2005. "My Nanny Was a Dreadful Snob." In *Class Matters*, ed. *New York Times*, 234–36. New York: Times Books.

Campbell, Karen E., Peter V. Marsden, and Jeanne S. Hurlbert. 1986. "Social Resources and Socioeconomic Status." *Social Networks* 8:97–117.

Castilla, Emilio J., George J. Lan, and Ben A. Rissing. 2013a. "Social Networks and Employment: Mechanisms (Part1)." *Sociology Compass* 7(12):999–1012.

———. 2013b. "Social Networks and Employment: Outcomes (Part 2). *Sociology Compass* 7(12):1013–26.

Coleman, James S. 1988. "Social Capital in the Creation of Human Capital." *American Journal of Sociology* 94:95–S120.

D'Antonio, Michael. 2016. T*he Truth about Trump*. New York: St. Martin's Press.

DiTomaso, Nancy. 2013. *The American Non-Dilemma: Racial Inequality without Racism*. New York: Russell Sage Foundation.

Domhoff, William G. 2009. *Who Rules America? Challenges to Corporate and Class Dominance*, 6th ed. Boston: McGraw-Hill.

Egerton, Muriel. 1997. "Occupational Inheritance: The Role of Cultural Capital and Gender." *Work, Employment and Society* 11:263–82.

Fabrikant, Geraldine. 2005. "Old Nantucket Warily Meets the New." In *Class Matters*, ed. *New York Times*, 166–81. New York: Times Books.

Fernandez, Roberto M., and Nancy Weinberg. 1997. "Shifting and Sorting: Personal Contacts and Hiring in a Retail Bank." *American Sociological Review* 62:833–902.

Fernandez, Roberto, Emilio J. Castilla, and Paul Moore. 2000. "Social Capital at Work: Networks and Employment at a Phone Center." *American Journal of Sociology* 105:1288–1356.

Field, John. 2017. *Social Capital*. London: Routledge.

Forbes. 2016. "*Forbes* 400: The Full List of the Richest People in America in 2016." www .forbes.com/sites/chasewithorn/2016/10/04/forbes-400-the-full-list-of-the-richest-people-in-america-2016/2/#1cf1dc667b17 (accessed March 31, 2017).

Frank, Robert. 2007. *Richistan: A Journey through the American Wealth Boom and the Lives of the New Rich*. New York: Crown.

Goffman, Erving. 1951. "Symbols of Class Status." *British Journal of Sociology* 2:294–304.

———. 1959. *The Presentation of Self in Everyday Life*. Harmondsworth, UK: Pelican.

———. 1967. *Interaction Ritual*. New York: Pantheon.

Granovetter, Mark S. 1973. "The Strength of Weak Ties." *American Journal of Sociology* 78:1360–80.

———. 1974. *Getting a Job: A Study of Contacts and Careers*. Cambridge, MA: Harvard University Press.

———. 1983. "The Strength of Weak Ties: A Network Theory Revisited." *Sociological Theory* 1:201–33.

Grugulis, Irena, and Dimitrinka Stoyanova. 2012. "Social Capital and Networks in Film and TV: Jobs for the Boys?" *Organization Studies* 33(10):1311–31.

Hirshi, Travis. 1969. *Causes of Delinquency.* Berkeley: University of California Press.

Johnston, David Cay. 2005. "Richest Are Leaving Even the Rich Far Behind." In *Class Matters,* ed. *New York Times,* 182–91. New York: Times Books.

———. 2016. *The Making of Donald Trump.* Brooklyn: Melville House.

Kendall, Diana. 2002. *The Power of Good Deeds: Privileged Women and the Social Reproduction of the Upper Class.* Lanham, MD: Rowman & Littlefield.

———. 2008. *Members Only: Elite Clubs and the Process of Exclusion.* Lanham, MD: Rowman & Littlefield.

Kerbo, Harold R. 2012. *Social Stratification and Inequality: Class Conflict in Historical, Comparative, and Global Perspective.* New York: McGraw-Hill.

Kranish, Michael, and Marc Fisher. 2016. *Trump Revealed: An American Journey of Ambition, Ego, Money, and Power.* New York: Scribner.

Lareau, Annette. 2000. *Home Advantage: Social Class and Parental Intervention in Elementary Education.* Lanham, MD: Rowman & Littlefield.

———. 2003. *Unequal Childhoods: Class, Race, and Family Life.* Berkeley: University of California Press.

Lewin, Tamar. 2005. "A Marriage of Unequals" and "Up from the Holler: Living in Two Worlds, at Home in Neither." In *Class Matters,* ed. *New York Times,* 51–62 and 63–72. New York: Times Books.

Lin, Nan. 1982. "Social Resources and Instrumental Action." In *Social Structure and Network Analysis,* ed. Peter V. Marsden and Nan Lin, 131–45. Beverly Hills, CA: Sage.

———. 1999. "Social Networks and Status Attainment." *Annual Review of Sociology* 23:467–88.

———. 2000. "Inequality in Social Capital." *Contemporary Sociology* 29:785–95.

Lin, Nan, and Dan Ao. 2008. "The Invisible Hand of Social Capital: An Exploratory Study." In *Social Capital: An International Research Program,* ed. Nan Lin and B. H. Erickson, 107–32. Oxford: Oxford University Press.

Lin, Nan, and Mary Dumin. 1986. "Access to Occupations through Social Ties." *Social Networks* 8:365–85.

Lin, Nan, and Bonnie Erickson, eds. 2008. *Social Capital: An International Research Program.* New York: Oxford University Press.

LinkedIn. 2017. "About Us." https://press.linkedin.com/about-linkedin?# (accessed March 1, 2017).

Lutter, Mark. 2015. "Do Women Suffer from Network Closure: The Moderating Effect of Social Capital on Gender Inequality in a Project-Based Labor Market, 1929–2010." *American Sociological Review* 80(2):329–58.

Massey, Douglas S. 2007. *Categorically Unequal: The American Stratification System.* New York: Sage.

McDonald, Steve. 2005. "Patterns of Informal Job Matching Across the Work Career: Entry-Level, Reentry-Level, and Elite Non-Searching." *Sociological Inquiry* 75(3):403–28.

———. 2011. "What's in the 'Old Boys' Network? Accessing Social Capital in Gendered and Racialized Networks." *Social Networks* 33(4):317–30

———. 2015. "Network Effects across the Earnings Distribution: Visible and Invisible Job Finding Assistance in the Labor Market." *Social Science Research* 49(1):299–313.

McDonald, Steve, and Jacob C. Day. 2010. "Race, Gender, and the Invisible Hand of Social Capital." *Sociology Compass* 8(2):307–31.

McDonald, Steve, and Glen Elder Jr. 2006. "When Does Social Capital Matter? Non-Searching for Jobs Across the Life Course." *Social Forces* 85(1):521–50.

McDonald, Steve, Lindsay Hamm, James R. Elliott, and Pete Knepper. 2016. "Race Place, and Unsolicited Job Leads: How the Ethnoracial Structure of Local Labor Markets Shapes Employment Opportunities." *Social Currents* 3(2):118–37.

McDonald, Steve, Nan Lin, and Dan Ao. 2009. "Networks of Opportunity: Gender, Race, and Job Leads." *Social Problems* 56 (3):385–402.

McDonald, Steve, and Christine A. Mair. 2010. "Social Capital across the Life Course: Age and Gender Patterns of Occupational Networks." *Sociological Forum* 25(2):335–59.

McGrath, Charles. 2005. "In Fiction, A Long History of Fixation on the Social Gap." In *Class Matters*, ed. *New York Times*, 192–201. New York: Times Books.

Mills, C. Wright. 1951. *White Collar*. New York: Oxford University Press.

Mohr, John, and Paul DiMaggio. 1995. "The Intergenerational Transmission of Cultural Capital." *Research in Social Stratification and Mobility* 14:167–99.

Packard, Vance O. 1959. *The Status Seekers*. New York: David McKay.

Parks-Yancy, Rochelle. 2006. "The Effects of Social Group Membership and Social Capital Resources on Careers." *Journal of Black Studies* 36:515–45.

Petersen, Trond, Ishak Saporta, and Marc-David Seidel. 2000. "Offering a Job: Meritocracy and Social Networks." *American Journal of Sociology* 106:763–816.

Reeves, Richard V. 2017. *Dream Hoarders: How the American Upper Middle Class Is Leaving Everyone Else in the Dust, Why That Is a Problem, and What to Do about It*. Washington, DC: Brookings Institution Press.

Rivera, Lauren. 2015. *Pedigree: How Elite Students Get Elite Jobs*. Princeton, NJ: Princeton University Press.

Scott, Janny, and David Leonhardt. 2005. "Shadowy Lines That Still Divide." In *Class Matters*, ed. *New York Times*, 1–26. New York: Times Books.

Sherwood, Jessica Holden. 2010. *Wealth, Whiteness, and the Matrix of Privilege: The View from the Country Club*. Lanham, MD: Rowman & Littlefield.

Stainback, Kevin. 2008. "Social Contacts and Race/Ethnic Job Matching." *Social Forces* 87(2):857–86.

Steinhauer, Jennifer. 2005. "When the Joneses Wear Jeans." In *Class Matters*, ed. *New York Times*, 134–45. New York: Times Books.

Tilly, Charles. 1998. *Durable Inequality*. Berkeley: University of California Press.

Veblen, Thorstein. 1953. *The Theory of the Leisure Class*. New York: Modern Library.

Wacquant, Loic, and William Julius Wilson. 1989. "The Cost of Racial and Class Exclusion in the Inner City." *Annals of the American Academy of Political and Social Sciences* 501:8–26.

Weber, Max. 1968. *Economy and Society*. Trans. and ed. Guenther Roth and Claus Wittich. Berkeley: University of California Press.

Wilson, William Julius. 1987. *The Truly Disadvantaged: The Inner City, the Underclass, and Public Policy*. Chicago: University of Chicago Press.

———. 1996. *When Work Disappears: The World of the New Urban Poor*. New York: Knopf.

Wilson, Kenneth L., and Alejandro Portes. 1980. "Immigration Enclaves: An Analysis of the Labor Market Experiences of Cubans in Miami." *American Journal of Sociology* 86:295–319.

5

Making the Grade

Education and Mobility

To those of you who received honors, awards, and distinctions, I say, well done. And to the C students, I say, you too can be president of the United States.

—George W. Bush, Yale commencement address,
thirty-three years after his graduation

In America, as in all contemporary industrial societies, education has come to play an important role in selecting people for positions in the occupational structure. The close connection between "getting ahead" and education, however, is relatively recent. In the mid-nineteenth century, the United States was a nation of small property owners, farmers, and shopkeepers. Many could read and write, but most had little formal education. Although opportunity has been an essential part of the American Dream since its beginnings, it meant the possibility for a person to grow to full potential, unfettered by the limits of class background or older feudal relations. The model for upward mobility was the "self-made man" (and most then were men) who started and grew his business or farm through hard work and determination, not by getting more education than his competitors.

The expansion of schooling was the result of major changes in the structure of occupational opportunities. With continuing industrialization, technological change, the rise of large corporations, and the closing of the frontier, by the end of the nineteenth century opportunities for becoming a self-made man had declined precipitously (see chapter 6). America was no longer a nation of small-scale entrepreneurs, farmers, and shopkeepers. More people were becoming employees in increasingly large, bureaucratically structured work organizations. These new conditions generated the development of new occupations, and with them new pathways to success.

After World War II, growth in white-collar service and professional jobs accelerated, and opportunities for upward mobility through various forms of entrepreneurship continued to decline. As this occurred, young people began to see diplomas and degrees as an alternate and less risky means to upward mobility—as tickets to the middle class and the newer white-collar jobs that had proliferated. These changes in the occupational structure created increasing incentives for investment in education, and led to an increasing proportion of Americans completing both high school and college. In 1940, less than 25 percent of adults had completed high school and less than 5 percent had completed at least a bachelor's degree. Rates of growth in educational attainment rapidly accelerated such that by 2015, almost nine in ten adults had completed high school, and one in three had earned at least a bachelor's degree (see table 5.1).

Part of what stimulated increased college enrollments following World War II was the Servicemen's Readjustment Act of 1944, more commonly referred to as the GI Bill. Under benefits provided after World War II, more than two million returning veterans attended US colleges and universities, sharply increasing the percent of the adult population that was college-educated. Higher education has not completely replaced entrepreneurship as an avenue to economic success. However, building one's own business is an arduous task with high risk for failure. Given the uncertainties of entrepreneurship, even many businesspeople prefer that their children pursue the less risky path of professional training rather than following in their footsteps as entrepreneurs.

In the modern era, parental investment in the futures of their children through formal education has thus largely replaced the inheritance of the family farm or the family business as the major form of intergenerational transfer of privilege. In preindustrial societies, the small family business and especially the small family

Table 5.1.   Educational Attainment by Persons Age 25 and Over, Select Years 1910–2015

Year	High School Completion (%)	BA or Higher (%)
1910	13.5	2.7
1920	16.4	3.3
1930	19.1	3.9
1940	24.5	4.6
1950	34.3	6.2
1960	41.1	7.7
1970	55.2	11.0
1980	68.6	17.0
1990	77.6	21.3
2000	84.1	25.6
2010	87.1	29.9
2015	88.4	32.5

Source: US Department of Education (2017a).

Table 5.2. Median Annual Income for Full-Time Workers, Age 25 and Older, by Educational Attainment (2016)

Education Level	Median Income ($)
Professional degree	90,740
Doctorate	86,528
Master's degree	71,760
Bachelor's degree	60,112
Associate's degree	42,588
Some college, no degree	39,312
High school graduate	35,984
Less than high school	26,208

Source: US Department of Labor (2017).

farm always had the disadvantage of being potentially reduced in value or sustainability when subdivided into smaller parts among multiple heirs, giving rise to the then-common inheritance practice of primogeniture (the eldest male child inherits everything). With industrialization, however, inheritance of privilege was much less likely to take on the tangible form of discrete farms or businesses, and more likely to be in the form of fungible assets such as savings, investments, and educational opportunities, in which there is no per-unit diminution of value in assets, and equal transfer of assets to multiple heirs is easier.

Overall, the relationship between education and future income is clear: the more education, the greater the chances of higher income (see table 5.2). What is less clear are the causal mechanisms responsible for this connection. Two rival theoretical perspectives on the relationship between education and social class position have emerged with correspondingly different views on the direction of causality between these life circumstances. The functionalist perspective posits that educational attainment is essentially a "cause" of one's social class position in society, whereas the conflict perspective posits that educational attainment is essentially an "effect" of social class position.

FUNCTIONAL VIEWS OF EDUCATION

The expansion of formal education has substantially increased the importance of schooling in the process of social selection. In modern corporate America, with increasingly complex and bureaucratized work structures, educational credentials have become a major determinant of an individual's life chances. According to the American Dream, the educational system provides substantial opportunities for able and hardworking children from lower-status families to move up, while requiring children from higher-status families to at least prove themselves in school if they want to maintain their advantages. Among those who take this view, schools are likened to an elevator in which everyone gets on at the same floor (equality of educational opportunity) but, depending on how well he or she does in school (merit), gets off at a different floor corresponding to a particular level of occupational prestige and income.

James Bryant Conant, while serving as president of Harvard University, wrote two articles (1938, 1940) that summarized his view of the role of education in the process of social selection. He argued that democracy does not require a "uniform distribution of the world's goods" or a "radical equalization of wealth." Instead, it requires a "continuous process by which power and privilege may be automatically redistributed at the end of each generation" (Conant 1940, 598). He and other "meritocrats" considered schools to be the primary mechanism of redistribution. Doubting that talent was concentrated at the top of the social-class structure, they believed it was instead rather evenly distributed throughout. By giving every student, from the most humble to the most privileged, an equal educational opportunity at the beginning of life, society would be in a position to select those most qualified by intelligence and hard work to occupy the command posts at the top. In this way, an "aristocracy of talent" would be re-created fresh in every generation. The argument, which some have called "meritocratic aristocracy," neatly combines a principle of an "aristocracy" based on merit with a principle of democratic selection, or equality of opportunity.

In this view, the meritocratic foundation of the American Dream is its educational system—the primary engine of equality of opportunity. The educational system recognizes and rewards with diplomas and certificates those who work hardest, have the most ambition and perseverance, and possess the most talent and intelligence. In short, according to this formulation, the educational system recognizes and rewards the meritorious, regardless of the circumstances into which they are born, thus reducing inequalities based on nonmerit factors like birth or inheritance.

Functional theory suggests that, in the interest of efficiency and productivity, the most important and demanding tasks of society need to be filled by the most capable and competent individuals. Increasingly, the most capable and competent individuals are identified by the educational system, which screens and sorts individuals presumably on these traits. The educational system in turn provides the training and skills needed to fill occupations in America's modern and changing industrial economy. The educational requirements of jobs in industrial society constantly increase as a result of technological change. The proportion of jobs that require low skill declines while the proportion that requires high skill increases. What is more, the same jobs are continually upgraded in their skill requirements. The result is need-driven educational expansion: Educational requirements for employment continually rise, and more and more people are required to spend longer and longer periods in school. The most obvious meritocratic aspect of this theory is its clear claim that the opportunity to acquire training and skills is directly proportional to individual merit: talent and ability. By implication, educational expansion should reduce socioeconomic inequality, since educational opportunity is apportioned presumably on the basis of individual merit, which is distributed equally among the social classes.

According to this theory, humans can invest in themselves to increase their human capital, thereby increasing their productive capacities (Schultz 1961; Becker 1993). As individuals invest in their own human capital, they can command a higher premium for their labor. It is not the educational credentials themselves that are of value, but the skills and knowledge certified by those credentials. In essence, educated workers are seen as "worth" more because they "know" more and can "do" more.

Following the advent of computer-assisted data analysis, research attempting to empirically specify the mechanisms and processes of individual achievement accelerated. Although there had been prior studies of "who gets ahead" in America, sociologists Peter Blau and Otis Dudley Duncan's 1967 *The American Occupational Structure* produced an avalanche of research on the subject of social mobility—the overall amounts and patterns of movement in the occupational structure—as well as what has come to be called *status attainment*, the process whereby a set of interrelated factors operate to determine which individuals get ahead educationally and occupationally. The latter research has produced the Wisconsin School, so named because the Department of Sociology at the University of Wisconsin became the most important site devoted to the elaboration and extension of Blau and Duncan's initial work. The Wisconsin School, which has dominated the formulation of the questions and methods used to address the issue of status attainment, uses complex multivariate statistical techniques to examine an ever-increasing number of individual-level psychological and attitudinal characteristics that would seem to make a difference in the levels of education, status of occupations, and incomes that people eventually attain. These "status-attainment" studies develop and test models that measure the independent effects of various attributes, such as socioeconomic background (parental education, occupation, income), measured mental ability (IQ, for example), educational and occupational aspirations, and the influence of significant others on these aspirations, by statistically holding other variables in the model constant.

In a nutshell, these studies indicate that a mixture of merit (or "achieved") and nonmerit (or "ascribed") factors explains variations in educational, occupational, and income attainment. Family background (socioeconomic status) is an important ascribed factor that indirectly affects educational attainment. In turn, educational attainment has a sizable effect on occupational attainment, but it is important to remember that educational attainment is itself influenced by ascribed factors, some of which are not included in these models.

Clearly, high-level educational credentials are an important key to obtaining prestigious and well-paid jobs, and research suggests that people who finish higher-level degrees have a "leg up" in the labor market, even if they are not otherwise advantaged. While status-attainment studies have made important contributions to our understanding of "who gets ahead," this essentially individualistic perspective has produced incomplete and sometimes misleading results. Individual-level psychological, attitudinal characteristics and "human capital" resources (e.g., intelligence, aspirations) are assumed by these models to be the most important factors relevant to the attainment of education, occupational status, and income. Status-attainment models, however, have tended to underestimate the effects of ascriptive factors; more importantly, they neglect the effects of impersonal economic forces—structures of occupational and industrial opportunity ("demand-side" variables)—that are beyond individuals' control and have a role in determining the payoff of human-capital resources (see chapter 7).

In short, individuals are subject to complex and shifting structures of demand, the vicissitudes of history, accident, employers' decisions (rational and irrational), and their own decisions (good and bad). While some of the unexplained variation in who gets ahead no doubt has to do with "being in the right place at the right time" and similar factors of good or bad fortune, we must remember that these are actually individual-level reflections of structurally based demand for talents, skills, and experience.

CONFLICT VIEWS OF EDUCATION

A vastly different view of the role of education sees education not as a cause but largely as an effect of social class. According to this view, children generally receive education in proportion to their social-class standing: Upper-class children tend to get upper-class educations (e.g., at elite private prep schools and Ivy League colleges); middle-class children tend to get middle-class educations (e.g., at public schools and public universities); working-class people tend to get working-class educations (e.g., at public schools and technical or community colleges); and poor people tend to get poor educations (e.g., inner-city schools that have high dropout rates, and usually no higher education). In these settings, students are in essence being groomed for future roles in the economy, with upper-class students being largely groomed for command positions in major social institutions, middle-class students being largely groomed for functionary positions as midlevel managers and administrators, and working-class students being largely groomed for technical and vocational roles. In this way, existing educational and class inequalities are largely "reproduced" across generations (Bourdieu 1973; Bourdieu and Passeron 1990; Bowles and Gintis 1976).

Social and Cultural Capital

Conflict theorists identify several ways in which educational advantages and disadvantages are passed on from parents to children. A primary mechanism for this transfer is through social and cultural capital (see chapter 4). Parents are the main purveyors of social and cultural capital to their children. Parents, for instance, are their children's first teachers. Affluent parents are typically much better prepared to act in this capacity than less-affluent parents. Affluent parents are typically better educated themselves, and therefore in a better position to convey basic cultural knowledge to their children. Research has consistently shown that even at early ages, affluent parents more often speak to their children, read to their children, and provide their children with more stimulating learning environments than less-affluent parents (Putnam 2015; Ballantine et al. 2017). Affluent parents are also more likely to have high expectations for their children and provide more encouragement to succeed (Pew Research Center 2015).

Research has long established class-based differences in child-rearing practices in which working-class parents more frequently emphasize conformance and compliance, whereas middle-class parents emphasize creativity and self-direction (Kohn 1963). Whereas working-class parents more often adopt a "natural growth" approach to childhood development, which minimizes parental intervention and direction, affluent parents more often adopt a "concerted cultivation" style of parenting, in which parents actively intervene to direct their children's futures (Lareau 2003).

Parental involvement can take many forms, including reading to children, assisting with homework, meeting with teachers, being involved in school organizations and activities, and even volunteering time to assist teachers in educational projects and activities. Privileged parents can also afford to invest more heavily in enrichment goods and services such as books, computers, high-quality child care, music lessons, and summer camps. Moreover, the spending gaps for such enrichment goods and services between high-income and low-income parents have increased over time (Kornrich 2016; Kornrich and Furstenberg 2013; Duncan and Murnane 2011).

Privileged parents are also more likely themselves to have high educational attainment and be familiar with "how the system works" and "how to work the system" to maximize advantages for their own children, intervening on their behalf sometimes aggressively with teachers, principals, and other administrators (Lareau 2000; Lareau and Weininger 2003). Such aggressive privileged parents are commonly referred to by teachers and school administrators as "helicopter" parents. As birthrates have declined, especially among the privileged, there is some speculation that privileged parents are even more aggressive in investing in the futures of the fewer children they now have compared to prior generations. In the past, more children meant an increase in the odds that at least some would succeed even without aggressive parental intervention. Parents may feel more pressure with fewer children to advance the futures of each of the one or two children they are likely to have. With fewer total children, they also have more resources available per child to do so.

By the time students enter formal elementary schools, there are already sharp class-based differences in "school readiness" related to both cognitive and social development. Increasing evidence shows that early childhood development is critical to later academic success (Ballantine et al. 2017; Reardon 2011; Duncan and Murnane 2011; Ermisch et al. 2012). Not only is the class achievement gap persistent as children move through the educational system, but research also shows that the class achievement gap has grown in recent decades (Reardon 2011).

French sociologist Pierre Bourdieu emphasized that schools are instruments of social and cultural reproduction, which are means of social-class reproduction (Bourdieu

1973; Bourdieu and Passeron 1990). According to Bourdieu, schools do not produce cultural capital, or even the means to appropriate it. Instead, they recognize it, reward the possession of it, and certify its possession by differentially awarding educational credentials in proportion to the amount of cultural capital possessed. Children from lower classes with less cultural capital are eliminated from the system because of their cultural-capital deficits, or they self-eliminate as they come to recognize their low objective chances of success within the system. Affluent students, on the other hand, with middle-class vocabularies, manners, and decorum, are seen to possess "behavioral repertoires" deemed desirable by teachers and school officials. These qualities, often referred to as "soft skills," may be perceived as meritorious individual character traits rather than as markers of social-class position. Thus, schools tend to reinforce the cultural-capital inequalities based on differences in family socioeconomic status.

School Quality and School Funding

While students from privileged backgrounds have social and cultural advantages regardless of which schools they attend, they are more likely to attend "good" schools that are staffed by competent and experienced teachers, provide an academic college-preparatory curriculum, and are populated by other privileged students (Ballantine et al. 2017; Duncan and Murnane 2011; Massey 2007). Jonathan Kozol, for instance, vividly characterizes the American system of education as one of "savage inequalities" (1991) that operates in effect as a system of "apartheid schooling" (2006). Kozol dramatically describes dilapidated school buildings and facilities, inadequate textbooks and teaching materials, and often unsafe and unsanitary conditions in poor school districts, with much cleaner and superior equipment and settings found in wealthy school districts. A large part of these differences can be attributed to unequal school funding. The public schools attended by children from higher-income families are better partially because a significant portion of school funding comes from local property taxes, which produce more revenue in privileged residential areas. Despite a growing body of research that repeatedly demonstrates the negative effects of reliance on local funding on student academic achievement, the reliance on local funding is increasing. For example, in the 1989–1990 school year, the proportion of total revenues for public elementary and secondary schools that came from local property taxes was 36 percent (US Department of Education 2007); by the 2013–2014 school year, that figure was 45 percent, an increase of 9 percent (US Department of Education 2017b). States also vary in the amount of funding made available to public schools.

But this is only part of the story. Schools in wealthier areas are "better" for reasons other than the amount of economic resources spent on students. Not only do high-income families, living in high-income residential areas, provide a strong tax base that can be tapped to fund quality schools, but such families also have the political clout needed to more effectively demand quality education for their children. Wealthy parents also often have the option of avoiding public schools altogether by sending their children to expensive elite private schools and academies. Further, as noted above, the children of high-income families bring considerable cognitive ability as well as social and cultural capital with them to the schools. Finally, the socioeconomic composition of the student body contributes to the formation of school climates or cultures that can prove beneficial or harmful to academic and subsequent occupational attainment. Students benefit from peers and "significant others" who exhibit high educational and occupational aspirations because they contribute to educational and occupational attainment. Thus, school quality varies not only by amounts and kinds of economic inputs, but also by the social, cultural, and intellectual composition of the student body, which varies according to the socioeconomic status of students' families.

These composition factors to some extent mitigate the effects of material conditions and school spending on academic performance. Early research by sociologists James Coleman et al. (1966) and Christopher Jencks et al. (1972), for instance, seemed to show that a number of measures of school quality did not show significant relationships with outcomes such as test scores and later college attendance. In other words, regardless of spending levels and the quality of schools, children from more privileged backgrounds do better than children from less privileged backgrounds. Parents with their own resources can to some extent compensate in other ways for inadequate schools to ensure their own children's academic success. Affluent parents, for instance, can provide private tutoring, additional enrichment activities, test preparation services, and the like, not otherwise available to students of lesser means. Even where funding per student is equivalent in poor and affluent school districts, it would likely take additional funding per student to address additional challenges encountered in poor school districts to produce equivalent learning experiences and outcomes (Putnam 2015; Lafortune et al. 2015). Although the findings of more than forty years of research are somewhat mixed, they generally show that differences in educational, occupational, and income attainment are at least partially attributable to differences in school quality, and that the net effects of school quality are substantial (Arroyo 2008; Altonji and Mansfield 2011; Condron and Roscigno 2003; Johnson 2006).

Parents themselves clearly believe that there are real differences in school quality and that these differences affect their children's chances for future academic and occupational success. Parents are impressed by the varying reputations that schools develop, and are willing to pay the higher costs of housing in residential areas served by "quality" schools (Lareau 2014). But, of course, variation in income means that not all parents can equally afford these higher housing costs.

School Tracking

Another practice that jeopardizes equality of educational opportunity and tends to reproduce existing inequalities across generations is school tracking. A majority of US public schools use some form of tracking in which children are placed in different groups, or tracks, that prepare some for college and others for vocations that do not require college. There has been much research on the factors that influence track placement and the outcomes of such placement, but conclusions are complex because of the variety of tracking systems in use. While measured intellectual skills are the factors most directly responsible for track placement, recall also that cognitive skills and academic performance are influenced by family socioeconomic status, especially in critical early stages of childhood development.

Tracking takes place through vocational education as well. Sociologists James Ainsworth and Vincent Roscigno (2005) found that there are significant class, race, and gender disparities in vocational educational placement, even after accounting for prior achievement and educational expectations. They found that vocational involvement increases the likelihood of dropping out of high school and significantly decreases college attendance. Their findings suggest that educational-institutional processes often assumed to be neutral have striking and negative effects on subsequent educational and occupational trajectories.

Regardless of the manner in which students are tracked within the educational system, the outcomes of tracking are fairly clear. First, track mobility is typically low. Once a child is placed in a low track, it is difficult to "move up," and for those placed in a high track, it is difficult to do poorly enough to "move down." In short, tracking affects teacher expectations as well as access to quality teachers and the courses needed for college eligibility. Tracking produces self-fulfilling prophecies. Children in higher college-preparatory tracks tend to improve in academic achievement over the years, while those in lower tracks tend to perform at levels that make them ineligible for higher education. Children in higher tracks are less likely to drop out of school, have higher educational aspirations, and are more likely to attend college. In short, tracking often works to reinforce class differences and has an independent effect of further differentiating children in terms of family background (Lewis and Cheng 2006; Oakes 1985, 1990).

Attempts at Reform

Various attempts to reduce the race/class "achievement gap" have produced several policy proposals with limited success. Head Start programs, for instance, are designed to address cultural and learning deprivations that low-income and minority children often have upon entry into the school system that puts them at a competitive disadvantage. Research on the long reach of these deprivations into adulthood suggests that such early childhood interventions would be effective in reducing the achievement gap (Duncan and Murnane 2011; Alexander et al. 2014). Magnet and charter schools, national standardized testing as a means of evaluating teacher and school performance, and proposed choice and voucher plans have also been advanced as ways to close the achievement gap. The cost, source of control, and effectiveness of these various reforms are highly controversial and for the most part still experimental. In the meantime, the opportunity/achievement gap persists.

Higher Education

The pattern that produces class-based inequality of educational opportunity in K–12 also extends to higher education. The inequalities reproduced across generations are substantial but far from complete. In part this is because some parents, regardless of class position, are more successful in promoting the futures of their children. And some children, regardless of class position, are more capable than others. Some of the most capable are also assisted by merit-based scholarship programs and concerted efforts by some institutions to diversify their student bodies. As a result, some rich kids fail, and some poor kids succeed. These exceptions, however infrequent, help to sustain at least the outward appearance of meritocracy and the American Dream.

The overall pattern of unequal access to higher educational opportunity is clear. Access to higher education is highly stratified by socioeconomic status (Weis et al. 2014; Pell Institute 2017). In 2015, 73 percent of students from the highest quartile of household income went on to attend a four-year college after high school, compared to only 21 percent from the lowest quartile of household income, a gap of 52 percent (Pell Institute 2017). Of course, not everyone who attends college graduates. Of students who attained a bachelor's degree in 2015 by age twenty-four, 58 percent were from the highest quartile of household income, compared to only 12 percent from the lowest quartile of household income (Pell Institute 2017).

These differences become even greater at greater income extremes, and at the most selective colleges (Chetty et al. 2017; Pell Institute 2017). In the most comprehensive study available of college access and mobility opportunities involving thirty million college students from 1999 to 2013, Raj Chetty and his associates (2017) found that among students who attend an "Ivy-Plus" college (Ivy League colleges plus University of Chicago, Stanford, MIT, and Duke), more are from the richest 1 percent of households than the bottom 50 percent of income distribution combined. Children whose parents are in the top 1 percent of the income distribution, for instance, are seventy-seven times more likely to attend an Ivy-Plus institution than parents who are in the bottom income quintile.

Access to elite institutions is important, since elite firms and corporations that pay the highest salaries focus their recruitment efforts among graduates of these select institutions (Rivera 2015), and top-ranking officers and directors of Fortune 500 companies are drawn substantially from alumni of these elite institutions (Zweigenhaft 2015). For instance, nearly 10 percent of CEOs of Fortune 500 companies are Harvard graduates (Zweigenhaft 2015). Of the nine current US Supreme Court justices, all are graduates of Ivy League law schools—five from Harvard Law School (Roberts, Kennedy, Breyer, Kagan, Gorsuch); three from Yale Law School (Thomas, Sotomayor, Alito); and one who first attended Harvard Law School, but completed her studies at Columbia Law School (Ginsburg). It is also noteworthy to point out that the last five American presidents were all graduates of Ivy League universities: Donald Trump (University of Pennsylvania); Barack Obama (Columbia and Harvard), George W. Bush (Yale and Harvard), Bill Clinton (Yale), and George H. W.

Bush (Yale). Not only do CEOs, Supreme Court justices, and presidents have very high salaries and very high occupational prestige, but they also occupy the most powerful positions in society as a whole.

Socioeconomic Status and Standardized Aptitude Tests

There are several ways in which the pattern of unequal access to educational opportunities in K–12 is extended to the university level. Initial advantages or disadvantages of class placement at birth not only create unequal starting points, but, as we have seen, they accumulate and are amplified over time. One of the ways this difference works to the disadvantage of those from lower socioeconomic backgrounds is the use of standardized aptitude tests, such as the SAT and ACT, as criteria of admission to colleges and universities. Research has consistently shown that scores on these tests are highly correlated with family income, encouraging an increasing number of institutions to drop them as a requirement, or to make them optional to avoid class bias in their admissions processes (Guinier 2015).

As we have seen, such tests were initially designed to promote meritocratic criteria for admission to colleges and universities. As the companies that produce these tests are careful to point out, they are not measures of innate intelligence, but instead are designed to measure one's "aptitude" for advanced study. However, research (Bowen et al. 2011) has shown that such tests are very poor predictors of college performance, or even of completing college. High school grades are far better predictors of successful college completion. On average, high school grades have five times more predictive power than test scores on college completion. For highly selective colleges and universities, test scores are better predictors of college completion, but still have only half the predictive power of high school grades. Moreover, the predictive power of high school grades is increased once controls are added for the quality of high school attended.

At one level, all of this stands to reason. Grades are measures of actual performance, and prior performance is a good measure of future performance. Standardized tests, on the other hand, do not capture intangibles such as creativity, motivation, leadership, or perseverance. What they do capture is socioeconomic background, since it is well known that scores on such aptitude tests are highly correlated with family income, probably to a large extent related to the effects of social and cultural capital described earlier. To the extent that colleges still use such tests as screening devices for admission, those from lower socioeconomic backgrounds are at a systematic disadvantage based on selection criteria that turn out to have little bearing on the actual likelihood of success.

Legacy Admissions and Demonstrated Interest

Another rather direct way in which social-class advantage at the college level is reproduced across generations is through legacy admissions (Soares 2007; Stevens

2007; Golden 2003, 2006; Karabel 2005; Espenshade et al. 2004; Radford 2013; Howell and Turner 2004). Legacy admissions refer to advantage or additional consideration extended to applicants because family members are alumni of the institution to which the student has applied. In essence, legacy admissions operate as a nonmerit affirmative action program for the already privileged. Studies of these practices generally reveal a roughly two-to-one admission advantage for legacies compared with overall rates (Bowen and Bok 2009; Howell and Turner 2004). In his study of admission practices at Yale University from 1920 to 2000, Joseph Soares shows that legacies comprised an average of 20 percent of the first-year class at Yale University, with more recent years (1990–2000) averaging somewhat less, at about 13 percent (Soares 2007, 91).

In *Creating a Class: College Admissions and the Education of Elites* (2007), sociologist Mitchell Stevens summarizes the findings of a particularly revealing study that shows how other more subtle mechanisms beyond legacy considerations operate to reproduce class advantage. Stevens gathered participant observation data working for a year and a half in the admissions office of an elite New England college. Unsurprisingly, Stevens found that admissions were highly competitive. He also found that creating a first-year class was quite complicated, and involved the use of criteria that favored the already privileged. He shows that this task cannot be completed without "systematic preferences," and that racial affirmative action is minimal.

For example, applicants are given preference if their parents can pay full tuition, if they attended a high school with a high-status zip code, if they are athletes (especially football players), and even if they are popular. Stevens thus explains how elite colleges and universities reproduce the nation's most privileged classes. He finds that individualized evaluation protocols do not create equal educational opportunity, but reproduce class privilege. In competing for the limited seats at these institutions, the goal of parents is to raise children with the attributes most sought by elite colleges and universities: measurable academic and extracurricular accomplishment and athletic prowess, good looks, a slender body, and an outgoing personality. Admission to such colleges is taken as evidence of excellent parenting, intellectual prowess, academic talent, and considerable accomplishment, and certifies elite status.

Besides the legacy advantage for the already privileged, another more subtle nonmerit affluent advantage in college admissions, particular to selective institutions, is the capacity for students to "demonstrate interest" in such institutions by making costly on-campus visits at student expense. Universities have a vested interest in reducing their "melt rate" of students who are accepted but do not attend. One way to do this is to gauge student interest and enthusiasm for a particular university in admission decisions by considering student follow-up with on- and off-campus contacts.

One recent case study of a medium-size highly selective university (Dearden et al. 2017), for instance, showed that both off-campus and on-campus contacts matter, but on-campus contact matters more, as evidenced by student personal appointments, attendance at information sessions, and campus visits. Moreover, the effect of making such contacts was highest when it came to those students with the highest SAT scores, as universities most often compete with each other for those students. Making both off-campus and on-campus contacts, for instance, increased the probability of admission by 20 percent, and by double that amount for applicants in the highest SAT quartile. Affluent students are better able to increase their probabilities for admission, especially to the most selective colleges, by being able to afford the costs of multiple application fees and costly on-campus visits, often to multiple universities.

Increasing College Costs and Student Debt

The cost of attending colleges and universities is also a major barrier to access for students and their families with modest means (Goldrick-Rab 2016; Armstrong and Hamilton 2013; Price 2004). As previously noted in chapter 1, the cost of higher education in the past several decades has risen much faster than the overall cost of living. For the 2013–2014 academic year, the average annual costs for tuition, fees, room, and board were $18,110 at public four-year colleges and $35,987 at private nonprofit and for-profit colleges (US Department of Education 2017c). Of course, these costs are averages. For commuter community colleges, annual costs can be as low as $5,000; for Ivy League institutions, annual costs can be as high as $90,000. Controlling for inflation, average costs have more than doubled over the past thirty years for both public and private institutions (US Department of Education 2017c).

Despite these higher costs, rates of college attendance in the past several decades have increased. This has been possible through increased student debt. Federal Pell Grants for low-income students have not kept pace with these rising costs. For the 1975–1976 academic year, the maximum Pell Grant covered 67 percent of the costs of attending a four-year public university; for the 2015–2016 academic year, that amount was reduced to 26 percent (Pell Institute 2017). Meanwhile, states have sharply reduced the subsidy for tuition at state universities and colleges, passing on a greater burden of cost to students. For the 1992–1993 academic year, 46 percent of students incurred some debt, with an average student debt upon graduation of $16,500 (in constant 2012 dollars); for the 2011–2012 academic year, 71 percent of students incurred some student loan debt, with an average student debt upon graduation of $29,400 (Pell Institute 2017). In 2017, total outstanding student debt reached $1.34 billion, more than double the amount in 2008, and almost double that for total credit card debt (Federal Reserve Bank of New York 2017).

Compared to the early 1900s, when less than 5 percent of Americans were college-educated, there has been a dramatic increase in the proportion of the adult population that is college-educated, which now is about one-third of all adults. More democratized access to higher education has been brought about through government funding of higher education, the GI Bill and its ongoing iterations, post–World War II expansion of state universities and community colleges, federal Pell Grant guaranteed student loans, and the willingness of private lenders to forego collateral loan requirements and instead to loan money to students against the prospects of future earnings. In other words, the expansion of higher education to a greater segment of the American population has been primarily accomplished through student debt.

At the same time there has been a debt-financed increase in students going to college, there has also been a depressed job market for college graduates, resulting in high rates of underemployment for college graduates, especially for new entrants in the labor market (Abel and Deitz 2016; Rose 2017; Vedder et al. 2013). Depending on how "underemployment" is measured, estimates are that roughly between 30 percent to 50 percent of college graduates are in jobs that either do not require a college degree, or that have below-average concentrations of college graduates doing those jobs. As a result, there are both inflationary pressures to seek more advanced degrees to gain a competitive edge and increased skepticism about the value of return in the investment in higher education.

CREDENTIAL INFLATION AND THE PAPER CHASE

Over the past century, educational requirements for entry to jobs have spread to a wide range of occupations, keeping step with advances in educational attainment. The desire for more opportunity may be enough to increase the numbers of students seeking higher levels of schooling, but it does not in itself increase the probability that such hopes will be realized. Only a tightening link between educational qualifications and jobs can do that. An important facet of the school's changing role in social selection has to do with the rise of what Randall Collins (1979) has called *credentialism*—the monopolization of access to the more rewarding jobs and economic opportunities by the holders of degrees and certificates.

In the process of credential inflation, higher degrees come to be required even for some jobs that may not be very intellectually demanding or for which an advanced degree would hardly seem necessary. For example, a college degree may not actually be needed to "manage" a retail franchise outlet. But if the pool of applicants for such a position comes to include holders of college degrees, they will tend to be selected over those without degrees, and soon a college degree will become a requirement. Once credentials are established as a requirement for hiring, inflationary pressures are strong, because students and their families have a strong interest in obtaining resources—in this case, educational credentials—that promise them greater opportunities. In short, the aspiration for upward mobility can "ratchet up" credential requirements above what they might otherwise be, producing credential inflation. The result has been the proliferation of specialized occupational jurisdictions that are off limits to anyone without the accepted educational credentials. Professional associations, governments, and educational institutions have each played a role in constructing occupations and carving the structure of occupations into a maze of occupational jurisdictions controlled by the holders of specialized credentials; all have a stake in the expansion of the "credential society" (Collins 1979; Brown 1995, 2001).

A related argument is that the growth of credentialism has been fueled primarily by the growth of large organizations and the incentives of those in positions of authority in these organizations to find efficient ways to process people and to fill positions. Those making hiring decisions can hardly have a deep knowledge of each of perhaps hundreds of applicants' job-relevant characteristics. Some "shorthand" is needed—objective "evidence" that can be presumed to indicate potential for success. Organizations have come to use educational credentials as an important component of this shorthand—as signals that their holders are more likely than other people to behave in organizationally valued ways. Thus, educational credentials have proven a cost-effective way to limit the pool of eligibles and to aid in the hiring of people presumed to have qualities that organizations value. For example, educational credentials may signal the ability of a job applicant to concentrate in a disciplined way on assigned problems, something that students must do repeatedly if they are to succeed in school. Other traits include reliability (simply showing up every day on time and in a work-ready state), the ability to handle nonroutine or self-directed work, and the ability to conform to the direction and desires of superiors. From the employers' point of view, it is a good bet that those who have survived all the paper writing and examinations of a college education, as well as its stifling bureaucratic organization, have developed these qualities to a greater degree than those who have not.

Today, higher educational credentials are required for professional, technical, and managerial occupations and for most other nonclerical white-collar jobs in large private- and public-sector work organizations. These jobs represent a very large proportion of the most prestigious and best-paying jobs available. Even in the less-credentialized sphere of business management, credentialism has grown rapidly. Almost no one is promoted up the ranks into top management today without a college degree, and an MBA from a top-ranked business school has become an important ticket of admission to the executive suite.

However, the widespread practice of using educational credentials as proxies for skills needed to do certain jobs is imperfect. Beyond literacy and basic computational skills, most of what people need to know to perform most work tasks is learned on the job, not in the classroom. Educational credentials are only an indirect means of assessing a person's capacity to perform such tasks. To the extent that educational signals used as convenient screening devices for job placement are inaccurate, true meritocracy is compromised. In such cases, education does not act as a vehicle of upward social mobility for the most deserving; instead, the *lack* of particular credentials operates as an artificial barrier to mobility.

SUMMARY

Education is both a merit and nonmerit factor in getting ahead in America. It is a merit factor in the sense that students "earn" grades, credits, and diplomas. It is a nonmerit factor in the sense that competition for success is structured by an educational system that does not provide equality of opportunity, because all the nonmerit advantages that accrue to students from more-privileged backgrounds—including inherited familial economic resources (which translate into "quality education" and high educational aspirations), social capital (which includes parental "connections" and positive peer influences), and cultural capital—collectively produce K–12 educational outcomes, including high grade-point averages, standardized and AP test scores, and SAT scores, which are important selection criteria for America's "best" colleges and universities. But additional advantages accrue to class privilege, ranging from the simple ability to pay for an elite private college or university education, to the financial ability to take advantage of "early-acceptance" programs at such institutions, to elaborate back-channel "slotting" operations in which highly connected and expert high school and prep school counselors work closely with admissions officials to virtually place higher-status students at these institutions.

Equality of educational opportunity is a crucial component of the American Dream, but it has never come close to existing in America. Family socioeconomic status and other ascribed characteristics directly and indirectly affect educational attainment. Schools both reflect and re-create existing inequalities in society. Schools reward children of the privileged by certifying and enhancing their social and cultural capital. On the other hand, schools punish children of lower socioeconomic status for their lack of such capital, consigning them to lower-quality teachers, curricula, tracks, and schools, as well as to the self-fulfilling prophecies of low expectations that these produce. As a result, less-privileged children are awarded fewer and lower-valued credentials, and inequality is largely reproduced across generations. Moreover, with increased job competition and increased credential inflation, class reproduction continues to occur, but at higher levels of educational attainment in the population as a whole.

Education is widely perceived as an "engine of mobility" and a primary way to get your ticket punched to middle-class status and fulfillment of the American Dream. The next chapter looks at what has historically been perceived as the major alternate pathway to economic success: starting and operating a business.

REFERENCES

Abel, Jaison R., and Richard Deitz. 2016. "Underemployment in Early Careers of College Graduates Following the Great Recession." Report 749, Federal Reserve Bank of New York. www.newyorkfed.org/medialibrary/media/research/staff_reports/sr749.pdf?la=en (accessed June 23, 2017).

Ainsworth, James W., and Vincent J. Roscigno. 2005. "Stratification, School-Work Linkages and Vocational Education." *Social Force* 84:257–84.

Alexander, Karl, Doris Entwisle, and Linda Olson. 2014. *The Long Shadow: Family Background, Disadvantaged Urban Youth, and the Transition to Adulthood.* New York: Russell Sage Foundation.

Altonji, Joseph G., and Richard K. Mansfield. 2011. "The Role of Family, School, and Community Characteristics in Inequality in Education and Labor-Market Outcomes." In *Whither Opportunity?: Rising Inequality, Schools, and Children's Life Chances,* ed. Greg. J. Duncan and Richard J. Murnane, 339–57. New York: Russell Sage Foundation.

Armstrong, Elizabeth A., and Laura T. Hamilton. 2013. *Paying for the Party: How College Maintains Inequality.* Cambridge, MA: Harvard University Press.

Arroyo, Carmen G. 2008. *The Funding Gap.* Washington, DC: Educational Trust.

Ballantine, Jeanne, Floyd M. Hammack, and Jenny Stuber. 2017. *The Sociology of Education: A Systematic Analysis*, 8th ed. New York: Routledge.

Becker, Gary S. 1993. *Human Capital: A Theoretical and Empirical Analysis with Special Reference to Education.* New York: Columbia University Press.

Blau, Peter, and Otis Dudley Duncan. 1967. *The American Occupational Structure.* New York: John Wiley.

Bourdieu, Pierre. 1973. "Cultural Reproduction and Social Reproduction." In *Knowledge, Education, and Cultural Change*, ed. Richard Brown, 71–112. London: Tavistock.

———. 1984. *Distinction.* Cambridge, MA: Harvard University Press.

Bourdieu, Pierre, and Jean-Claude Passeron. 1990. *Reproduction in Education, Society, and Culture.* London: Sage.

Bowen, William G., and Derek Bok. 2009. *The Shape of the River: Long-Term Consequences of Considering Race in College and University Admissions.* Princeton, NJ: Princeton University Press.

Bowen, William G., Matthew M. Chingos, and Michael S. McPherson. 2011. *Crossing the Finish Line: Completing College at America's Public Universities.* Princeton, NJ: Princeton University Press.

Bowles, Samuel, and Herbert Gintis. 1976. *Schooling in Capitalist America.* New York: Basic Books.

Brown, David K. 1995. *Degrees of Control: A Sociology of Educational Expansion and Occupational Credentialism.* New York: Teachers College Press.

———. 2001. "The Social Sources of Educational Credentialism: Status Cultures, Labor Markets, and Organizations." *Sociology of Education* (extra issue):19–34.

Chetty, Raj, John N. Friedman, Emmanuel Saez, Nicholas Turner, and Danny Yagan. 2017. "Mobility Report Cards: The Role of Colleges in Intergenerational Mobility." Equality of Opportunity Project. Stanford University. www.equality-of-opportunity.org/papers/coll_mrc_paper.pdf (accessed June 23, 2017).

Coleman, James S., Ernest Q. Campbell, Carol J. Hobson, James McPartland, Alexander M. Mood, Frederic D. Weinfold, and Robert L. Link. 1966. *Equality of Educational Opportunity.* Washington, DC: US Government Printing Office.

Collins, Randall. 1979. *The Credential Society: A Historical Sociology of Education and Stratification.* New York: Academic Press.

Conant, James Bryant. 1938. "The Future of Our Higher Education." *Harper's Magazine* 176 (May): 561–70.

———. 1940. "Education for a Classless Society: The Jeffersonian Tradition." *Atlantic* 165 (May): 593–602.

Condron, Dennis J., and Vincent J. Roscigno. 2003. "Disparities Within: Unequal Spending and Achievement in an Urban School District." *Sociology of Education* 76 (January): 18–36.

Dearden, James A., Suhui Li, Chad D. Meyerhoefer, and Muzhe Yang. 2017. "Demonstrated Interest: Signaling Behavior in College Admissions." *Contemporary Economic Policy* 35(4):630–57.

Duncan, Greg J., and Richard J. Murnane. 2011. "Introduction: The American Dream: Then and Now." In *Whither Opportunity?: Rising Inequality, Schools, and Children's Life Chances*, ed. Greg J. Duncan and Richard J. Murnane, 3–23. New York: Russell Sage Foundation.

Entwisle, Doris R., Karl L. Alexander, and Linda S. Olson. 2010 "The Long Reach of SES in Education." In *Handbook of Research in Schools, Schooling, and Human Development*, ed. Jacquelynne S. Eccles and Judith L. Moore. New York: Routledge.

Ermisch, John, Markus Jangtti, and Timothy Smeeding, eds. 2012. *From Parents to Children: The Intergenerational Transmission of Advantage.* New York: Russell Sage Foundation.

Espenshade, Thomas J., Chang Y. Chung, and Joan L. Walling. 2004. "Admission Preferences for Minority Studies, Athletes, and Legacies at Elite Universities." *Social Science Quarterly* 84(2):612–23.

Federal Reserve Bank of New York. 2017. "Quarterly Report on Household Debt and Credit, May 2017." www.newyorkfed.org/medialibrary/interactives/householdcredit/data/pdf/HHDC_2017Q1.pdf (accessed June 23, 2017).

Golden, Daniel. 2003. "Family Ties: Preference for Alumni Children in College Admission Draws Fire." *Wall Street Journal*, January 15.

———. 2006. *The Price of Admission: How America's Ruling Class Buys Its Way into Elite Colleges—And Who Gets Left Outside the Gates.* New York: Crown Publishers.

Goldrick-Rab, Sara. 2016. *Paying the Price: College Costs, Financial Aid, and the Betrayal of the American Dream.* Chicago: University of Chicago Press.

Guinier, Lani. 2015. *The Tyranny of the Meritocracy: Democratizing Higher Education in America.* Boston: Beacon Press.

Howell, Cameron, and Sarah E. Turner. 2004. "Legacies in Black and White: The Racial Composition of the Legacy Pool." *Research in Higher Education* 455(4):325–51.

Jencks, Christopher L., Marshall Smith, Henry Acland, Mary Jo Bane, David K. Cohen, Herbert Gintis, Barbara Heyns, et al. 1972. *Inequality: Reassessment of the Effect of Family and Schooling in America.* New York: Harper & Row.

Johnson, Heather Beth. 2006. *The American Dream and the Power of Wealth: Choosing Schools and Inheriting Inequality in the Land of Opportunity.* New York: Routledge.

Karabel, Jerome. 2005. *The Chosen: The Hidden History of Admission and Exclusion at Harvard, Yale, and Princeton.* New York: Houghton Mifflin.

Kohn, Melvin L. 1963. "Social Class and Parent-Child Relationships: An Interpretation." *American Journal of Sociology* 68(4):471–80.

Kornrich, Sabino. 2016. "Inequalities in Parental Spending on Young Children: 1972–2010." *AERA Open.* 2(2):1–12.

Kornrich, Sabino, and Frank Furstenberg. 2013. "Investing in Children: Changes in Parental Spending on Children, 1972–2007." *Demography* 50:1–23.

Kozol, Jonathan. 1991. *Savage Inequalities: Children in America's Schools.* New York: Crown.

———. 2006. *The Shame of the Nation: The Restoration of Apartheid Schooling in America.* New York: Crown.

Lafortune, Julien, Jesse Rothstein, and Diane Whitmore Schanzenbach. 2015. *School Finance Reform and the Distribution of Student Achievement.* Cambridge, MA: National Bureau of Research.

Lareau, Annette. 2000. *Home Advantage: Social Class and Parental Intervention in Elementary Education*. Lanham, MD: Rowman & Littlefield.

———. 2003. *Unequal Childhoods: Class, Race, and Family Life*. Los Angeles: University of California Press.

———. 2014. "Schools, Housing, and the Reproduction of Inequality." In *Choosing Homes, Choosing Schools*, ed. Annette Lareau and Kimberly Goyette, 169–206. New York: Russell Sage Foundation.

Lareau, Annette, and Elliot B. Weininger. 2003. "Cultural Capital in Educational Research." *Theory and Society* 32(5–6):567–606.

Lewis, Theodore, and Shih-Yu Cheng. 2006. "Tracking, Expectations and the Transformation of Vocational Education." *American Journal of Education* 113(1):67–99.

Massey, Douglas S. 2007. *Categorically Unequal: The American Stratification System*. New York: Russell Sage Foundation.

Oakes, Jeannie. 1985. *Keeping Track: How Schools Structure Inequality*. New Haven, CT: Yale University Press.

———. 1990. *Multiplying Inequalities: The Effects of Race, Social Class, and Tracking on Opportunities to Learn Mathematics and Science*. Santa Monica, CA: Rand.

Pell Institute. 2017. "Indicators of Higher Education Equity in the United States: 2017 Historical Trend Report." Pell Institute for the Study of Opportunity in Higher Education: Washington, DC. http://pellinstitute.org/downloads/publications-Indicators_of_Higher_Education_Equity_in_the_US_2017_Historical_Trend_Report.pdf (accessed June 23, 2017).

Pew Research Center. 2015. *Parenting in America: Outlooks, Worries, Aspirations*. www.pewsocialtrends.org/2015/12/17/parenting-in-america/ (accessed June 22, 2017).

Price, Derek V. 2004. *Borrowing Inequality: Race, Class, and Student Loans*. Boulder, CO: Lynne Rienner Publishers.

Putnam, Robert D. 2015. *Our Kids: The American Dream in Crisis*. New York: Simon & Schuster.

Radford, Alexandra Walton. 2013. *Top Student, Top School? How Social Class Shapes Where Valedictorians Go to College*. Chicago: University of Chicago Press.

Reardon, Sean. 2011. "The Widening Academic Achievement Gap Between Rich and Poor: New Evidence and Possible Explanations." In *Whither Opportunity: Rising Inequality, Schools and Children's Life Chances*, ed. Greg J. Duncan and Richard J. Murnane, 91–115. New York: Russell Sage Foundation.

Rivera, Lauren. 2015. *Pedigree: How Elite Students Get Elite Jobs*. Princeton, NJ: Princeton University Press.

Rose, Stephen J. 2017. "Mismatch: How Many Workers with a Bachelor's Degree Are Overqualified for Their Jobs?" Washington, DC: Urban Institute. www.urban.org/sites/default/files/publication/87951/college_mismatch_final_0.pdf (accessed June 20, 2017).

Schultz, Theodore W. 1961. "Investment in Human Capital." *American Economic Review* 51:1–17.

Soares, Joseph. 2007. *The Power of Privilege: Yale and America's Elite Universities*. Stanford, CA: Stanford University Press.

Stevens, Mitchell L. 2007. *Creating a Class: College Admissions and the Education of Elites*. Cambridge, MA: Harvard University Press.

US Department of Education. 2007. *National Center for Education Statistics, Common Core of Data (CCD)*, "National Public Education Financial Survey," 1989–1990 and 2004–2005. Washington, DC: US Government Printing Office.

———. 2017a. *Digest of Educational Statistics: National Center for Education Statistics*. Table 104.10. https://nces.ed.gov/programs/digest/d15/tables/dt15_104.10.asp (accessed July 2, 2017).

———. 2017b. "The Condition of Education: Public School Revenue Sources." National Center for Education Statistics. https://nces.ed.gov/programs/coe/indicator_cma.asp (accessed June 23, 2017).

———. 2017c. "Tuition Costs of Colleges and Universities." National Center for Education Statistics. https://nces.ed.gov/fastfacts/display.asp?id=76 (accessed January 16, 2017).

US Department of Labor. 2017. "Unemployment Rates and Earnings by Educational Attainment." www.bls.gov/emp/ep_chart_001.htm (accessed July 2, 2017).

Vedder, Richard, Christopher Denhart, and Jonathan Robe. 2013. "Why Are Recent College Graduates Underemployed? University Enrollments and Labor Market Realities." Washington, DC: Center for College Affordability and Productivity. http://centerforcollegeaffordability.org/uploads/Underemployed%20Report%202.pdf (accessed June 23, 2017).

Weis, Lois, Kristin Cipollone, and Heather Jenkins. 2014. *Class Warfare: Class, Race, and College Admissions in Top-Tier Secondary Schools*. Chicago: University of Chicago Press.

Zweigenhaft, Richard L. 2015. "The Role of Elite Education for White Men, White Women and People of Color in the US Corporate Elite." Paper Presented at Elite Education Conference, June 29, 2015, Toronto, Ontario. www2.ucsc.edu/whorulesamerica/power/elite_education.html (accessed June 23, 2017).

6

I Did It My Way

The Decline of Self-Employment and the Ascent of Corporations

> I ate it up, and spit it out. I faced it all and I stood tall, and did it my way.
>
> —Lyrics from "My Way," cowritten by Paul Anka
> and Frank Sinatra, as performed by Frank Sinatra

Apart from higher education, the major alternate route to upward mobility in America has historically been through owning and operating one's own business. An important part of the American Dream is the opportunity to strike out on your own, be your own boss, and own your own business. Self-employment, in many ways, epitomizes the American Dream. Being self-employed exemplifies independence, initiative, self-reliance, and rugged individualism—virtues held in high regard in American society. The entrepreneur who builds a business from scratch and turns it into a success is an American icon.

The image of the rugged individualist fit well with conditions in early American society. Estimates are that in colonial America over 80 percent of the labor force was self-employed (Phillips 1958, 2). Most were farmers who owned their small family farms. Others were craftsmen, shopkeepers, and artisans. A few were fee-for-service professionals such as lawyers and physicians. Even the most prosperous of businesses employed relatively few workers, at least by modern standards. Among the small segment that was not self-employed, the largest contingent comprised slaves and indentured servants.

Wealth and property were primarily tied to the land, and the land was vast and only sparsely populated. After independence, the federal government acquired vast tracks of land on its Western frontier. The government had acquired so much land that it was willing to give some of it away to white settlers who would stake a claim. For example, as a result of the Homestead Act of 1862, the US government gave nearly 1.5 million families title to 246 million acres of land, nearly the size of California and Texas combined (Shapiro 2004, 190). At least for white settlers, America was literally the land of opportunity. The idea of rugged pioneers setting out against all the odds to stake their own claims and conquer the West became a deep and abiding image in the American psyche.

Self-employment also fit well with the principles of free-market capitalism. Economic self-interest, individual ownership, and unbridled competition became the cornerstones of the new economy. Self-employment resonated with the experience of the new nation. Since those early days, however, economic conditions have changed dramatically. Large bureaucratically organized corporations now dominate the American economic landscape. Despite these colossal shifts in the economy, many Americans continue to cling to the romantic image of the lone inventor and the individual entrepreneur as backbones of the American economy. In this chapter, I chronicle these changes and discuss their impact on the prospects for meritocracy.

MOM AND POP, WHERE ART THOU?
THE DECLINE OF SELF-EMPLOYMENT

Estimating historical rates of self-employment can be a tricky business (Aronson 1991, 137–42; Wright 1997, 142–45). Despite problems of comparability, counting, and classification, the overall historical pattern is clear. No matter how you calculate them, rates of self-employment in America have declined sharply. Self-employment as a percentage of the total labor force has plummeted from an estimated 80 percent in 1800 (Phillips 1958, 2) to an official rate of just 6.2 percent in 2017 (US Department of Labor 2017a). Since 1967, the Bureau of Labor Statistics "official" count of self-employed workers includes only those whose businesses are not incorporated. However, 40 percent of self-employed workers form corporations in which they become wage and salary employees in their own companies (Hipple and Hammond 2016). While the "official" self-employment rate in 2015 was 6.2 percent, the combined rate that includes both incorporated and unincorporated self-employed workers was slightly higher, at 10.1 percent, still well below earlier levels.

Among the incorporated self-employed are owners of franchised businesses. Individuals who own franchises licensed through major corporations strongly identify as self-employed (Bills 1998). Franchises operate in such diverse areas as motels, restaurants, convenience stores, gas stations, clothing outlets, and even traditionally locally owned and operated businesses such as plumbing services and funeral homes. One example of the trend toward chains or franchise business is pharmacies, traditionally a locally owned and operated business. As late as 1966, 40 percent of pharmacists were self-employed, with most working in independent pharmacies. By 2011, only 5 percent of pharmacists were self-employed, with most working in national pharmacy chains such as CVS, Walgreens, and Rite-Aid (Goldin and Katz 2016).

According to the International Franchise Association (2016), in 2016 there were over 800,000 franchise businesses in the United States, generating $868 billion in revenue. An estimated 40 percent of retail sales are made through franchise outlets (Everett 2006; Dant et al. 2011). One-fourth of these outlets are owned by the parent franchisor company, while the majority are owned or partly owned by franchisees (Blair and Lafontaine 2005). Although franchisees may be owners or part owners of such establishments, they are not entrepreneurs in the traditional sense. They do not create new business concepts or develop new products. They often rely on the franchisor to provide training, financing, and marketing. Most franchisees are contractually bound to follow standardized procedures and operations established by the franchisor. Franchisees are therefore neither fully independent owners nor fully dependent wage employees. Instead, they represent a kind of in-between status most often referred to as "dependent self-employment" (Bills 1998; Muehlberger 2007).

Another dependent type of self-employment includes those who are self-employed but have only one client. Such enterprises may be spin-offs of parent businesses that are established separately for tax purposes. Instead of representing true entrepreneurial activity, such employment may be a new way for employers to hire outsourced workers under arrangements of homework, freelancing, or subcontracting (Wright 1997, 140). Large construction firms, for instance, frequently subcontract trade work to individuals or small companies, often for less pay and benefits than the firm would pay its own full-time employees. Increasingly, large farmers in Texas and the Southwest use subcontractors to supply labor in an effort to avoid legal problems hiring undocumented Mexican immigrants (Massey 2007). Although individual craft workers or owners of the subcontracting companies may be "self-employed," they are often largely or wholly dependent on a single client, reducing their leverage and true autonomy.

Professionals in group practices may also identify themselves as self-employed and often incorporate for tax purposes, but they are not sole practitioners in the classical sense. There are clear advantages for professionals who work in these settings, such as taking turns being "on call" for the practice, having colleagues immediately available to consult, sharing expensive equipment and overhead costs, and hiring accountants, receptionists, nurses, and billing agencies. But their work and conditions of employment are increasingly bureaucratized and subject to control by others.

Those who work "under the table" or "off the books" in what is alternately referred to as the "irregular economy," "the shadow economy," or the "black market" also confound the estimates for self-employment in the labor force (Dallago 1990; Greenfield 1993; Leonard 1998; Naylor 2002; Schlosser 2003; Venkatesh 2006; Williams 2006; Williams and Windebank 1998). Individuals who work in the irregular economy may be self-employed or work for someone else. They may be in the irregular economy involuntarily because of lack of regular employment, or they may be voluntarily engaged in "hidden" entrepreneurial activity. Much of the economic activity that occurs in this sector is intentionally engaged in illegally to avoid taxation and regulation. Forms of work in this sector are varied, ranging from housewives watching other people's children in their homes for undeclared pay, to undocumented immigrants working in a variety of settings, to handymen doing home improvement and repair, to people participating directly in criminal activities, such as theft, fencing, drug dealing, gambling, prostitution, loan sharking, smuggling, or, more recently, Internet or cybercrime. The full extent of these activities is unknown.

In many ways, the irregular economy is a bastion of unadulterated free enterprise. It is, in effect, unregulated and untaxed and creates opportunities for ambitious, risk-taking entrepreneurs. For some, the irregular economy has long been one of the few sources of employment or mobility in economically depressed areas (Fusfeld 1973; Naylor 2002; Venkatesh 2006). Some research, for instance, indicates that successful drug dealing early in life increases the likelihood of legitimate self-employment in later years (Fairlie 2002). Although employment in the irregular economy may, for some, be a vehicle of upward mobility and, in some cases, a pathway to eventual employment in the regular economy, it is not generally considered a legitimate part of the American Dream.

Early declines in self-employment were mainly the result of the Industrial Revolution and the mechanization of agriculture, which displaced many small family farms. At the same time, opportunities for wage employment increased in the growing industrial sector. Although the decline of self-employment was most rapid in agriculture, self-employment declined in the nonagricultural sector as well. Goods manufactured in smokestack factories replaced handmade goods produced in craft shops. Supermarkets and chain convenience stores replaced family-owned groceries and dry-goods stores. Giant suburban malls with "big-box" corporate chain outlets replaced the family-owned shops and specialty stores. Chain motels and hotels replaced family-owned roadside inns. Fast-food and franchise restaurants replaced family-owned diners. HMOs and joint specialty practices replaced the "hang-out-a-shingle" solo family doctor. While remnants of traditional local independent businesses remain, each of these arenas of the economy has become increasingly bureaucratized, moving gradually away from sole proprietorships to partnerships to larger corporate establishments.

BETWIXT AND BETWEEN: THE CONTRADICTORY CLASS POSITION OF THE SELF-EMPLOYED

The class position of self-employed workers is at best ambiguous. Karl Marx initially distinguished two main social classes in capitalist societies: those who own the means of producing wealth (bourgeoisie) and those who sell their labor to others (proletariat). The bourgeoisie, however, include several subcategories (Wright 1997). One group of bourgeoisie, *rentier capitalists*, own businesses and hire the labor of others but do not themselves work for an income. Another group of bourgeoisie, *entrepreneurial capitalists*, both work in the businesses they own and hire the labor of others.

Petty bourgeoisie, on the other hand, own their own businesses and work in them but do not hire the labor of others.

The vast majority of the self-employed in the United States are true petty bourgeoisie; that is, they do not have paid employees. In 2015, for instance, 85.6 percent of unincorporated self-employed workers and 58 percent of incorporated employees had no paid employees (Hipple and Hammond 2016). Of self-employed workers who did have paid employees, most had very few. Seventy percent of unincorporated self-employed workers and 52 percent of incorporated self-employed workers had four or fewer employees. Only 6.1 percent of unincorporated self-employed workers and 12.5 percent of incorporated self-employed workers had more than twenty employees.

Petty bourgeoisie and entrepreneurial capitalists occupy what sociologist Erik Olin Wright refers to as "contradictory" locations within the class structure. In some ways these groups share characteristics with capitalists, and in some ways they share characteristics with wage laborers. Like capitalists, the petty bourgeoisie own their own businesses, but unlike capitalists, the petty bourgeoisie do not hire or control the labor of others. Entrepreneurial capitalists and the petty bourgeoisie share with the proletariat the characteristic of working for an income. But unlike the proletariat, the work of entrepreneurial capitalists and the petty bourgeoisie is not supervised or controlled by others.

In later stages of industrial development, these class divisions become even more blurred. Some sociologists, for instance, make a distinction between the "old middle class" and the "new middle class" (Mills 1951). The old middle class consisted mostly of entrepreneurial capitalists and the petty bourgeoisie—that is, small-business owners, family farmers, and solo fee-for-service professionals. The old middle class was considered generally respectable, mostly well-to-do, and fiercely independent. However, in later stages of industrialization, a new middle class of managers, administrators, and technicians emerged. The new middle class came about with the advent of the "managerial revolution" and the "separation of ownership from control" (Berle and Means 1932). In the early part of the twentieth century, more and more owners withdrew from day-to-day control of their businesses and began to hire managers to run them. As businesses became larger and more complex, layers of bureaucracy were added, and the ranks of management grew. Remnants of the old middle class remain, but it is outnumbered and overshadowed by the ascendance of the new middle class.

CHARACTERISTICS OF THE SELF-EMPLOYED

With the notable exceptions of farmers, ranchers, and construction workers, most self-employed workers today are clustered in the service sector of the economy. The US Department of Labor (2014a) reports that for 2012, the occupations with the highest number of self-employed workers included farmers and ranchers (680,500); supervisors of retail salespersons (390,00); child-care workers (374,100); carpenters

(325,400); construction managers (275,000); hairdressers, hairstylists, and cosmetologists (254,500); landscapers and groundskeepers (253,000); construction laborers (251,500); maids and housekeeping cleaners (177,200); and real estate agents (176,300). Significantly, the US Department of Labor projects that farmers and ranchers, who are the largest group of self-employed workers, are expected to decline by 18,000 workers between 2014 and 2024, as the result of continued automation in agriculture, and the continued displacement of traditional small family farms with large "agribusiness" corporations (US Department of Labor 2017b).

Compared to the wage-labor force, self-employed workers tend to be older, white, and male. Age differences in rates of self-employment are especially acute in both upper and lower age groups. In 2015, rates of self-employment were highest for workers over sixty-five years of age (15.5 percent for unincorporated self-employed, and less than 10 percent for incorporated self-employed), and lowest for workers under twenty-four years of age (1.9 percent for unincorporated self-employed, and less than 1 percent for incorporated self-employed workers) (Hipple and Hammond 2016). Moreover, rates of self-employment for workers under the age of thirty have declined over the past several decades (Wilmoth 2016), indicating less entrepreneurial opportunity for recent generations of workers. Older workers are more likely than younger workers to have both the work experience and the accumulated capital required to start businesses. Also, in some cases older workers may opt for self-employment as an alternative to retirement, or as a way to control the amount and pace of work as their physical stamina declines.

Self-employed workers are somewhat more likely to be male than female. In 2015, 7.4 percent of male workers were among the unincorporated self-employed compared to 5.2 percent of women workers; the corresponding rates of self-employment among incorporated self-employed workers were 4.9 percent for men and 2.3 percent for women (Hipple and Hammond 2016).

Overall rates of self-employment among women have increased over time, especially in the 1980s and through the mid-1990s, but have remained steady since then (US Bureau of Labor 2014b; Patrick et al. 2016). While rates of self-employment have remained steady for married women, rates of self-employment among unmarried women have continued to increase (Patrick et al. 2016). This difference may reflect a divergence of motivations for self-employment for married and unmarried women. Patrick et al. (2016) found, for instance, that family commitments and more-traditional attitudes about women's roles may push married women into self-employment, but that unmarried women are more influenced by favorable perceptions of local business climates as well as perceptions of their own abilities and more progressive attitudes about women's roles in their decision to pursue self-employment.

Although self-employment is often seen as a vehicle of upward social mobility for ethnic minorities, whites have higher rates of self-employment than these groups. In 2015, for instance, the rate of unincorporated self-employment for whites was 6.9 percent, compared to 6.4 percent for Hispanics, 5.6 percent for Asians, and 3.6 percent for blacks. The rates of incorporated self-employment were 4 percent for whites, 4 percent for Asians, and less than 2 percent for both blacks and Hispanics (Hipple and Hammond 2016). The generally lower rates of self-employment among minorities may be attributed in part to reluctance among white customers to patronize minority-owned businesses, and whites' assumption that minority-owned businesses produce inferior products or services (Feagin and Sikes 1994; Parker 2004). Also, on average, people of color, especially blacks, have much less wealth than whites, and therefore have less capital to start businesses and more difficulty securing business loans (Parker 2004; Shapiro 2017).

Some studies suggest that the self-employed tend to have different psychological characteristics than wage workers (cf. Thornton 1999 and Parker 2004). These studies suggest, for instance, that need for achievement, internal locus of control, risk-taking propensity, and independence are associated with the likelihood of self-employment. Other studies suggest that self-employment disproportionately attracts workers with low productivity who might otherwise have difficulty finding suitable employment in the wage sector. Such "trait" studies, however, are plagued by methodological problems, especially the basic issue of separating cause and effect. In short, do certain psychological characteristics or predispositions lead to self-employment, or does self-employment create such characteristics in individuals? Also, such traits are not unique to the self-employed, creating problems of demarcation. Not surprisingly, the results of these studies have been very mixed. Regardless of specification and the direction of causality, the idea that individual characteristics alone account for self-employment or entrepreneurship has largely been abandoned in favor of more multidimensional models that take into consideration the influence of organizational, market, and environmental influences.

At least some self-employment, for instance, occurs not as a matter of individual choice or desire to start a new business or strike out on one's own, but as the result of unemployment (e.g., a downsized white-collar executive who freelances as a self-employed "consultant"), subemployment (the laid-off factory worker who works as a self-employed "handyman"), or outsourced employment (a former wage employee who contracts with an employer to perform the same services as a contract laborer, often for less pay and little or no benefits) (Wright 1997, 139–42). In addition, some employment in the "irregular" economy is also involuntary; that is, individuals may resort to working "off the books," often in illegal activities, when stable wage employment is not available or is difficult to secure (Fusfeld 1973; Naylor 2002; Venkatesh 2006). The full extent of these various forms of nonvoluntary self-employment is difficult to estimate. Most studies, however, show that self-employment tends to decline during periods of economic expansion and increase during periods of economic decline (Hipple 2010), further indicating that at least some self-employment is reluctantly entered into when wage employment is otherwise not available or is difficult to secure.

The income of self-employed workers is also difficult to assess. Overall, self-employed workers earn less on average than wage and salary workers (Astebro and Chen

2014; Blanchflower 2015; Roche 2014; Hamilton 2000). However, there are important internal distinctions among the self-employed regarding income. First, there is a much greater range of income differences among the self-employed than among wage and salary workers. Among self-employed workers, a few do very well, but most earn very little, which skews overall averages. Self-employed hedge-fund managers, for instance, may make millions, but there are relatively few of them compared to hundreds of thousands of self-employed child-care workers and hairdressers, most of whom earn very little. Second, and relatedly, there are considerable differences in average income for unincorporated and incorporated self-employed. The smaller segment of incorporated self-employed, who include more prosperous business owners and fee-for-service professionals, such as doctors and lawyers, earn more on average than either unincorporated self-employed or wage and salary workers. Comparing full-time workers in the United States in 2013, the average annual income for wage and salary workers was $47,232, compared to $37,014 for unincorporated self-employed and $79,817 for incorporated self-employed (Blanchflower 2015).

Assessing the real income of self-employed workers is further complicated because self-employed workers, in an attempt to reduce tax liability, are more likely to under-report income than are wage workers (Aronson 1991; Hurst et al. 2014). Or, as in the case of the illegal irregular segment of the economy, self-employment earnings may be disguised or not reported at all. What is more, self-employed workers who own their own businesses tend to work many more hours than wage laborers, which effectively reduces the hourly rate of return among the self-employed. In addition, income alone does not tell the whole story, since self-employed workers must fund their own retirements, medical insurance, and vacation time, which reduces the effective value of total earnings. The recent inflationary surge in the costs of private medical insurance and the lack of pooled risks for self-employed people have especially eroded effective wage benefits for the self-employed.

Another characteristic of self-employment is that it is associated with very high risks for workplace injury and death. Self-employed workers, for instance, are four times more likely to be victims of fatal work injuries than wage and salary workers (US Bureau of Labor 2016a). This higher rate of on-the-job fatalities among the self-employed is primarily associated with the disproportionate tendency for self-employed workers to work in industries with higher injury and fatality rates, especially agriculture, forestry, fishing, and construction. However, the self-employed are also more likely to have higher fatality rates even when working in the same occupations as their wage and salary counterparts (Pegula 2004). This difference may be related to several factors associated with the conditions of work among self-employed workers, including fewer workplace safety measures (self-employed workers may ignore safety concerns to try to stay competitive, or have fewer resources to spend on safety education and equipment), longer hours worked among self-employed (increasing the risk of fatigue while operating hazardous machinery), and the older ages among self-employed workers (increasing risks of more strenuous physical activities) (Pegula 2004).

Self-employed workers are not only at greater risk for fatal on-the-job injuries, but also are more likely to be murdered on the job. The higher risk for homicide among self-employed workers is primarily in retail sales. Small family-owned retail and lodging establishments are often located in marginal or low-income areas and may be more attractive targets for armed robberies than larger stores or national retail chains (Pegula 2004, 34), which are also more likely to be located in suburban malls and use electronic surveillance, private police, and other more elaborate security measures.

Another type of risk for self-employed workers is the high risk of business failure, especially for those striking out alone to start a new business. Rates of survival for new businesses are notoriously low. According to time series data tracked by the US Bureau of Labor (2016b), only two-thirds of new businesses survive for two years, half close within five years, and only about one-third make it ten years or more.

This is nothing new; self-employment and new business starts have always been very high-risk ventures. But the presence of large corporations makes such ventures even more risky, reflected in sharp declines in new business starts in recent decades (Hathaway and Litan 2014). Small businesses that take on established corporations for market share are at a distinct disadvantage. Small-business starts that have the best chance of success are those that find new, localized, or unique market niches. Even then, such establishments run the risk of being swallowed up by larger concerns seeking entry into niche markets, especially if these niches yield high returns and offer opportunities for national or global expansion.

SWIMMING WITH THE SHARKS: THE ASCENT OF THE MODERN CORPORATION

The historical decline of self-employment has taken place alongside the related growth and increasing dominance of large-scale corporations. At the time of the American Revolution, corporations did not exist. During colonial times, a handful of joint stock companies, such as the East India Company, the Massachusetts Bay Company, and the Hudson Bay Company, were chartered by the British Crown to reap the bounty of the New World (Derber 1998). With the establishment of American independence, a few establishments were granted corporate charters by states and sometimes the federal government to provide specific public services, such as roads, bridges, canals, or colleges. In exchange for these expressly public services, such private entities were granted powers normally delegated to governments, such as the power to collect tolls.

At first, corporate charters were granted only under strictly delimited conditions. In addition to requiring that corporations explicitly serve the public interest, corporate charters were granted for limited periods, and restricted the amount of assets corporations could accumulate (Derber 1998, 122). These restrictions were consistent with the distrust that early legislators had of all large organizations, including the new corporate entities (Perrow 2002, 33–35). Individual states, however, competed with one another for corporate revenue by offering increasingly lenient statutes for incorporation. One small state, Delaware, host to a particularly large and important corporation, DuPont, ultimately offered the most lenient statutes for incorporation and became the darling of large corporations everywhere. Roughly half of today's Fortune 500 companies, regardless of where they conduct business, are incorporated in the state of Delaware. With most government restrictions lifted, the modern corporate form emerged (Derber 1998; Miller 1977; Perrow 2002; Roy 1997). By 2012, corporations accounted for 82.1 percent of all business revenue, while partnerships accounted for only 14.1 percent, and sole proprietorships, only 3.4 percent (US Internal Revenue Service 2017).

Crucial to the establishment of the modern corporation was a series of legal decisions that redefined the essence of the corporation. These decisions allowed corporations to operate for private gain without explicitly serving the public interest, established the principle of limited liability, and extended the legal rights of individuals to corporations. The elimination of the requirement for public service enabled an unrestricted profit motive. Under the principle of limited liability, investors would risk only the amount of money they invested in a corporation, and would not be liable for whatever other debts the corporation acquired. Especially critical to these court rulings was the extension of the legal rights of individuals to corporations. These rulings allowed the pooling of enormous amounts of capital from multiple investors in single companies, a phenomenon that has been described as the "socializing of capital" (Roy 1997).

When ratified in 1787, the Constitution of the United States did not contain the word *corporation*, nor does it today. It is understandable that its framers, otherwise concerned about concentrations of power not directly accountable to the public, overlooked corporations, since the corporate-like entities of the day were neither numerous nor powerful. As corporations became more numerous and powerful, constitutional issues related to corporations arose. Since the Constitution recognizes only two legal entities, the government and the individual, the courts in essence had to decide which of these applied to corporations. In a series of key US Supreme Court decisions in the early 1800s, corporations were interpreted legally as individuals under the provisions of the Constitution. As such, corporations were extended the legal rights of individuals, especially with regard to the Fourteenth Amendment, which provides for "equal protection" under the law.

Among the rights granted to corporations was the right to buy and sell property. With the legal ability to buy and sell property like individuals, corporations ferociously bought and sold each other. The history of corporations in America is the history of the big fish eating the little fish, and eventually the big fish eating each other. Most major markets in the United States became dominated by a few big fish. The 1880s and 1890s marked an era of rapid consolidation. Through trade associations, pools, trusts, cartels, and other organizational devices, turn-of-the-century capitalists managed to consolidate economic power to an alarming degree. Widespread consolidation led to artificially inflated prices, which provoked organized efforts to reinstate more competitive conditions. Political agitation from farmers and small-business owners, who were caught in the grip of railroad combinations, prompted the establishment of the Interstate Commerce Commission in 1887, the government's first major attempt to regulate trade, and the Sherman Antitrust Act of 1890, the government's first organized effort to control monopolies.

Although monopolies were illegal, the major "smokestack" industries in the United States that made America an industrial giant—autos, steel, chemicals, and oil—became dominated by a few large corporations and settled into their current oligopolistic structure (Suarez-Villa 2015). Numerous other familiar industries became similarly highly concentrated (see table 6.1). Overall, the largest five hundred corporations in America are responsible for two-thirds of the US gross domestic product (*Fortune* 2017). The largest one hundred manufacturing firms account for over 26 percent of the value of all manufactured products in America (US Census Bureau 2012).

Retail outlets are now also rapidly becoming oligopolized. By 2012, the largest fifty retail firms were responsible for 37 percent of all retail sales (US Census Bureau 2012), a substantial sum considering that small-business establishments tend to be located in the retail sector of the economy. The newest development in retail sales has been the growth of e-commerce or online shopping, led by industry giant Amazon, which has itself become a threat to shopping malls and large retailers such as Walmart, Sears, Kmart, and Target, which previously displaced many small and locally owned retail shops. Amazon was established in 1994 as an online bookseller and quickly expanded into retail sales in general. In 2016 Amazon announced plans to open its first "brick and mortar" stores, and in 2017 acquired Whole Foods, a high-end grocery chain.

At the top of the pyramid chain of corporate dominance in the US economy are big banks and other major financial institutions, such as insurance, securities, credit, and mortgage companies. This is the "paper-tiger" sector of the economy involved not in the making of things but in moving money around—that is, in buying and selling money, credit, insurance, or financial risk. At over 20 percent of US gross domestic product by 2005, the financial sector had become the largest sector of the US economy, exceeding manufacturing, health care, and wholesale/retail trade (Phillips 2008). Like other sectors of the economy, the financial sector has become increasingly consolidated. In 1996, the largest five US commercial banks held 23 percent of total industry assets; by 2014, the largest five US banks held 48 percent of total industry assets, or more than double the earlier level of concentration (Federal Reserve Bank of St. Louis 2016). The rapid consolidation of US industry in general, and especially the financial sector, has led to increasing concerns that these corporate entities are "too big to fail." That is, because of their sheer size and the potential ripple effects should they fail, they could drag the rest of the economy down with them, risking the collapse of the economy as a whole, as was evident in the events leading to and precipitating the Great Recession of 2008.

The Great Recession was brought about by changes in banking regulations that encouraged speculative and undercapitalized lending practices. With these changes,

Table 6.1. Examples of Highly Concentrated Industries, 2012

	Market Share of Four Largest Firms (%)
Manufacturing industries	
Electric lightbulbs and parts	84
Petrochemicals	78
Aircraft manufacturing	80
Automobile manufacturing	60
Tire manufacturing	69
Household appliances	65
Plastic bottles	55
Paper mills	54
Soap and detergents	81
Iron and steel mills	49
Household refrigerators and freezers	93
Electric computers	51
Cigarette manufacturing	88
Food production industries	
Breweries	88
Distilleries	65
Breakfast cereals	81
Cookies and crackers	60
Chocolate confectioneries	51
Snack food	52
Soft drinks	63
Coffee and tea	58
Ice cream and frozen desserts	46
Flour milling	55
Dog and cat food	72
Retail sales outlets	
Variety stores	89
Office supply and stationery	85
Hobby, toy, and game stores	77
Department stores	73
Bookstores	70
Athletic footwear stores	70
Cosmetics, beauty supplies, and perfume	56
Pet and pet supply stores	69
Computer and software stores	73
Pharmacies and drugstores	70
Electronics and appliance stores	54
Optical goods stores	57
Financial institutions	
Credit card issuing firms	78
Central banks	79
Consumer lending firms	52

	Market Share of Four Largest Firms (%)
Information	
TV broadcasting	52
Radio broadcasting	50
Motion picture theaters (except drive-ins)	56
News syndicates	60
Cellular and other wireless communications	89
Cable and other program distribution	71

Source: US Census Bureau (2012).

the paper tiger eventually became a house of cards. In the 1960s and 1970s, the federal government set up programs to help low-income families become homeowners. These programs insured mortgage loans against default under relaxed rules for eligibility. These "subprime" loans were "packaged" with conventional loans and resold to investors. Once the conventional mortgage market was saturated, banks—anxious to earn fees and turn quick profits—increasingly turned to the subprime market (Fligstein and Goldstein 2011). By 2007, 70 percent of all loans made were unconventional mortgages (Fligstein and Goldstein 2011). The buying and selling of these so-called "ninja" loans in the subprime market occurred in an economic climate of both deregulation and corporate consolidation.

Commercial banks previously restricted from investments of this type entered the frenzy with zeal. The largest of these soon dominated the mortgage-backed securities market. Market confidence in these securities eventually eroded, and the credit supply dried up. Housing prices fell sharply, and large numbers of American homeowners defaulted on mortgages. Investment companies were then stuck with large amounts of "toxic assets" in loans that exceeded the value of homes and the capacity of homeowners to make payments, and the economy as a whole went into free fall. By late 2007, the financial sector was on the edge of economic collapse, reminiscent of the banking collapse that triggered the Great Depression in 1929. The federal government, itself deeply in debt, was reluctantly forced to step in and bail out the credit market at a staggering sum of over $700 billion. All of these events had devastating effects for individuals, including job loss, mortgage defaults, and personal bankruptcy quite independent of the merit of discrete workers. Although there was some talk about breaking up the big banks to reduce chances of similar economic vulnerabilities in the future, the big banks emerged from the crisis with an even larger market share of banking assets than before the onset of the Great Recession.

Megamergers

The historically high level of market consolidation in all sectors of the economy has been fueled by a frenzy of megamergers occurring in recent decades (see table 6.2). Huge sums of money are taken out of the credit economy to finance such mergers without typically creating any new products or new jobs (as combined entities

Table 6.2.   Examples of Recent Megamergers

Megamergers	Price ($ billions)	Date
AOL + Time Warner	165.0	2000
Verizon Com + Verizon Wireless	130.0	2013
Dow Chemical + DuPont	130.0	2017
InBev + SAB Miller	117.4	2015
Heinz + Kraft	100.0	2015
Glaxo + SmithKline	76.0	2000
BellSouth + AT&T	73.0	2006
Royal Dutch Shell + BG Group	70.0	2015
JPMorgan + Bank One	58.0	2004
Pfizer + Wyeth	68.0	2009
Pfizer + Pharmacia	60.0	2002
Procter & Gamble + Gillette	57.0	2005
InBev + Anheuser-Busch	52.0	2008
Bank of America + Merrill Lynch	50.0	2009
Cingular + AT&T Wireless	41.0	2005
Sprint + Nextel	35.0	2005
Duke Energy + Progress Energy	32.0	2012
Microsoft + LinkedIn	26.2	2016
Facebook + WhatsApp	19.0	2014
Time Warner + Adelphia	17.7	2006
Texaco + Unocal	16.8	2005
Bank of New York + Mellon	16.5	2007
First Union + Wachovia	14.4	2003
Wells Fargo + Wachovia	12.7	2009
Sears + Kmart	11.0	2005
Microsoft Corporation + Skype	8.5	2011
Molson + Coors	4.0	2005
Adidas + Reebok	3.8	2006

benefit from various economies of scale). Most of these are horizontal mergers in which large firms acquire other large firms in the same industry group, resulting in even higher levels of market consolidation.

With name changes as well as acquisitions of new product lines, the average consumer simply cannot keep up with who owns what. For instance, grocery stores in America often devote an entire glassed-in wall with numerous brands of beer available for purchase. Presumably, this involves a variety of consumer "choices," but what most consumers do not realize is that only a handful of companies are behind those brand names. Just two companies—Anheuser-Busch InBev and MillerCoors—control 69 percent of market share, with Anheuser-Busch InBev alone responsible for 43.5 percent market share (National Beer Wholesalers Association 2017). Anheuser-Busch InBev has more than two hundred brands of beer globally, including such popular brands as Budweiser, Busch, Michelob, Corona, Stella Artois, Becks, Rolling Rock, and O'Doul's. In recent years, small craft breweries have grabbed a larger share of the total beer market. The larger breweries have responded by buying out formerly independent craft breweries, along with their local brand names. Between 2011 and 2016, Anheuser-Busch InBev acquired eight such craft breweries (*Forbes* 2017).

As a result of such mergers and acquisitions and the retention of brand names, there is the illusion of more consumer choice and competition than actually exists. In classical economics, the consumer is seen as "king," and every purchase is seen as a "vote" in the economic marketplace. As the story goes, if customers are dissatisfied with the products or policies of any particular company, they are free to take their business elsewhere (including using boycott as an organized form of protest). However, if choices are limited or nonexistent, or if the consumer does not know what the choices represent (who owns what), then this form of restraint on the marketplace is severely compromised.

The largest corporation in America (and the world) is now Wal-Mart Stores, Inc., the largest retailer in the United States, and emblematic of the postindustrial shift from goods production to retail and service industries. As measured by both total annual revenues ($485 billion) and total number of employees (2.3 million) (*Fortune* 2017), Walmart Superstores and Walmart Sam's Clubs discount retail warehouses are a long way away from the mom-and-pop corner grocery stores of the 1950s.

Despite the expansion in size and power of corporate goliaths, small business is often heralded as the backbone of the American economy. Small businesses are often thought to be responsible for most employment, most business activity, and most innovation in the economy. However, the data indicate otherwise. While businesses with no paid employees (most of which are self-employed businesses) represent about 80 percent of all business establishments, they account for only about 3 percent of total business receipts (US Small Business Administration 2015). Among business establishments that have at least one paid employee, those with fewer than twenty employees account for 18 percent of such businesses, employ 18 percent of all paid employees, and generate 12 percent of total business receipts for such businesses. At the other end of the continuum, business establishments with over five hundred employees account for less than 1 percent of all businesses with at least one employee, but employ 52 percent of all paid employees and generate 64 percent of total business receipts among businesses with paid employees (US Census Bureau 2015).

Even these numbers underestimate the dominance of large firms in the American economy. While separate business establishments are defined as single physical locations where business is conducted, these include branch offices and franchise sites for larger corporations. In addition, many smaller establishments are tied to the larger firms as suppliers or retailers of products and services provided by the megacorporations. Larger corporations often create "vertical networks" of smaller contractor firms under their control, while at the same time downsizing their own labor forces (Harrison 1994, 47).

Not only are small businesses not dominant in the economy as a whole, but they are also not the major source of product innovation. In 1901, 80 percent of US patents were issued to individuals (Caplow et al. 2001, 258). By 2015, only 12.3 percent of all patents were issued to individuals (US Patent and Trademark Office

2016). The remaining patents were issued to organizational entities, most of which are corporations. While some new technologies may originate with individuals and small businesses, most individuals or small companies do not have the capital to set up large-scale production facilities or market new technologies. As a result, larger established corporations often buy out small-time players. Buying out promising new technologies from individuals and smaller companies is often a way for large corporations to stay technologically competitive without heavily investing in expensive basic research programs that may not yield tangible results. Other major sources of technological innovation occur outside the private sector altogether through government- and university-sponsored research.

All of this is far removed from the self-employed entrepreneur. The ascendance of large-scale corporations affects self-employment in several ways. First, large corporations create barriers of entry for small businesses, especially sole proprietorships. Thus, small businesses neither have the capital, nor can they generate the volume of business needed to challenge large businesses operating in similar markets. In technologically advanced societies, some forms of production require large-scale operations that preclude self-employed or small-business operations. As large companies increasingly dominate markets, barriers to entry reduce business dynamism and discourage new business starts. For instance, a Brookings Institute study showed that the firm entry rate in the United States (firms less than one year old as a share of all firms) fell by nearly half in the thirty-year period between 1978 and 2011 (Hathaway and Litan 2014). Second, compared to employment in large corporations, employment in the small-business sector is generally less stable, does not pay as well, and usually does not provide the same quality of benefits. Third, the ascendance of large corporations has reduced opportunities for rapid social mobility. When sole proprietors had no corporations to compete against, it was more possible for individual entrepreneurs to establish new market niches and grow their businesses rapidly. Rags-to-riches scenarios, while never common, are now even less common.

The decline of self-employment and the dominance of large bureaucratic corporations changes mobility in another way. Starting a new business requires different individual characteristics than maintaining an established one. The "entrepreneurial personality"—supposedly bold, visionary, risk-taking, and ruggedly individualistic—while perhaps well suited for launching new business ventures, is probably not as well suited for running large bureaucratic organizations. Once you are already ahead, the idea is to stay ahead, and the best way to do that is to play it safe.

Bureaucracies generally reward compliance, not defiance. In bureaucratic settings, one does not typically advance by being the defiant, rugged, and fiercely independent individualist of American folklore, but by going along to get along, being a team player, following rules and procedures, and slowly climbing the bureaucratic ladder one step at a time. Clearly, some individual entrepreneurs who strike out on their own manage to defy the odds and do very well. Those who succeed do not necessarily work harder than those who fail, nor are they necessarily more inherently capable or meritorious.

SUMMARY

Americans embrace the ideal of the self-made person. It is quintessentially American to "go your own way," "do your own thing," and "be your own boss." In economic life, this ideal is best exemplified by self-employment. Since colonial times, however, the self-employed as a proportion of the total American labor force have steadily and drastically declined. Despite the entrepreneurial mystique surrounding the image of self-employment, the reality for many who are self-employed is often less than glamorous. The vast majority of jobs held by self-employed workers are either physically demanding jobs, such as farmer or construction worker, or service jobs such as hairdresser, child-care worker, or retail shopkeeper. Such jobs carry high risks for workplace fatality, including becoming a victim of workplace homicide. Compared to their wage-worker counterparts, the self-employed tend to work longer hours, often for effectively lower earnings after having to fund their own health care, vacations, and retirement plans. Some reluctantly resort to involuntary forms of self-employment when wage or salaried jobs are unavailable, including self-employment in the irregular and often illegal "underground" economy. And while some do overcome the odds and do very well, striking out on one's own to start a new business is clearly an extremely high-risk pursuit.

The rapid historical decline in self-employment corresponds to the ascendance of large corporations in the American economy. The collective assets and associated economies of scale of the corporate behemoths tend to undercut competition from smaller companies and discourage new entrants. Despite the reality of an economy dominated by increasingly large corporations, many Americans cling to the imagery of the go-it-alone entrepreneurial spirit as the backbone of the American economy. Such language, however, no longer accurately describes an economy dominated by very large corporate bureaucracies and a labor force composed of individuals who mostly work for somebody else.

Which new businesses succeed and which fail has more to do with than just the imagination and determination of entrepreneurs. The next chapter examines the impact of another important but often overlooked factor in getting ahead or falling behind in America—the effect of luck or being in the right place at the right time.

REFERENCES

Aronson, Robert L. 1991. *Self-Employment: A Labor Market Perspective*. New York: ILR Press.

Astebro, T., and J. Chen. 2014. "The Entrepreneurial Earnings Puzzle: Mismeasurement or Real?" *Journal of Business Venturing* 291(10):88–105.

Berle, Adolf A., and Gardiner C. Means. 1932. *The Modern Corporation and Private Property*. New York: Macmillan.

Bills, David B. 1998. "A Community of Interests: Understanding the Relationships between Franchisees and Franchisors." In *Research in Stratification and Mobility*, Vol. 16, ed. Kevin T. Leicht, 351–69. Greenwich, CT: JAI Press.

Blair, Roger, and Francine Lafontaine. 2005. *The Economics of Franchising*. New York: Cambridge University Press.

Blanchflower, David G. 2015. "Self-Employment across Countries in the Great Recession of 2008–2014." Yearly Report on Flexible Labor and Employment commissioned by Ranstad, Dartmouth College. www.dartmouth.edu/~blnchflr/papers/flexibilitywork_2015.pdf (accessed July 12, 2017).

Caplow, Theodore, Louis Hicks, and Ben J. Wattenberg. 2001. *The First Measured Century: An Illustrated Guide to Trends in America, 1900–2000*. Washington, DC: AEI Press.

Dallago, Bruno. 1990. *The Irregular Economy: The "Underground Economy" and the "Black" Labour Market*. Hants, UK: Dartmouth Publishing.

Dant, Rajiv, Marko Grünhagen, and Josef Windsperger. 2011. "Franchising Research Frontiers for the Twenty-First Century." *Journal of Retailing* 87(3):253–68.

Derber, Charles. 1998. *Corporation Nation: How Corporations Are Taking Over Our Lives and What We Can Do about It*. New York: St. Martin's Griffin.

Everett, Wallace C. 2006. "Using State and Local Programs to Fuel Franchise Growth." *Franchising World* 38(12):63–64.

Fairlie, Robert W. 2002. "Drug Dealing and Legitimate Self-Employment." *Journal of Labor Economics* 20(3):538–76.

Feagin, Joe R., and Melvin P. Sikes. 1994. *Living with Racism*. Boston: Beacon Press.

Federal Reserve Bank of St. Louis. 2016. "Five Bank Asset Concentration in the United States." https://fred.stlouisfed.org/series/DDOI06USA156NWDB (accessed July 27, 2017).

Fligstein, Neil, and Adam Goldstein. 2011. "The Roots of the Great Recession." In *The Great Recession*, ed. David B. Grusky, Bruce Western, and Christopher Wimer, 21–55. New York: Sage.

Forbes. 2017. "The Year That Was: Anheuser-Busch InBev." www.forbes.com/sites/greatspeculations/2017/01/26/the-year-that-was-anheuser-busch-inbev/#531206211558 (accessed July 27, 2017).

Fortune. 2017. "Fortune 500." http://fortune.com/fortune500/list/ (accessed July 18, 2017).

Fusfeld, Daniel. 1973. *The Basic Economics of the Urban Racial Crisis*. New York: Holt, Rinehart & Winston.

Goldin, Claudia, and Lawrence F. Katz. 2016. "A Most Egalitarian Profession: Pharmacy and the Evolution of a Family-Friendly Occupation." *Journal of Labor Economics* 24(3):75–147.

Greenfield, Harry I. 1993. *Invisible, Outlawed, and Untaxed: America's Underground Economy*. Westport, CT: Praeger.

Hamilton, Barton H. 2000. "Does Entrepreneurship Pay? An Empirical Analysis of Returns to Self-Employment." *Journal of Political Economy* 108(3):604–31.

Harrison, Bennett. 1994. *Lean and Mean: The Changing Landscape of Corporate Power in the Age of Flexibility*. New York: Guilford Press.

Hathaway, Ian, and Robert E. Litan. 2014. "Declining Business Dynamism in the United States: A Look at States and Metros." Economic Studies at Brookings. www.brookings.edu/wp-content/uploads/2016/06/declining_business_dynamism_hathaway_litan.pdf (accessed July 19, 2017).

Hipple, Steven. 2010. "Self-Employment in the United States." *Monthly Labor Review*, September, 17–32.

Hipple, Steven F., and Laurel A. Hammond. 2016. "Self-Employment in the United States." Bureau of Labor Statistics. www.bls.gov/spotlight/2016/self-employment-in-the-united-states/pdf/self-employment-in-the-united-states.pdf (accessed July 11, 2017).

Hurst, Erik, Geng Li, and Ben Pugsley. 2014. "Are Household Surveys Like Tax Forms: Evidence from Income Underreporting of the Self-Employed." *Review of Economics and Statistics* 96(1):19–33.

International Franchise Association. 2016. "The Economic Impact of Franchised Businesses: Vol. IV, 2016." www.franchise.org/sites/default/files/Economic%20Impact%20of%20Franchised%20Businesses_Vol%20IV_20160915.pdf (accessed July 11, 2017).

Leonard, Madeleine. 1998. *Invisible Work, Invisible Workers: The Informal Economy in Europe and the US.* New York: St. Martin's.

Massey, Douglas S. 2007. *Categorically Unequal: The American Stratification System.* New York: Sage.

Miller, Arthur Selwyn. 1977. *The Modern Corporate State: Private Governments and the American Constitution.* Westport, CT: Greenwood Press.

Mills, C. Wright. 1951. *White Collar: The American Middle Class.* New York: Oxford University Press.

Muehlberger, Ulrike. 2007. *Dependent Self-Employment: Workers on the Border between Employment and Self-Employment.* New York: Palgrave Macmillan.

National Beer Wholesalers Association. 2017. "Industry Fast Facts." www.nbwa.org/resources/industry-fast-facts (accessed July 27, 2017).

Naylor, R. T. 2002. *Wages of Crime: Black Markets, Illegal Finance, and the Underworld Economy.* Ithaca, NY: Cornell University Press.

Parker, Simon C. 2004. *The Economics of Self-Employment and Entrepreneurship.* New York: Cambridge University Press.

Patrick, Carlianne, Heather Stephens, and Amanda Weinstein. 2016. "Where Are All the Self-Employed Women: Push and Pull Factors Influencing Female Labor Market Decisions." *Small Business Economics* 46(3):365–90.

Pegula, Stephen M. 2004. "Occupational Fatalities: Self-Employed Workers and Wage and Salary Workers." *Monthly Labor Review,* March, 30–40. www.bls.gov/opub/mlr/2004/03/art2full.pdf (accessed July 27, 2017).

Perrow, Charles. 2002. *Organizing America: Wealth, Power, and the Origins of Corporate Capitalism.* Princeton, NJ: Princeton University Press.

Phillips, Joseph D. 1958. *Little Business in the American Economy.* Urbana: University of Illinois Press.

Phillips, Kevin. 2008. *Bad Money: Reckless, Finance, Failed Politics and the Global Crisis of American Capitalism.* New York: Viking.

Roche, Kristin. 2014. "Female Self-Employment in the United States: An Update to 2012." US Bureau of Labor Statistics. www.bls.gov/opub/mlr/2014/article/female-self-employment-in-the-united-states-an-update-to-2012.htm (accessed July 13, 2017).

Roy, William. 1997. *Socializing Capital: The Rise of the Large Industrial Corporation in America.* Princeton, NJ: Princeton University Press.

Schlosser, Eric. 2003. *Reefer Madness: Sex, Drugs, and Cheap Labor in the American Black Market.* Boston: Houghton Mifflin.

Shapiro, Thomas M. 2004. *The Hidden Cost of Being African American: How Wealth Perpetuates Inequality.* New York: Oxford University Press.

———. 2017. *Toxic Inequality: How America's Wealth Gap Destroys Mobility, Deepens the Racial Divide, and Threatens Our Future.* New York: Basic Books.

Suarez-Villa, Luis. 2015. *Corporate Power, Oligopolies and the Crisis of the State.* Albany: State University of New York Press.

Thornton, Patricia. 1999. "The Sociology of Entrepreneurship." In *Annual Review of Sociology*, Vol. 25, ed. Karen S. Cook and John Hagan, 19–46. Palo Alto, CA: Annual Reviews.

US Census Bureau. 2012. Economic Census Tables. www.census.gov/programs-surveys/economic-census/data/tables.2012.html.html (accessed July 26, 2017).

US Census Bureau. 2015. "Private Firms, Establishments, Employment, Annual Payroll, and Receipts by Firm Size, 1988–2014." www.sba.gov/advocacy/firm-aize-data (accessed July 19, 2017).

US Department of Labor. 2014a. "Self-Employment: What to Know to Be Your Own Boss." Career Outlook. www.bls.gov/careeroutlook/2014/article/self-employment-what-to-know to-be-your-own-boss.htm (accessed July 10, 2017).

———. 2014b. "Female Self-Employment in the United States: An Update to 2012." www.bls.gov/opub/mlr/2014/article/female-self-employment-in-the-united-states-an-update-to-2012-1.htm (accessed July 13, 2017).

———. 2016a. "National Census of Fatal Occupational Injuries in 2015." www.bls.gov/news.release/pdf/cfoi.pdf (accessed July 12, 2017).

———. 2016b. Table 7. "Survival of Private Sector Establishments by Opening Year." www.bls.gov/bdm/us_age_naics_00_table7.txt (accessed July 12, 2017).

———. 2017a. Table A-9. Selected Employment Indicators. www.bls.gov/news.release/empsit.t09.htm (accessed July 10, 2017).

———. 2017b. "Farmers, Ranchers and Other Agricultural Managers." Occupational Outlook Handbook, 2016–2017. www.bls.gov/ooh/management/farmers-ranchers-and-other -agricultural-managers.htm (accessed July 11, 2017).

US Internal Revenue Service. 2017. "Table 1, Number of Returns, Total Receipts, Business Receipts, Net Income and Deficit by Form of Business: 1980 to 2012." www.irs.gov/uac/soi-tax-stats-integrated-business-data (accessed July 17, 2017).

US Patent and Trademark Office. 2016. *Patenting Trends Calendar Year 2015*. www.uspto.gov/web/offices/ac/ido/oeip/taf/pat_tr15.htm (accessed July 18, 2017).

US Small Business Administration. 2015. "Table: Private Firms: Establishments, Employment, Annual Payroll and Receipts by Firm Size, 1988–2014." www.sba.gov/advocacy/firm-size -data (accessed July 19, 2017).

Venkatesh, Sudhir Alladi. 2006. *Off the Books: The Underground Economy of the Urban Poor.* Cambridge, MA: Harvard University Press.

Williams, Colin. 2006. *The Hidden Enterprise Culture: Entrepreneurship in the Underground Economy.* Cheltenham, UK: Edward Elgar.

Williams, Colin, and Jan Windebank. 1998. *Informal Employment in the Advanced Economies: Implications for Work and Welfare.* New York: Routledge.

Wilmoth, Daniel. 2016. "The Missing Millennial Entrepreneurs." US Small Business Administration. www.sba.gov/sites/default/files/advocacy/Millenial_IB.pdf (accessed July 11, 2017).

Wright, Erik Olin. 1997. *Class Counts: Comparative Studies in Class Analysis.* New York: Cambridge University Press.

7

The Luck Factor

Being in the Right Place at the Right Time

> I think we consider too much the good luck of the early bird, and not enough the bad luck of the early worm.
>
> —Franklin Delano Roosevelt

> My aspiration now is to get by luck what I could not get by merit.
>
> —Mason Cooley, US aphorist

Merit hard-liners tend to deny or downplay the role of luck in getting ahead in America. Defenders of meritocracy often claim, "Individuals make their own luck," or, sarcastically, "The harder I work, the luckier I become." For Americans who are at the top of the system especially, there is often a deep denial that luck had anything to do with it. In a culture that extols meritocracy, individuals tend to retrospectively fashion their own biographical narratives consistent with the values of that culture. Economist Robert Frank (2016) notes that in such a culture, Americans are often quick to acknowledge the "headwind" factors that otherwise might prevent them from getting ahead based on individual merit, but are much less inclined to acknowledge "tailwind" factors that propelled them forward beyond merit, or even despite the lack of it. Starting with the "birth lottery" of initial parental social-class placement in the relay race to get ahead (see chapter 3) and whatever innate endowments we receive from the genetic roll of the dice that our parents provide us, factors entirely outside of our control play a major factor in who ends up with what of what there is to get. If people are honest, it is difficult to deny that chance events and many twists and turns along the way are at least partially responsible for where one ends up in the system.

But the effects of luck are hard to determine. Luck is hard to pin down precisely because its effects are random. Social scientists are trained to empirically look for and account for explanatory factors that occur beyond random chance. The scientific community has very high thresholds for ascribing any level of causality to factors that could otherwise be due to random chance. As any beginning statistics student knows, the minimally acceptable scientific threshold for ascribing any level of confidence that "x" might related to "y" is that such an empirical relationship would occur at least 95 times out of 100 beyond random chance alone. Known as a "confidence interval," the 95 percent threshold is the "gold" standard in scientific research, but 99 percent, or 99.9 percent, is even better. Using the minimum 95 percent threshold, the best statistical models used to account for how income and wealth are distributed, for instance, "explain" only about half of the total variance. Some of the "unexplained" or "residual" variance in these models could come from a combination of leaving out factors that matter, and from less-than-perfect measures of the factors included. But some of the unexplained variance is also likely due to random variation—or, in more everyday language, "just plain dumb luck."

There are ways, however, that social scientists can factor some forms of luck into our models, at least indirectly. For instance, adding measures for "economic inheritance" or "family background" into statistical models may partially account for the "birth lottery" effect, although these effects are not usually labeled as luck per se. This chapter examines other factors related to luck—in particular, the effect of being in the "right" place at the "right" time.

THE DEMAND SIDE

In thinking about who ends up with what jobs, Americans tend to first think about what economists call the "supply side." In labor economics, the supply side refers to the pool of workers available to fill jobs. The ideology of meritocracy leads Americans to focus on the qualities of individual workers: how smart they are, how qualified they are, how much education they have, and so on. These "human capital" factors, however, represent only half of the equation. The other half, the "demand side," is about the number and types of jobs available. How many jobs are available, their location, how much they pay, and how many people are seeking them are important but often neglected considerations in assessing the impact of merit on economic outcomes.

The history of the American labor force can be summarized by tracing the evolution of three jobs: farmer, factory worker, and retail sales clerk. Figure 7.1 depicts historical changes in the American labor force comparing farming, manufacturing, and service occupations. In colonial times, the vast majority of American workers were farmers. Many worked their own small family farms. Corporations did not exist. America for the most part was an agrarian and land-based society. With the beginning of the Industrial Revolution in the mid-nineteenth century, what the

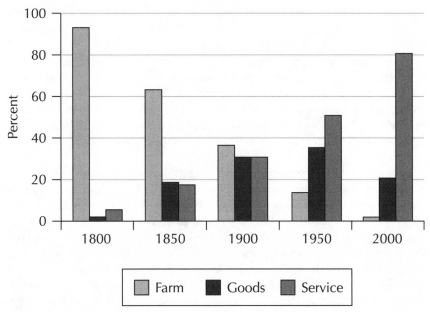

Figure 7.1.   Employment by Industry (*Source*: US Bureau of the Census, 1975, 2001)

average worker did for a living began to change. Farming became progressively more mechanized. Herbicides, pesticides, tractors, harvesters, and other heavy equipment gradually replaced field hands. America could grow more food with less human labor. By the end of the nineteenth century, urban factories were booming. Displaced farm laborers moved in large numbers from the rural countryside to urban centers in search of factory jobs.

More Americans became factory workers, operating machines that turned raw goods into finished products. Most were machine operators; some were skilled craftsmen—electricians, millwrights, tool and die makers, and the like. Corporations replaced family businesses, and the rate of self-employment sharply declined. By the middle of the twentieth century, manufacturing had reached its peak. Manufacturing jobs, while still employing a significant proportion of the labor force in the United States, began to decline. The rate of decline accelerated in the latter part of the twentieth century with the increased automation of production processes and an increased shift to production sites outside of the United States, where labor was cheaper, less unionized, and less regulated. At the same time, farming occupations as a proportion of the total labor force fell off even more precipitously.

In the wake of these changes, the growth of the service sector of the economy exploded and now far outstrips farming and manufacturing as a source of employment. The service sector includes a mixed bag of occupations ranging from hairstylists, to insurance agents, to sales clerks, to computer programmers—all having to do in some way with processing either information or people, or both. Instead of being a field hand on the farm or a machine operator in the factory, the typical worker in America is now a sales clerk in a department store.

These changes are significant in terms of how people "experience" intergenerational mobility. Each generation encounters a different array of "slots" to be filled. The changes in the "tasks" that need doing are not a reflection of individual merit. They are the result of changes in technology and concomitant changes in the division of labor, in economic and political policy, and in the global economy. Sociologists refer to mobility caused by changes in the division of labor in society as "structural mobility."

For most of the twentieth century, the types of slots available represented a generalized occupational upgrading. Unskilled farm labor, the backbone of an agrarian economy, was being replaced by factory and office work. Factory work included many blue-collar skilled and semiskilled jobs—an upgrade in terms of both earnings and social status. Compared to farming and manufacturing, office work in the service sector was cleaner, less dangerous, and less physically demanding, and often conferred higher social status. The general standard of living also rapidly increased. Most of the upward "movement" individuals experienced compared to their parents and grandparents was the result of these structural changes, not individual merit. The college-educated computer programmer whose father was a factory worker with a high school education, whose father before him was a farmer with a grade school education, is not necessarily smarter, more motivated, or of higher moral caliber than his father or grandfather. Each faced very different opportunity structures. Fueled by the ideology of meritocracy, however, individuals swept up in these waves of social change are often quick to falsely attribute their rise in social standing to individual merit alone.

Beginning in the early 1970s, the ground shifted. Several trends coalesced to radically alter the American occupational landscape. First, US industrial corporations were beginning to feel the pinch of increasing foreign competition. In the immediate aftermath of World War II, the United States emerged from the conflict as the only industrialized nation that had not had its industrial infrastructure damaged or destroyed. Under these conditions, the United States easily dominated global markets. As part of the postwar recovery effort, the United States helped rebuild Germany and Japan. Germany and Japan, among other nations, were now emerging as serious global competitors. In 1973, an oil embargo imposed by the Organization of the Petroleum Exporting Countries (OPEC) sharply increased production costs, which was especially detrimental to nations and industries with the oldest and least-efficient production facilities. The automobile industry in the United States, which had been the backbone of America's postwar industrial might, suffered dramatically from these changes. Using the most modern production facilities, Japan and Germany, producing smaller, more fuel-efficient, and higher-quality automobiles, made significant inroads into the American automobile market. Similar scenarios were played out as well in other industries, including steel, textiles, and chemicals, all of which had been part of America's postwar industrial strength.

To compensate for these losses, American industry sought new strategies. In what economists Bennett Harrison and Barry Bluestone (1988) characterize as "the Great U-Turn," American corporations responded to these new competitive pressures through massive corporate "restructuring." Several strategies were pursued simultaneously, including shifting sites of production, encouraging supply-side government policy, "outsourcing," and "downsizing." To reduce production costs, corporations aggressively shifted production and technical-support services abroad. New communications technologies and declining transportation costs accelerated the globalization of markets. The trade deficit for the United States dramatically increased as imports exceeded exports, placing downward pressure on wages and benefits. Domestically, factory production shifted away from the urban industrial centers in the north-central and northeastern parts of the United States to the South and Southwest. All of these moves reduced production costs by relocating factory production, as well as many technical-support services, to new domestic and international locations with lower wages, less unionization, and less government regulation.

As part of the pressure to keep factories and service-support centers open or operating in the United States, those that did remain often extracted wage and benefit "concessions" and "givebacks" from workers. Corporations aggressively moved to break up existing unions and to prevent new ones from forming, further depressing wages and benefits, especially for blue-collar workers. As part of "downsizing" campaigns, corporations replaced permanent, higher-paid workers with "outsourced" contract labor and dramatically increased part-time temporary and contingent labor, partly as a strategy to avoid the benefit compensation otherwise mandated for full-time workers (Katz and Krueger 2016; Hatton 2011).

At the same time, corporations pressed for changes in government policy. Corporate America found a sympathetic sponsor for these changes in Republican presidential administrations, which lowered corporate and personal income taxes for the wealthy, deregulated large segments of the economy, trimmed the nonmilitary federal workforce, and sharply reduced welfare and other government programs targeted toward the poor. Operating in a new climate of relaxed government regulation, big business entered into a frenzy of megamergers, takeovers, and acquisitions. Most mergers resulted in layoffs, as combined entities realized savings from increased economies of scale. Billions of dollars were taken out of the economy to finance megamergers. With increased profits, corporations also increasingly bought back stock in their own companies, artificially inflating the value of stock and thereby also increasing CEO compensation based on stock options (Leopold 2016; Kahle and Stulz 2017). In addition, a much higher proportion of corporate profits were paid out as dividends to shareholders (Kahle and Stulz 2017). All of these maneuvers further expanded overall economic inequality between those living primarily off investments and those who primarily worked for a living. Through mergers and stock manipulations, investors could make money without necessarily increasing production or creating new jobs. When the dust cleared, there were fewer but bigger corporations. Investment income increased. Wages and benefits decreased or remained stagnant.

Corporate profits and the salaries of corporate CEOs soared. Inequality increased. Social mobility declined. Job and income instability increased.

CREATIVE DESTRUCTION

Millions of American workers were caught up in the tidal force of these structural changes. The American economy was being transformed from auto, steel, and oil to fast food, day care, and retail outlets. Hardest hit were male blue-collar factory workers. Between 2000 and 2010, the manufacturing sector lost 5.6 million jobs, the largest decline in manufacturing employment history (Hicks and Devaraj 2015). Some of the loss of these jobs was due to outsourcing and the resulting trade imbalance, but most of the job loss in manufacturing was the result of automation. One study estimates that approximately 13 percent of the job loss in manufacturing was due to increasing trade imbalance, while approximately 88 percent of the job loss was due to automation and resulting gains in productivity (Hicks and Devaraj 2015). In the post–World War II period, it had been possible for many working-class Americans with only a high school diploma to realize the American Dream by working in factories with good pay, good benefits, and long-term job stability. With advancing globalization and automation, this pathway to fulfillment of the American Dream has been progressively cut off. New jobs are being created, but these are mostly in the "soft," low-wage, low-skill service sector.

The growth of the low-wage service sector is illustrated by the US Department of Labor's list of the fifteen fastest-growing jobs in America that are expected to produce the most new job slots between 2014 and 2024 (see table 7.1). Included in the list are low-pay service jobs such as personal care aides, home health aides, food preparation and service workers, retail salespersons, restaurant cooks, and janitors and cleaners. Most of these jobs are very low-tech and require little formal education. Of these fastest-growing jobs in America, eight, or more than half, minimally require "no formal educational credential," including four of the five fastest-growing jobs. One requires at least a high school diploma (customer service representative); two minimally require some training beyond high school, but no college degree; four minimally require a bachelor's degree (registered nurses, accountants and auditors, general and operations managers, and software developers). None require a graduate or professional degree. Reflecting the continued anticipated aging of the population and the difficulty of either outsourcing or automating hands-on care, five of these jobs are in medical services, including the top three. It is also instructive to note that eleven of the fifteen fastest-growing jobs (all those that did not minimally require at least a bachelor's degree) are jobs that have median incomes below the median for all occupations (US Bureau of Labor 2015).

The process by which some jobs are reduced or eliminated and other slots are increased or new ones are created is known among economists as *creative destruction*, a term coined by Harvard economist Joseph Schumpeter in the 1950s. There has

Table 7.1. Occupations with Highest Projected Growth, 2014–2024

2014 National Employment Matrix Title and Code		Employment Number[a]		Projected Change, 2014–2024		Median Annual Wage, 2014 ($)	Typical Education Needed for Entry
		2014	2024	Number[a]	Percent		
Total, all occupations	00-0000	150,539.9	160,328.8	9,788.9	6.5	35,540	—
Personal care aides	39-9021	1,768.4	2,226.5	458.1	25.9	20,440	No formal educational credential
Registered nurses	29-1141	2,751.0	3,190.3	439.3	16.0	66,640	Bachelor's degree
Home health aides	31-1011	913.5	1,261.9	348.4	38.1	21,380	No formal educational credential
Combined food preparation and serving workers, including fast food	35-3021	3,159.7	3,503.2	343.5	10.9	18,410	No formal educational credential
Retail salespersons	41-2031	4,624.9	4,939.1	314.2	6.8	21,390	No formal educational credential
Nursing assistants	31-1014	1,492.1	1,754.1	262.0	17.6	25,100	Postsecondary nondegree award
Customer service representatives	43-4051	2,581.8	2,834.8	252.9	9.8	31,200	High school diploma or equivalent
Cooks, restaurant	35-2014	1,109.7	1,268.7	158.9	14.3	22,490	No formal educational credential
General and operations managers	11-1021	2,124.1	2,275.2	151.1	7.1	97,270	Bachelor's degree
Construction laborers	47-2061	1,159.1	1,306.5	147.4	12.7	31,090	No formal educational credential
Accountants and auditors	13-2011	1,332.7	1,475.1	142.4	10.7	65,940	Bachelor's degree
Medical assistants	31-9092	591.3	730.2	138.9	23.5	29,960	Postsecondary nondegree award
Janitors and cleaners, except maids and housekeeping cleaners	37-2011	2,360.6	2,496.9	136.3	5.8	22,840	No formal educational credential
Software developers, applications	15-1132	718.4	853.7	135.3	18.8	95,510	Bachelor's degree
Laborers and freight, stock, and material movers, hand	53-7062	2,441.3	2,566.4	125.1	5.1	24,430	No formal educational credential

[a] Numbers in thousands.
Source: US Bureau of Labor Statistics (2015).

always been some "churning" of jobs in the labor force, but the pace of these changes has accelerated with advancing technology.

As prior waves of automation replaced millions of agriculture and manufacturing jobs, information- and people-processing jobs in the service sector are now also increasingly subject to substantial job loss through automation. A recent Oxford University study of the American labor force concluded that 47 percent of current jobs in the American labor force are at risk of being automated in the next twenty years (Frey and Osborne 2017). Computerization is at the forefront of these projected job losses, especially for low-level information- and people-processing jobs. Job displacement occurring with such rapidity and on such a scale would be historically unprecedented.

Although low-level information- and people-processing jobs are most subject to automation, higher-level service and professional jobs are not immune (Ford 2015). Many commercial aircraft, for instance, are now programmed to take off and land at all the major airports of the world, potentially rendering pilots as human backup systems. Remotely controlled drones are already replacing piloted aircraft for many military aircraft missions. Computer software programs can "read" and "diagnose" X-rays, CT, and MRI scans. Intricate surgeries are now "performed" by surgical robots. Computer software programs can "write" accurate sports stories drawing on box scores of completed games. Much of the routine background work of lawyers, such as writing briefs and identifying relevant case law, can be automated. The university classroom professor with chalk and a blackboard—the technology of instruction that persisted for centuries essentially unchanged—is rapidly being supplemented by online computer-assisted "distance education," aided by interactive "PowerPoints," "machine grading," and computer programs designed to detect student plagiarism. Textbook publishers are rapidly designing software programs for self-paced interactive modules that largely automate the routine work of teaching, reducing the professorial role to mostly answering occasional questions that might arise.

Although professional jobs might not be entirely eliminated, automation may reduce the numbers of workers required to do them. One example of this trend is pharmacy, a profession that formerly required a bachelor's degree as the first degree for pharmacy practice. Since 1990, however, a graduate doctoral-level degree (PharmD) has been designated by the American Association of Colleges of Pharmacy as the new first professional degree. Although pharmacists sometimes prepare or compound medications, most drugs now are prepared by manufacturers and prepackaged. Pill counters count out pills, and computer records check for warnings, side effects, dispensing protocols, and possible drug interactions. Pharmacy technicians often do much of this routine work, which is then "checked" by the licensed pharmacist before dispensing. While an important part of the health-care delivery system, the majority of what most pharmacists do in their jobs is often highly routinized.

What slots that will need to be filled in the division of labor of the future remains unclear. With prior waves of automation, as part of the "creative destruction" process, new slots were created as others were eliminated. As agriculture was mechanized, manufacturing was booming. As manufacturing jobs declined, jobs in the service sector expanded. If service jobs are eventually automated in the manner that agriculture and manufacturing jobs have been, what happens next? There is not now a clear set of replacement positions on the horizon. A pessimistic scenario is one in which society experiences mass unemployment and even more severe economic inequality. An optimistic scenario is one in which as-yet-undeveloped labor-intensive technologies, products, or services emerge to absorb job losses in other sectors. An alternate optimistic alternative is one in which society could enter a new leisure age in which productivity gains would be high enough and equally shared enough to allow everyone to work less, resulting in the gradual erosion of the standard forty-hour workweek. In the long term, the shape and contour of a future division of labor is uncertain. In the meantime, how do we match training for current jobs with the need for individuals to fill them?

ALL DRESSED UP AND NOWHERE TO GO

Even if every adult in America were currently college-educated, the "demand" for college-level jobs would remain the same. We would simply have more college-educated workers filling jobs that do not require college degrees, and higher rates of underemployment in society as a whole. As levels of educational attainment in the population have increased, and as the economy has fallen short of producing jobs that require more education, rates of underemployment have increased. Several social scientists have documented a trend toward higher levels of underemployment among college graduates (Rose 2017; Vedder et al. 2013; Abel et al. 2014; Schmitt and Jones 2012; Livingstone 2004). Depending on different empirical definitions of "overqualified" or "underemployed," estimates of the extent of underemployment among college graduates range from about 25 percent to 50 percent.

Economist Richard Vedder and his associates (2013), for instance, found that by 2010, 48 percent of employed US college graduates were in jobs that require less than a four-year college education. They note that many occupations that require less than a college degree already have significant percentages of college graduates in them, such as office clerks (17.6 percent), retail sales clerks (24.6 percent), secretaries and administrative assistants (16.8 percent), cashiers (10.2 percent), bartenders (16.5 percent), and waiters and waitresses (14.3 percent). Between 2010 and 2020, using Department of Labor estimates, they anticipate that jobs requiring at least a bachelor's degree will grow by 14.3 percent, but the number of college graduates will increase by 31 percent; in other words, there will be nearly three new college graduates for every new job requiring a college degree (Vedder et al. 2013).

The story of the "overeducated/underemployed" college graduate is somewhat complicated, in that college graduates in these jobs often have higher incomes than non–college graduates in those same positions, with the college graduates also having better mobility opportunities over time. That is, some college graduates may start out in positions that do not require a college degree, but may over time transition to jobs requiring college degrees. In this sense, there is still a long-term "college" premium for lifetime earnings compared to non–college graduates, even for "underemployed" college graduates. Nevertheless, it is clear that compared to prior generations, there has been a steady upgrading of human capital on the supply side of the labor market, but the creation of "good jobs" on the demand side has not kept pace with higher levels of educational attainment in the population as a whole. The implications of these findings are clear: There is no general shortage of talent or skill in the labor force. In fact, the situation is exactly the opposite. The economy is not producing enough jobs that match the skill and talent available in the labor force.

In *The Education–Jobs Gap* (2004), sociologist David W. Livingstone provides a comprehensive study of this general trend. Livingstone identifies five different types of underemployment: the talent-use gap, subemployment, credential underemployment, performance underemployment, and subjective underemployment. The *talent-use gap* refers to the opportunity gap between rich and poor to attain university degrees. Assuming equal levels of potential talent in the population as a whole, those from wealthier backgrounds are at least twice as likely to receive college degrees. In other words, long before people enter the labor force, potential talent is already wasted through differential access to higher education. *Subemployment* refers to a variety of nonvoluntary substandard conditions of employment, such as being unemployed but looking for work, discouraged workers who are unemployed but have given up actively looking for work, and those working part-time but wanting to work full-time. An estimated 14 to 24 percent of the US labor force, depending on cyclical variation, falls into this category. *Credential underemployment*, which refers to the condition in which a person's level of formal education exceeds that which is required for the job, affects an estimated 20 percent of the labor force. This type of underemployment, however, is constantly adjusted as employers raise educational requirements for positions, often beyond their real skill demands. A better measure of the overall extent of underemployment in the labor force is *performance underemployment*, which refers to the gap between the skills of the job holder and the actual skill demands of the job. This type of underemployment affects an estimated 40 to 60 percent of the employed labor force and has been steadily increasing for the past twenty-five years. Finally, Livingstone considers *subjective underemployment*, which refers to workers' perceptions that they hold jobs beneath their ability levels. Livingstone estimates that 20 to 40 percent of the labor force holds this view.

In a careful early study of labor-force changes through the 1970s, sociologist Randall Collins (1979) estimated that only 15 percent of the increase in educational requirements for new jobs could be attributed to the need for a more educated workforce. Most of the rest of the increase in educational requirements could be attributed to credential inflation—requiring higher levels of educational attainment unrelated to the actual skill demand of jobs (see chapter 5). As the labor force became more educated, employers simply increased their educational requirements. The result was an inflationary spiral of educational credentials.

Not having a credential (as opposed to the skills required to do a job) can be a nonmerit barrier to mobility. That is, if employers require a college degree for jobs that do not actually need a college graduate for their performance, then not having the credential per se can operate against more-experienced or -skilled candidates. The vast majority of jobs that college graduates hold, in reality, require literacy and not much else. The formal credentials people hold, as Livingstone states, represent only "the tip of the learning iceberg"; fully 70 percent of what people need to know to do their jobs they learn informally on the job (2004).

As the pace of technological change increases, continuing and on-the-job training becomes even more important. To this extent, credentials, which are more available to those from more privileged backgrounds, become artificial barriers to true meritocracy. Collins notes that even some of the most technically demanding jobs—physician, engineer, lawyer—could be learned, and historically were, through apprenticeship training. For practical purposes, there is no evidence to suggest that learning about something by seeing it diagrammed on a blackboard in a classroom is superior to learning the same thing through direct observation and application on the job. Indeed, learning theory suggests that the reverse is probably the case. Colleges have begun to respond to employers' pleas for more practical occupational training by offering more "vocational" majors and embracing more "active" modes of learning, including internships and practica.

One of the problems in matching educational credentials with job demands is the length of training and the changing nature of the job market. The job market is difficult to predict in the long run, and this is a problem for those pursuing jobs that require long periods of formal training. Current "vacancies" and "high demand" may diminish by the time the training period is over. The market has ebbs and flows on both the supply and demand side. When demand is high, the market responds by attracting new entrants. Large numbers of new entrants can glut a market, resulting in oversupply, particularly if demand also dries up. In essence, people can be all dressed up with no place to go. One could argue that the truly meritorious would read market trends correctly and respond accordingly. The reality, however, is that markets, particularly long-term markets, are highly unpredictable. As rates of change increase, predictability declines. Most job experts agree that the job market is much more fluid now than it was for prior generations. Over a lifetime, the average worker now makes many more job changes both in terms of type and place of employment than his or her predecessors. In short, any one worker's location in the labor force at any one point is at least as much the result of market demands as individual merit.

THE NONREVENGE OF THE NERDS

The rapid expansion of low-skill jobs in the service sector and the related extent of underemployment in the labor force are inconsistent with the arguments of the postindustrial-society thesis first advanced by American sociologist Daniel Bell

(1976). Observing a shift toward more white-collar employment, Bell theorized that American society had moved beyond industrialization. The emergent "postindustrial" society placed a high premium on formal and technical knowledge. According to this thesis, technical experts would come to dominate America and other advanced societies. Science and technology would be the key to the postindustrial future. In short, the future would belong to the nerds. In some ways, Bell's predictions seem to have been realized with the advance of the computer age. The computer has become the leading edge of the information society. Computer-related industries, populated by young, technically competent experts, flourished in the digital e-boom of the 1980s and 1990s.

While it is true that the computer age ushered in a new genre of occupational specialties, it is also true that the bulk of the expansion of new jobs, as we have seen, has actually been very low-tech. The assumption of the need for a more highly educated labor force has outpaced the reality.

BABY BOOMERS AND BABY BUSTERS

When a person is born matters for his or her life chances. Malcolm Gladwell begins his highly acclaimed book *Outliers: The Story of Success* (2008) with a description of a study of the birth dates of professional hockey players. The study, by psychologists Roger Barnsley and A. H. Thompson (1988), found that professional hockey players disproportionately had birth dates in the early months of the year, especially January, February, and March. As it turns out, the birth date for age placement in youth hockey leagues in Canada is January 1. So that means that players playing in the same league at the same "age" could actually be as much as a year apart, with those being born in the earlier months nearly a year older than those being born in later months. At preadolescence, the age difference means a lot in terms of size, coordination, and maturity. At successive levels of advancement, the "best" players are selected for more competitive teams. Initially, the older players have a significant competitive advantage over younger players and advance more quickly. As they are advanced, they receive more advanced coaching and are encouraged to continue further. In this sense, success begets success, which is built upon an initially nonmerit advantage. Gladwell refers to this multiplier of initial advantage using a term coined by sociologist Robert Merton—"the Matthew effect"—referring to a biblical verse in the Gospel of Matthew: "For unto everyone that has shall be given, and he shall have abundance. But from him that has not shall be taken away even that which he hath."

Being in the right place at the right time is partly a matter of when people are born and when they enter the labor market. Quite apart from individual ability, how many people are chasing how many and what kind of jobs in what location is of major consequence. The best scenario is one in which a person is part of a small birth cohort and enters the labor force during a period of economic expansion; the worst scenario is one in which a person is part of a large cohort entering the labor force during a period of economic retrenchment. Consistent with the Matthew effect described earlier, the first full-time job after completion of formal education matters for future mobility, since first jobs set career trajectories. Getting started on a branch higher up the tree in the first place will likely put one higher up from the ground at the end.

Despite its relatively large size, the baby-boomer cohort has done better than the smaller baby-buster cohort that followed it. Although there is some disagreement about the causes of the recent job changes, all are in agreement that the ground has shifted, and there are fewer opportunities for good jobs now than for prior generations of workers. Simply put, beyond considerations of individual merit, it matters when you were born and what the labor force looks like when you enter it.

But timing is only part of the story; being in the right place also matters.

THE GEOGRAPHY OF ECONOMIC INEQUALITY

Throughout the first half of the twentieth century, the South lagged well behind other regions of the country. In 1947, for instance, family incomes in the South were 40 percent smaller than in other regions (Levy 1998, 127), partially because portions of the South were still largely underdeveloped industrially. This large gap was also due in part to the long history of racial discrimination that depressed the wages of a high proportion of poor rural blacks who lived there. But wages were also lower for Southern whites compared to whites living in other regions with similar jobs and similar levels of education.

Beginning in the 1960s, the South began to close the income gap on the rest of the country, and by the early 1990s, the gap between the South and other regions had closed to within about 20 percent (Levy 1998, 136). Economist Frank Levy (1998) points to several factors responsible for this change: the civil rights movement, which reduced economic discrimination; the extension of the interstate highway system and the development of network television, which helped link the South to other regions; and the spread of air-conditioning, making the South more amenable to the "climatically challenged." The availability of cheap land, low wages, low taxes, and low levels of unionization also encouraged industrial development in the South. During the same period, deindustrialization of the Northeast and Midwest (the Rust Belt) depressed wages, especially in the manufacturing sectors. Despite these changes, significant regional gaps in income and poverty rates remain. Among the ten states with the lowest median household income, nine are in the South, and among the ten states with the highest rates of poverty, eight are in the South (Frohlich et al. 2016). In short, despite recent trends toward closing gaps, how much one is likely to earn and the likelihood of being poor still depend significantly on the region of the nation in which one happens to live.

Differences in pay based on place can be illustrated by comparing salaries of public school teachers. Teachers perform fundamentally the same job regardless of where they teach, requiring for the most part the same qualifications—a bachelor's degree and a teaching certificate—but rates of teacher pay vary considerably by state. The average public school teacher pay during the 2012–2013 school year in the United States was $56,383 (US Department of Education 2017). However, the range of pay was considerable. Table 7.2 shows the states with the five highest average teacher salaries and those with the five lowest average teacher salaries. Average 2012–2013 public school K–12 teacher salaries ranged from a high of $75,279 in New York to a low of $39,580 in South Dakota (US Department of Education 2017). In other words, teachers in South Dakota earn only about half of what teachers in New York earn for doing the same job, requiring essentially the same qualifications. Even adjusting for cost-of-living differences among states, substantial pay differentials remain.

Defenders of meritocracy might suggest that the really good teachers will gravitate to New York, where the pay is higher, and the least meritorious teachers will gravitate to South Dakota, where the pay is the lowest. Pay, however, is not the only motivating factor in where people choose to work. Ties to family and community, personal preference, access to information about job openings (social capital), and local labor markets generated by employer preferences to hire locally are all also clearly factors.

Recent research on the geography of inequality further shows that place matters not just for wages but also for chances of upward mobility. In a comprehensive US mobility study using county-level data, Raj Chetty and his associates (2014) empirically identified overall rates of intergenerational mobility within local communities. They found that children whose household income was in the bottom quartile but who grew up in high-mobility neighborhoods were more than twice as likely to reach the highest income quartile as adults than children who grew up in low-mobility neighborhoods.

Table 7.2. Average Teacher Salary, 2012–2013

Rank	State	Average 2012–2013 Salary ($)	Percent of US Average
Highest Five States			
1	New York	75,279	134
2	Massachusetts	73,129	130
3	Connecticut	69,766	124
4	California	69,324	123
5	New Jersey	68,797	122
Lowest Five States			
46	West Virginia	46,405	82
47	North Carolina	45,947	81
48	Oklahoma	44,128	78
49	North Dakota	41,994	74
50	South Dakota	39,580	70

Source: US Department of Education (2017).

In follow-up studies, Chetty and his associates (2017a, 2017b) further focused on the subsequent adult earnings of individuals who as children moved from low-mobility neighborhoods to high-mobility neighborhoods, and vice versa. They found annual incremental effects on adult incomes of childhood exposure in these different neighborhood contexts. That is, every year growing up in "low-mobility neighborhoods" produced adverse effects on adult incomes, and similarly positive effects for every year of childhood exposure to "high-mobility neighborhoods." The longer the exposure, the greater the cumulative effect on adult incomes. They found that high-mobility neighborhoods were characterized by low rates of neighborhood racial segregation, low levels of economic inequality, high quality of K–12 schools, low rates of violent crime, and a low proportion of single-headed households. These effects were independent of individual variation on these measures; for instance, even if a child grew up in an intact family, his or her chances for upward mobility were adversely affected if that child grew up in a neighborhood with a high proportion of single-headed households. While such low-mobility communities exist throughout the United States, it is significant that they are especially concentrated in Southern states. In short, the data overwhelmingly confirm that place matters, independent of the characteristics of discrete individuals.

SPLIT LABOR MARKETS

In addition to the community in which the work is performed, the characteristics of the employing organization and the industrial location of the job also matter. Beyond the characteristics of individual workers, pay, benefits, and working conditions also vary across employers and industries (Cobb and Lin 2017; Averitt 1968; Kwon 2014; Stainback and Tomaskovic-Devey 2012; Dwyer 2013; Kalleberg 2011). Large, capital-intensive, high-profit firms with large market shares tend to pay employees the most. Government employment offers less pay but often provides high levels of job security. Level of government (federal, state, county, municipal) also makes a difference, with the federal level generally providing the best packages for employees.

The small-business sector, by contrast, generally offers the lowest pay, the fewest benefits, and the poorest working conditions. A janitor, for instance, who works in an office building for a major corporation, is likely to earn more than a janitor who works in a county public school building, who, in turn, is likely to earn more than a janitor who works in a local restaurant. Again, defenders of meritocracy might argue that the "best" and the hardest-working janitors will end up working for the major corporations, but there is no evidence to support such a claim. This is because such a claim assumes far more predictability and rationality in how workers are matched with jobs than actually exists. Workers do not systematically work for employing organizations that will pay the most for what they can do. For a variety of reasons—such as a job's availability at a particular place, at the particular time someone is seeking it—many people somewhat haphazardly end up working for whom they are working and doing the work they are doing (McDonald 2009).

Christopher Jencks et al. (1979, 306–11) identified three sources of wage variation among otherwise indistinguishable workers. First, the business cycle can create market uncertainties, making it impossible for workers to know in advance how many weeks in a year they may end up working in any given job. In this scenario, among similarly skilled workers doing the same kind of work, some might be laid off and others not. Second, large firms often create pay scales for occupational slots, not the people who fill them. A firm's complicated wage structure is not especially responsive to market changes, so at any point, some individual workers may be paid over and others under the real market rate. Finally, neither employing organizations nor individual workers have all the information necessary to optimize decisions that affect wages. Employing organizations do not always know the minimum they can pay to attract workers with sufficient skill to do the job, and workers do not always know how high a wage they can command. As a result, some employers pay more than necessary, and some workers accept less than they could get. As Jencks et al. note, "These suboptimal bargains mean that identical workers do not always earn identical amounts" (1979, 310).

THE RANDOM-WALK HYPOTHESIS

So far in this chapter, the discussion has revolved around education, jobs, and income. I have argued that the "going rate" of return for the jobs that people hold depends, to a large extent, on factors that lie outside the control of individual workers themselves. Getting ahead in terms of the occupations people hold and the pay they receive involves an element of luck—being in the right place at the right time. There is also an element of luck in the acquisition of great wealth. Indeed, luck may be even more of a factor in wealth attainment than income attainment. The luck factor in wealth acquisition, as we have seen, begins at birth. By an "accident of birth," some are born into great wealth while most are not. Since no one "chooses" their parents, those born into privilege may be thought of as "lucky." But what of "self-made" individuals who acquire great wealth without being born into it? In *Building Wealth* (1999), economist Lester Thurow identifies thirteen "rules" for wealth building. Rule number thirteen states, "Luck is necessary. Talent, drive, and persistence by themselves aren't enough to get wealthy."

Thurow's point is clear enough: Luck matters. Thurow observes that wealth creation comes from taking advantage of "disequilibriums," or shake-ups, in market conditions. Change brings about conditions of disequilibrium, and those conditions in turn create new opportunities for the creation of new wealth. Thurow identifies three types of disequilibrium: technological, sociological, and developmental. Technological disequilibrium refers to forms of new wealth created through advances in technology (e.g., computers) or the development of related products and services surrounding the advance of new technologies (e.g., computer software). Sociological disequilibriums are those created by behavioral or social change unrelated to technology. Thurow offers the example of the aging of the American population and how this demographic change creates new economic opportunities in products and services disproportionately consumed by the elderly (e.g., medical and assisted-living services). Finally, developmental disequilibrium refers to unequal conditions of development in different countries that create opportunities to introduce products and services available in one place that are not yet available in another place.

To some extent, those who are the most clever or most insightful might be better able to anticipate various market shake-ups. However, the "random-walk hypothesis" developed by economists seems to best account for who ends up with the right idea, the right product, or the right service. The argument is simply that striking it rich tends to be like getting struck by lightning: Many are walking around, but only a few get randomly struck. Large fortunes tend to be made quickly, taking early advantage of market shake-ups. The window for striking it rich is very narrow, since once it is open, others quickly rush in.

LOTTERY LUCKY

Another way to strike it rich in America is to win a lottery. The odds of getting rich by hitting the lottery jackpot, however, are long indeed. Lotteries offer the worst odds of any form of legalized gambling (Gudgeon and Stewart 2001). The odds of winning a multistate jackpot lottery, for instance, are roughly 1 in 150 million (Sweeney 2009). While odds are long, winning large jackpots can be lucrative. The largest lump-sum payments to a single ticket winner on a government-sponsored lottery went to Mavis Wanczyk in Massachusetts in 2017, who opted to take the $758.7 million winnings in a one-time lump-sum payment of $480 million, or $336 million after taxes, a considerable amount for most people, but still not nearly enough to place one on the Forbes 400 list of wealthiest Americans.

For a handful of very lucky Americans, then, winning the lottery can mean the fulfillment of the "rags-to-riches" American Dream. It is a nonmerit form of rapid mobility, but mobility nevertheless. The media hype surrounding this type of mobility encourages the idea that America is a land of opportunity in which anyone at any time might become instantly wealthy. As pointed out in chapter 1, having at least a chance to get rich has been one of the central themes of Americans' sense of the fulfillment of the American Dream. Advertisements for the purchase of state lottery tickets echo this theme, with slogans such as "Give Your Dream a Chance," "Get Rich Quick: Play the Lottery," and in one controversial billboard advertisement that appeared in a poor Chicago neighborhood, "This could be your ticket out" (Cohen 2016).

Both conservatives and liberals have opposed lotteries. Conservatives sometimes oppose lotteries as a form of vice along with all other forms of gambling; liberals sometimes oppose lotteries because they exploit the poor. The poor are the least able to afford tickets and the most vulnerable to the lure of instant wealth. Despite these reservations, lotteries hold great romantic appeal and have become a popular American pastime. As of 2016, forty-four states, the District of Columbia, and Puerto Rico have lotteries. As weeks go by without winners, the pots increase in value, which in turn attracts more players. An estimated 50 percent of Americans have purchased a lottery ticket at least once, and an estimated 25 percent of Americans buy a lottery ticket at least once a week (Cohen 2016). Americans spend over $70 billion annually on lottery tickets, more than they spend on music, books, sports tickets, video games, and movie tickets combined (Cohen 2016).

State-sponsored lotteries are only one form of "gaming." Legalized gambling in casinos is available in Las Vegas and Atlantic City and on some Native American reservations. Offshore cruise lines whose sole purpose is to provide sites for gambling have flourished. They all market the same product: the hope of instant wealth. Among hopefuls, a few do win big, with great fanfare and excitement. The longer the odds, the larger the purse. The hoopla surrounding the "winners" is part of the marketing strategy to encourage players to play more. But the reality is that most players either lose or, occasionally, win just a little. The odds favor the house, ensuring over the long run that the house is ultimately the biggest winner of all. The house edge is the difference between the true odds of winning and the odds that the house actually pays when someone wins. The difference is usually in the neighborhood of 10 percent, assuring a profit stream for the house in the long run. A toss of the coin, for instance, has a fifty-fifty chance of winning. If you bet a dollar to win, the house would pay 90 cents on the dollar for the bet.

Perhaps the largest but least recognized forum for legalized gambling in the United States is the stock market. For all practical purposes, investing in stocks and bonds is equivalent to gambling. The biggest difference between playing the stock market and other forms of gambling is that the odds for winning in the stock market are much better, although the return is usually much less. The odds of "winning" in the stock market can be increased beyond random chance by knowing as much as possible about the companies in which one invests, and by being able to predict market changes. Knowing about companies and markets, in part, is a matter of social and cultural capital—being in a loop composed of people with accurate and current information. As recent investment scandals have underscored, these odds can be increased illegally through insider trading. Apart from such schemes, however, there is still an element of investor risk. Indeed, the willingness to take chances and to risk capital is the primary justification for capitalism. If it were possible to predict the future with certainty, then there would be no risk. But as long as the future remains unpredictable, luck is a factor.

Having money to invest or gamble in the first place is also a factor—and an important one. Small investments, no matter how good the rate of return, are unlikely to generate great wealth. Like many other aspects of getting ahead in America, it takes money to make money. And the really big money in America, as we have seen, comes not from working for a living but from return on capital investments.

SUMMARY

In this chapter, several chance factors beyond individuals' immediate control that affect their life chances have been identified. While individuals do have some control over how skilled they are, they have no control over what kinds of jobs are available, how many, and how many individuals are seeking those jobs. These labor-market conditions occur independently of the capacities of discrete individuals—how smart or talented they are, how hard they work, or how motivated they are to get ahead. Most economists agree that labor-market conditions have fundamentally shifted since the early 1970s. A combination of circumstances prompted American corporations to sharply reduce manufacturing facilities in the United States, relocate facilities to the Sun Belt and overseas, consolidate through mergers, avoid unionization, "downsize" operations, "outsource" labor, and engage in other sweeping changes that collectively had a dramatic impact on the American labor force.

Although more Americans are getting more education, the economy is not producing enough jobs with good pay, good benefits, security, and opportunities for advancement commensurate with the higher levels of education attained. Compared to previous generations of workers entering the labor force, the most recent generation of workers faces fewer opportunities, greater job instability, and a greater chance of being stuck in dead-end jobs.

Beyond occupational success, being in the right place at the right time also matters for acquiring wealth. Striking it rich—be it through inheritance, entrepreneurial ventures, investments, or the lottery—necessarily involves at least some degree of just plain dumb luck. The simple fact is that there is far more intelligence, talent, ability, and hard work in the population as a whole than there are people who are lucky enough to find themselves in a position to take full advantage of these qualities.

After individuals complete their formal educational training and enter the labor force, the usual next step is to get married. In the next chapter, we examine the effects of marriage on economic inequality and chances for mobility.

REFERENCES

Abel, Johnson, Richard Dietz, and Yakin Su. 2014. "Are Recent College Graduates Finding Good Jobs?" *Current Issues in Economics and Finance* 20(1). Federal Reserve Bank of New York. www.newyorkfed.org/medialibrary/media/research/current_issues/ci20-1.pdf. New York.

Averitt, Robert T. 1968. *Dual Economy*. New York: W. W. Norton.

Barnsley, Roger, and A. H. Thompson. 1988. "Birthdate and Success in Minor Hockey: Key to NHL." *Canadian Journal of Behavioral Science* 20(2):167–76.

Bell, Daniel. 1976. *The Coming of Post-Industrial Society*. New York: Basic Books.

Chetty, Raj, Nathaniel Hendren, Patrick Kline, and Emmanuel Saez. 2014. "Where Is the Land of Opportunity? The Geography of Intergenerational Mobility in the U.S." *Quarterly Journal of Economics* 129(4):1553–1623.

Chetty, Raj, and Nathaniel Hendren. 2017a. "The Effects of Neighborhoods on Intergenerational Mobility I: Childhood Exposure Effects." www.equality-of-opportunity.org/assets/documents/movers_paper1.pdf (accessed August 4, 2017).

———. 2017b. "The Effects of Neighborhoods on Intergenerational Mobility II: County-Level Estimates." www.equality-of-opportunity.org/assets/documents/movers_paper2.pdf (accessed August 4, 2017).

Cobb, J. Adam, and Ken-Hou Lin. 2017. "Growing Apart: The Changing-Size Wage Effect and Its Inequality Consequences." *Administrative Science Quarterly* 82(2):304–40.

Cohen, Jonathan D. 2016. "State Lotteries and the New American Dream." Occasional Paper Series. University of Las Vegas–Nevada: Center for Gambling Research.

Collins, Randall. 1979. *The Credential Society: A Historical Sociology of Education and Stratification.* New York: Academic Press.

Dwyer, Rachel E. 2013. "The Care Economy? Gender, Economic Restructuring, and Job Polarization in the US Labor Markets." *American Sociological Review* 78(3):390–416.

Ford, Martin. 2015. *The Rise of the Robots: Technology and the Threat of a Jobless Future.* New York: Basic Books.

Frank, Robert H. 2016. *Success and Luck: Good Fortune and the Myth of Meritocracy.* Princeton, NJ: Princeton University Press.

Frey, Carl Benedikt, and Michael A. Osborne. 2017. "The Future of Employment: How Susceptible Are Jobs to Computerisation." *Technological Forecasting and Social Change* 114:254–80.

Frohlich, Thomas C., Michael B. Sauter, and Samuel Stebbins. 2016. "America's Richest (and Poorest) States." 24/7 Wall Street: Special Report. September 15. http://247wallst.com/special-report/2016/09/15/americas-richest-and-poorest-states-4/2/ (accessed August 8, 2017).

Gladwell, Malcolm. 2008. *Outliers: The Story of Success.* New York: Little, Brown.

Gordon, Robert J. 2017. *The Rise and Fall of American Growth: US Standard of Living since the Civil War.* Princeton, NJ: Princeton University Press.

Gudgeon, Chris, and Barbara Stewart. 2001. *Luck of the Draw: True-Life Tales of Lottery Winners and Losers.* Vancouver, WA: Arsenal Pulp Press.

Harrison, Bennett, and Barry Bluestone. 1988. *The Great U-Turn: Corporate Restructuring and the Polarizing of America.* New York: Basic Books.

Hatton, Erin. 2011. *The Temp Economy: From Kelly Girls to Permatemps in Postwar America.* Philadelphia: Temple University Press.

Hicks, Michael J., and Srikant Devaraj. 2015. "The Myth and the Reality of Manufacturing in America." Ball State University Center for Business and Economic Research. http://conexus.cberdata.org/files/MfgReality.pdf (accessed August 8, 2017).

Jencks, Christopher, Susan Bartlett, Mary Corcoran, James Crouse, David Eaglesfield, Gregory Jackson, Kent McClelland, et al. 1979. *Who Gets Ahead? The Determinants of Economic Success in America.* New York: Basic Books.

Kahle, Kathleen M., and Rene M. Stulz. 2017. "Is the U.S. Public Corporation in Trouble?" *Journal of Economic Perspectives* 31(3):67–88.

Kalleberg, Arne L. 2011. *Good Jobs, Bad Jobs: The Rise of Polarized and Precarious Employment Systems in the United States, 1970s to 2000s.* New York: Sage.

Kaplan, Roy. 1978. *Lottery Winners: How They Won and How Winning Changed Their Lives.* New York: HarperCollins.

Katz, Lawrence F., and Alan B. Krueger. 2016. "The Rise of Alternative Work Arrangements in the United States, 1995–2015." National Bureau of Economic Research. Working Paper No. 22667. www.nber.org/papers/w22667 (accessed August 8, 2017).

Kwon, Hyun Soo. 2014. "Economic Theories of Low-Wage Work." *Journal of Human Behavior in the Social Environment* 24(1):61–70.

Leopold, Les. 2016. *Runaway Inequality*. New York: Labor Institute Press.

Levy, Frank. 1998. *The New Dollars and Dreams: American Incomes and Economic Change*. New York: Sage.

Livingstone, D. W. 2004. *The Education-Jobs Gap: Underemployment or Economic Democracy*, 2nd ed. Clinton Corners, NY: Eliot Werner.

McDonald, Steve. 2009. "Right Place, Right Time: Serendipity and Informal Job Matching." *Socio-Economic Review*, 1–25.

Rose, Stephen J. 2017. "Mismatch: How Many Workers with a Bachelor's Degree Are Overqualified for Their Jobs?" Urban Institute: Income and Benefits Policy Center. www.urban.org/research/publication/mismatch-how-many-workers-bachelors-degree-are-over qualified-their-jobs/view/full_report (accessed August 8, 2017).

Schmitt, John, and Janelle Jones. 2012. "Where Have All the Good Jobs Gone?" Center for Economic and Policy Research. www.cepr.net/documents/publications/good-jobs-2012-07 .pdf (accessed January 20, 2013).

Stainback, Kevin, and Donald Tomaskovic-Devey. 2012. *Documenting Desegregation: Racial and Gender Segregation in Private-Sector Employment since the Civil Rights Act*. New York: Sage.

Sweeney, Matthew. 2009. *The Lottery Wars: Long Odds, Fast Money, and the Battle over an American Institution*. New York: Bloomsbury.

Thurow, Lester C. 1999. *Building Wealth: The New Rules for Individuals, Companies and Nations in a Knowledge-Based Economy*. New York: HarperCollins.

US Bureau of Labor. 2015. "Occupational Employment Projections through 2024." *Monthly Labor Review*, December. www.bls.gov/opub/mlr/2015/article/occupational-employment-projections-to-2024.htm (accessed January 20, 2017).

US Census Bureau. 1975. *Historical Statistics of the United States: Colonial Times to 1970*. Washington, DC: US Government Printing Office.

———. 2001. *Statistical Abstract of the United States 2001*. Washington, DC: US Government Printing Office.

US Department of Education. 2017. *Digest of Education Statistics, 2017*. Table 211.60, Estimated Average Annual Salary of Teachers in Public Elementary and Secondary Schools, by State: Selected Years 1969–1970 through 2012–2013. https://nces.ed.gov/programs/digest/d13/tables/dt13_211.60.asp (accessed August 4, 2017).

Vedder, Richard, Christopher Denhart, and Jonathan Robe. 2013. *Why Are Recent College Graduates Underemployed?* Washington, DC: Center for College Affordability and Productivity. http://files.eric.ed.gov/fulltext/ED539373.pdf (accessed August 8, 2017).

Wattles, Jackie. 2017. "Biggest Lottery Jackpots in US History." CNN Money. June 11. http://money.cnn.com/2016/05/01/news/largest-lottery-jackpots/index.html (accessed August 4, 2017).

Weeden, Kim. 2002. "Why Do Some Occupations Pay More Than Others? Social Closure and Earnings Inequality in the United States." *American Journal of Sociology* 108:55–101.

Wilson, William Julius. 1987. *The Truly Disadvantaged: The Inner City, the Underclass, and Public Policy*. Chicago: University of Chicago Press.

Wolf, Alison. 2003. *Does Education Matter? Myths about Education and Economic Growth*. London: Penguin Global.

8

Mobility through Marriage

The Cinderella Effect

With the Collaboration of Catherine B. McNamee

> The hall rang with the loudest acclamations of applause, and the company, all in
> one voice, pronounced her the most elegant creature that had ever been seen. And
> this was the little girl who had passed a great part of her life in the kitchen, and
> had always been called a "Cinder-wench."
>
> —Henry W. Hewet, *Cinderella; Or, The Little Glass Slipper*

Marrying up is an indirect form of social mobility. By marrying someone of higher social standing, one can become upwardly mobile not directly on one's own characteristics but through an attachment to another. Some might contend that marrying into money has an element of individual merit attached to it. That is, someone who marries up in social status is someone who is attractive enough, talented enough, charming enough, or shrewd enough to attract someone of higher social standing. Americans have a mixed view on this type of upward mobility. On the one hand, most Americans would not approve of marrying for money as a specific strategy for social advancement. On the other hand, if someone marries for love to a person of great wealth where love is the essential motivation for marriage, and wealth is incidental to the relationship, then so much the better. In this sense, marriage as a means of upward social mobility is like inheritance or luck—not as extolled or admired as mobility based on individual achievement, but nevertheless viewed as socially acceptable. Because men historically have had greater access to economic resources than women, this particular pathway of upward mobility has been generally more available to women than men.

In this chapter, we will examine the process of mate selection and how that factors into prospects for social mobility. That is, what factors are associated with who marries or partners with whom? Marriage matters in terms of social-class position in society. Marriage creates opportunities for economies of scale in living expenses and opportunities to combine financial assets. In general, married adults are more economically secure than unmarried adults and better positioned to pass on economic advantages to children.

A BRIEF HISTORY OF MATE SELECTION
AND THE ORIGIN OF CLASS ENDOGAMY

Despite the randomness of the fabled story that Cupid's arrow can strike anyone at any time or at any place, the human mating process is anything but random. Humans have always tended to marry people socially like themselves. *Homogamy* refers to the selection of mates with the same social or personal characteristics as themselves. *Heterogamy* is the obverse, referring to marriage between couples with differing social or personal characteristics. Homogamy is reinforced through social norms of endogamy. *Endogamy* refers to social expectations that encourage or require persons to marry within their own social group. *Exogamy* is the obverse, referring to social expectations or requirements that persons marry outside one's own group.

Marriage has existed in some form in all known human societies aside from one (the Na people of China) (Coontz 2005). However, the specific form that marriage takes has varied widely and wildly across different societies over time, so much so that it is difficult for social scientists to agree on a universal definition of marriage itself. With some exceptions, marriage is generally viewed as a socially approved arrangement regarding sexuality and reproduction. No known human society has been without rules or expectations about who could have sex with whom or who could marry whom. For the most part, such rules are formalized in the social institution of marriage. In addition to sexuality, marriage may also include expectations regarding child rearing, relationships with in-laws and other family members, household division of labor, and rules for inheritance of property. Variation in mate selection, marriage, and family organization are closely tied to economic and stratification systems and how these have changed over time.

Hunters and Gatherers

For the vast majority of human history, humans lived in hunting and gathering societies. Our hunter and gatherer ancestors lived off the land, foraging for game and wild vegetation. Foragers needed to move frequently, as food sources became exhausted once game was killed off or run off and vegetation was consumed. The rule of thumb for foragers is that you need a range of territory of about one square mile per person to sustain the group. Since foragers traveled by foot, their maximum range was limited. For this reason, the size of such groups was also limited, usually to around a few dozen individuals.

Since foragers lived off the land and traveled by foot to do so, there was a premium on traveling light and no point in hoarding perishable goods. Foragers lived a communal existence in which everyone had essentially the same standard of living. Sharing whatever was available was an essential survival strategy. Since everyone had essentially the same as everyone else, there were no social-class divisions. In these settings all marriages were by default economically homogenous.

Information regarding marriage and mate-selection practices in hunting and gathering societies is limited. Since most of these societies existed prior to written history, what we know about them comes from a combination of the archaeological record and observations of more contemporary hunting and gathering groups. From the information we do have, it appears that rules for who could marry whom vary among different forager groups, ranging from strict prescriptions and arranged marriages in some to less-regulated courtship in others (Walker et al. 2011). In the majority of these societies, marriages are arranged by parents or kinship groups, although changing partners or the equivalent of divorce and remarriage by choice is also common (Coontz 2005; Sanderson 2001). As these groups are small in number, and some form of incest taboo against marrying close relatives appears universal, marriage partners are frequently exchanged between forager groups. Since foragers do not accumulate property to any great extent, there is very little incentive for warfare among neighboring groups; having blood relatives in these groups further reduces the incentive for such conflicts (Levi-Strauss 1969). Creating alliances across groups through marriage could also be beneficial for survival in lean times or in the face of common threats.

Agricultural Revolution

Marriage and mate-selection practices changed with the onset of the agricultural revolution. About twelve thousand years ago, humans adopted planted cultivation as a primary means of acquiring resources, gradually giving up their nomadic existence and establishing permanent settlements. Eventually, communities were able to grow more crops than were minimally necessary to sustain the members of the group. Ever since this "surplus" was produced, some have managed through whatever means to get more of it than others. Land from which crops were produced was no longer just there as a natural resource but declared as private property by those who controlled the surplus. Those who controlled the surplus could use it to free some from working in the fields to do other things. Full-time occupations came into being, such as peasants to grow the crops, artisans to make things, scribes to keep track of things, and soldiers to protect the property of those who claimed ownership of it. With a reliable food source in one place, permanent and increasingly larger settlements could be developed. With permanent settlements, those with access to surplus could store and accumulate material goods. Rules of inheritance were established about who had legitimate claim to the accumulated property of those who died.

All of these developments gave rise to the feudal order and a stratification system based on ownership and control of the land, which was the major source of wealth. Once the inheritance of property was at stake, marriage rules became much more rigid and restrictive. In order to prevent the dilution of accumulated property and to maintain class divisions in society, class endogamy became the norm, as well as rules to ensure it. In land-based societies, marriage outside one's class or caste was exceedingly rare and often prohibited outright. Marriages were primarily arranged by parents as economic swaps between families, often including bride price and dowries.

Among the aristocracy in the feudal era, rules regarding marriage were especially strict since property and title were at stake. Most marriages were arranged by royal households as a means of solidifying property and creating economic, political, and military alliances among ruling families. Commoner marriages were less strict and less regulated, but still mostly arranged by parents. Even among commoners, parents had a vested interest in establishing alliances with other families for their own well-being (Coontz 2005). Where romantic love operated as a consideration for marriage, it was a secondary consideration at best, and not viewed as essential to the marriage. Through most of human history, marriage was fundamentally a social arrangement organized around property relations.

We do not ordinarily think of marriage as a set of property relations. Sociologist Randall Collins (1982), however, points out that even modern marriage can be interpreted as a set of property relations organized around marriage partners as erotic property, children as generational property, and material goods as household property. Even where romantic love is viewed as the primary basis of mate selection in modern Western societies, romantic attachments are seen in possessive terms. Love talk is talk of possession—"You are mine," "I am yours," and so on. Adultery can be viewed as a form of trespass on someone's claim to exclusive access to erotic property. In some states, married people can sue their straying spouse's paramour for alienation of affection. In modern societies, we do not think of children as property, but cases of child custody disputes following divorce look a lot like property disputes, to say nothing of material property disputes—both of which often end up in protracted court battles.

Industrialization

Romantic love as a relevant criterion for mate selection did not emerge in Western societies to any significant extent until the beginnings of the Industrial Revolution in the late eighteenth century (Coontz 2005; Abbott 2010). The industrial age shifted the primary basis of wealth production from agriculture to manufactured goods. The major factors related to this change were a combination of the development of a wage-labor market economy and a new emphasis on liberty and individual rights associated with the Enlightenment (Coontz 2005). In feudal systems, everyone essentially works for the landed aristocrat. The development of market economies and wage labor meant that workers could secure paid employment outside of familial obligations, reducing the dependence on parents and extended kin networks. The liberating ideas of the Enlightenment provided justification for respect for individual rights and freedom of choice, including in matters of the heart. These developments reduced but did not eliminate parental influence on mate selection. As with other forms of social change, the premium on romantic love as a primary and ultimately a necessary precondition for marriage only gradually took hold. In a system in which parental "blessing" was still often expected or required as a precondition for marriage, parents retained effective veto power regarding suitable mates, although parentally arranged marriages became less common.

The adoption of greater freedom of choice in mate selection and the emerging cultural ideal of romantic love as the primary criterion for marriage created the space in which it was possible for individuals to choose marriage partners outside their own social class. Although marrying outside one's social class became possible, it did not mean that it was particularly likely. Marrying someone of like economic standing was still the norm, although less prohibited. Beyond social class, restrictions surrounding marrying outside one's religion—and particularly outside one's race—were still in place, and usually even more restrictive.

Between a system of parentally arranged marriages and an altogether free market for mate selection, an intermediate chaperone system often emerged. Under the chaperone system, male suitors would "call" on prospective female partners under the watchful eyes of parents or other designated third parties. This chaperone system was a method of prevention against out-of-wedlock births, and provided parents with a measure of screening potential marriage partners, at least for daughters. In America, the chaperone system was largely broken up by the automobile, which provided a means to escape such third-party scrutiny.

The advent of the age of the automobile in the early 1900s also corresponded with the first wave of the women's liberation movement in America. In the Victorian period that preceded it, sexual inhibitions dominated. In the Victorian age, romance was distinct from sexual passion. The basis of romantic love was not sexual passion but emotion and sentimentality. Early American colonists brought these puritanical values of the period with them. As noted in chapter 1, the Protestant ethic of diligence and asceticism, however, led to an unsustainable contradiction for free-market capitalism; the ascetic restrictions on luxuries and self-indulgence limited market demand, while the "work hard" ethic enhanced it. Something had to give, and Americans chose to shed the asceticism ethic, and ultimately, the sexual inhibitions associated with it. In the first phase of the women's movement in America, as exemplified by the "flappers" of the "Roaring Twenties," women sought both the right to vote as well as their right to sexual fulfillment. These developments further solidified expectations for a free market for mate selection.

As industrialization took hold, societies became less organized around families and communities for survival. The transition to wage labor in the industrial society fostered separate spheres, with women working within the home in (mostly) unpaid labor, and men working for wages outside the home. Societal changes related to urbanization and industrialization occurring in the mid-twentieth century shifted marital unions into a new version of companionate marriages that emphasized partnership, love, and similar interests (Burgess and Locke 1945). This was driven by a stronger influence of the state that encouraged greater female empowerment, and individuals becoming more mobile, being able to move away from the watchful eyes of parents. While economic considerations were not entirely removed from mate selection decisions, an increased standard of living associated with industrialization meant that even young couples could reasonably expect that their economic futures would be secure and that a single male wage earner could provide adequately. Under these conditions, a more relaxed "love is all you need" mentality with regard to marriage flourished, reflected and culturally reinforced through novels, films, and music of the period.

Postindustrialization

Toward the end of the twentieth century, further gains in women rights, the development of the contraception pill (allowing women to control fertility, providing more flexibility to stay in the workforce), and the declining earning power of men's wages increased the number of women in the workforce. Dual-worker households developed into the norm, with women far more likely to gain higher levels of education (women in the United States now surpass men in both baccalaureate and post-baccalaureate degrees) and to earn personal income (albeit still less than men). With rising inequality and declining wages, economic futures became less secure. The emphasis on romantic love as a basis of mate selection has not declined, but has become less exclusive a consideration for marriage. In addition to maximizing personal satisfaction in relationships, potential marriage partners increasingly adopt what futurist Alvin Toffler (1980) described as a "love plus" attitude toward mate selection. Romantic love as a basis of mate selection is still important and necessary but no longer sufficient. For a marriage to take place, couples increasingly feel that they need to be economically secure before entering marriage.

MATE SELECTION IN CONTEMPORARY AMERICA

Despite a free market for mate selection and the steady erosion of parental influence, it is still the case that Americans are likely to marry people who replicate their own social profile in excess of random chance. That is, people tend to marry people of similar age, residence, education, race, and social-class background far beyond random chance alone. There are three primary possible reasons for this non-random convergence (Kalmijn 1998): 1) Everything else being equal, people may prefer to marry people like themselves; 2) third parties (e.g., friends, family, and sometimes institutions such as religious groups or the state) may encourage or even require such convergence; and 3) apart from intentional personal preference or outside pressure, people may tend to marry people from within their own social milieu or social circles of acquaintances, which in turn would substantially increase the probability of marrying someone like themselves.

The contemporary mate-selection process can be understood as a filtering system in which the range of eligible marriage partners is gradually narrowed in generally predictable ways. The various filters that shift and sort potential marriage partners do not operate in a rigid sequence but have an overall effect on who ends up marrying whom. Among those filters is propinquity, which refers to both geographic and social proximity. Mating requires meeting, and people are likely to draw their partners from a subset of people with whom they regularly come into contact. The propinquity effect does not itself directly imply either personal or social preferences, although individuals may purposely place themselves in geographic places or social circumstances that reflect personal or social preferences.

Research shows an increasing degree of residential segregation by income in the United States (Reardon and Bischoff 2011). As people increasingly live among those of similar levels of income and wealth, the potential for class-based homogamy increases. As noted in chapter 3, the upper class in America has historically been particularly geographically and socially isolated. The superwealthy live in exclusive communities, travel in exclusive social circles, and interact mostly with people like themselves. Upper-class institutions and rituals such as debutante balls, designed to introduce young women of marriageable age to "society"—meaning, upper-class society—encourage and reinforce the prospects class for endogamy among the wealthy. The social isolation of the wealthy has been replicated on a somewhat smaller scale with the "white flight" of middle- and upper-middle-class Americans to suburbs, beginning in the 1950s, and the more-recent popularity and expansion of gated communities and restrictive neighborhood covenants. These developments increase the likelihood that people of similar social backgrounds will be similarly geographically and socially situated.

Kalmijn and Flap (2001) have identified five potential "meeting settings" that highly structure the prospects of marriage: work, school, residence, common family networks, and voluntary associations (such as religious, political, and other cultural organizations that individuals voluntarily belong to). In a preliminary study conducted in the Netherlands, Kalmijn and Flap (2001) found, for instance, that 42 percent of married couples had met in one of these five institutional settings. Of these settings, the one in which couples were most likely to have initially met was educational settings. Moreover, the higher the level of education achieved, the more likely couples would have met in those settings.

These findings are consistent with other research conducted in the United States that show high rates of educational endogamy, especially at very high and very low levels of educational attainment (Fu and Heaton 2008; Rosenfeld 2008; Schwartz and Mare 2005). To the extent that educational endogamy occurs and to the extent that access to education is class-based (see chapter 5), the likelihood of class endogamy also increases. Class endogamy through education can occur in two ways. One way is that those of the same social-class background (class of origin) are more likely to go to the same kinds of schools and have the same levels of educational attainment. A second way is that those who are from lower social-class origins who are upwardly mobile are more likely to end up in educational and work settings that increase the prospect of marrying someone from a higher social class of origin compared to those who are not upwardly mobile.

Geographic and social propinquity, therefore, is likely to reduce the pool of eligible marriage partners in a manner that increases the prospects for marriage homogamy. The recent emergence of social media and Internet dating, however, may affect these outcomes. Internet dating is on the rise, and is rapidly becoming one of the most likely avenues for meeting your partner. An estimated 20 percent of newlyweds found their partner through the Internet (Rosenfeld and Thomas 2012). Internet dating has at least the potential to weaken or even negate the effect of geographic or social proximity, since prospective partners may be "screened" online outside these parameters.

On the other hand, self-selected online screening options could promote homogamy. Many Internet dating sites provide screening options that could replicate and perhaps even enhance the effects of geographic or social proximity. Some dating sites, for instance, are restricted to persons seeking partners with particular interests (e.g., dog lovers) or specific occupations (e.g., farmers) or particular religious or political affiliations. Other dating sites that market more to a general audience will often still attempt to "match" those with similar or preferred characteristics.

The extent to which potential partners are screened based on socioeconomic characteristics is difficult to determine. Most dating sites rely on mathematical algorithms based on a combination of personal characteristics and preferences to optimize the prospects of successful matches. How these algorithms work is difficult to determine, as many sites do not reveal their algorithms, but there is little doubt that socioeconomic characteristics and preferences are taken into account (Lewis 2015; Slater 2013). In other cases, socioeconomic matching may be a "by-product" related to other preferences (Lewis 2016). For instance, lower socioeconomic status is related to higher smoking rates (Hiscock et al. 2012), and Internet daters have shown a preference for someone with similar smoking habits (Hitsch et al. 2010b); therefore, matching on smoking behavior could also have the unintended effect of sorting on socioeconomic status. In other cases, sorting on the basis of socioeconomic status is more explicit—for instance, on dating sites that explicitly target or restrict users who have high socioeconomic standing, such as "The League" and "Luxy."

Research on Internet dating provides a unique platform to distinguish between preferences and opportunity to meet a person with different characteristics. It also provides information on the type of preferences people hold that could play into homogamy. That is, do people want matches with persons who share similar characteristics, or do people seek the best match possible with people with traits such as wealth and attractiveness that would be preferred by all? Studies support that both are occurring. Overall, people are seeking out partners like themselves, but those with desirable traits, such as high socioeconomic status, also receive the most attention (Hitsch et al. 2010a; Kreager et al. 2014; Lewis 2016; Lin and Lundquist 2013). This competition still results in endogamy, as those with "desirable traits" are more likely to get the most attention and filter interactions to those who similarly possess "desirable traits."

Research on Internet dating, however, also suggests that preferences regarding socioeconomic status are likely to be gendered, often reflecting traditional gender roles (Abramova et al. 2016; Hitsch et al. 2010a; Hitsch et al. 2010b; Kreager et al. 2014; Lewis 2016). That is, women tend to prefer matching with men of equivalent or higher socioeconomic status, and place a higher preference on this than men. Men, on the other hand, tend to prefer matching with women who have equal status, and show a disinterest in women with higher socioeconomic status, specifically women with higher education.

Beyond social class, individuals are encouraged or are likely to marry someone of their own race or ethnic group, religion, and someone similar in age. Although interracial marriage is less restricted and more common than in the past, there is still a high rate of overall racial homogamy. A recent Pew Research Center study (Livingston and Brown 2017) found that among newlyweds married in the United States in 2015, 17 percent married someone of a different race, compared to only 3 percent in 1967. Asians were most likely to marry outside their race (29 percent), followed by Hispanics (27 percent), blacks (18 percent), and whites (11 percent). Among all married persons in the United States in 2015, 90 percent were married to someone of their own race. High rates of race endogamy may be a reflection of a combination of geographic and social isolation among racial minorities and personal or social preference (Choi and Tienda 2017).

Although Americans as a whole are becoming less religious, a majority of married persons are married to someone within their own faith. According to a Pew Research Center Study (2015), 69 percent of married Americans have spouses with the same religion (counting Protestants as a single religious group). As is the case with interracial marriages, however, rates of interfaith marriages have increased sharply in recent decades. Among Americans married since 2010, 39 percent report being married to a spouse of a different religious group.

In addition to the tendency toward likeness on the bases of class, race, and religion, most Americans marry people of similar ages. In general, men are slightly older than women at the age of their first marriage, with the gender gap between ages at first marriage narrowing over time. In 1890 the median gender age gap was 4.1 years (men, 26.1, and 22.0 for women), but this gap had fallen to 2.1 years by 2016 (29.5 for men, and 27.4 for women) (US Census Bureau 2017). The decline is occurring as education and employment expectations for both sexes have become more similar.

Another filter in the mate-selection process is attractiveness. Here, free-market conditions tend to apply. That is, people tend to marry people of similar levels of physical attractiveness (Fugere et al. 2015). Criteria for attractiveness are related to biological markers for youth, health, and fertility (Buss 2016). But criteria for attractiveness may also in part be culturally defined and related to markers that overlap with other social categories, such as class and race. Physical attraction can overlap with class in another way as well. To the extent that looks matter in mate selection, as well as prospects for economic success (see chapter 9), the affluent are best po-sitioned to maximize whatever physical attributes they may possess through greater access to more expensive clothing and accessories, as well as the time and expense of appearance-altering strategies, such as the use of cosmetic surgery, gyms, spas, personal trainers, and such.

A fourth marriage filter is psychological characteristics and personal compatibility. In some cases, this may mean that partners share similar characteristics; in other cases, or in other respects, this may mean that partners have different but comple-mentary characteristics (Fisher 2009). What "works" is typically determined more by trial and error and how well couples get along than by couples consciously seeking out particular traits in prospective mates.

SOCIAL MOBILITY THROUGH MARRIAGE

For all of the reasons summarized above, most marriages are class-homogamous, meaning that most people marry someone of their own (or similar) social-class background. Cross-class or class-heterogamous marriages, however, do occur. His-torically, the prospect for upward mobility through marriage has been greater for women than men. In what might be referred to as the "Cinderella effect," early re-search seems to show that women could sometimes trade desirable traits, specifically attractiveness in a marriage market, for access to higher-status men (Elder 1969). This type of cross-class marriage is likely to occur with greater frequency in societies with high levels of gender inequality and highly gendered division of labor between husband-breadwinner and wife-homemaker roles.

An intentional strategy of "marrying up" for money or social status could be seen as a specific form of social climbing (see chapter 3), and subject to all of the risks as-sociated with it. Those who purse such a strategy risk social derision, including being undesirably labeled as "gold diggers" or "trophy wives." How extensive an intentional marrying-for-money strategy of upward mobility is, or how successful it might be, is unknown. Because of the social stigma attached to it, few would admit to it. The strategy itself, however, is not unknown. Those in pursuit of such a strategy can find ample advice on "how to marry rich" from a plethora of self-help books, YouTube videos, magazine articles, blogs, and even professional coaches. Such a strategy would generally not be considered a legitimate part of the American Dream.

Regardless of intent, determining the extent to which cross-class marriages occur greatly depends greatly on how "class" or "socioeconomic status" is conceptualized and measured. Class or socioeconomic status can be measured on the basis of oc-cupation, income, wealth, education, or some combination of those. Different rates of mobility can result depending on which dimensions of socioeconomic status are used, and how each of those is measured. In social science research, level of educa-tion is often considered a convenient proxy measure of social class or socioeconomic standing. There are several practical reasons for this. First, reliable income data are more difficult to get, and reliable wealth data are even more difficult to get. Second, education level (as opposed to years of education completed) can be broken down into meaningful categories for comparison much more easily and less arbitrarily than income or wealth. For instance, the one-year difference between sixteen years of education completed and fifteen years of education completed is the difference between having a college degree and not, whereas the one-year difference between fifteen years of education completed and fourteen years is less meaningful, both representing a level of educational attainment equivalent to "some college." Income and wealth are ratio variables with no natural categorical distinctions, although their distributions are highly skewed (see chapter 3). And unlike other measures of class, respondents' education levels tend to be stable once reaching adulthood. Although education level is most often used in studies of "assortative mating," educational level does not tell the whole story. For instance, there is likely a large class difference overall between graduates of Ivy League universities and graduates of much less prestigious institutions, although they would be considered "class-homogamous" on educational level alone.

Because the range of variation in income and wealth is much greater than education—and because there are no clear-cut categories of difference—income or wealth homogamy (and social mobility) is even more difficult to determine. Occupation is sometimes used in mobility studies, but it also has limitations. For instance, "manager" may be seen as a high-ranking occupational category, but there may be a large effective class difference between a manager of a local shoe store and a manager (CEO) of a major corporation. Occupations can also be scaled on the basis of prestige scores, but as with income, what would constitute homogamy in comparing "similar" matches would ultimately be arbitrarily determined.

Another important distinction in mobility studies concerns the bases of comparison in determining whether mobility has occurred. In determining whether someone has married up or down, is the critical basis of comparison between the current socioeconomic status of husbands and wives, or between the family background of one spouse compared to the family background of the other spouse? Relying just on spouses' education levels, current jobs, or current incomes at time of marriage might suppress significant class differences—for instance, between two accountants from the same firm who marry each other, one a "trust-fund baby" who has inherited great wealth, and one who was born into poverty but was intergenerationally mobile. These differences are significant, since couples raised in different social-class backgrounds bring different class-based orientations and sensibilities regarding money, work, play, housework, parenting, and emotions to their combined relationships (Streib 2015).

Despite challenges in measuring class homogamy/heterogamy, the overall evidence suggests that most Americans tend to marry persons with the same or similar socioeconomic standings, although there is some debate about the direction of change in recent decades. In one comprehensive study of educational homogamy in the United States since the early twentieth century, sociologist Robert Mare (2016) compared educational levels of spouses with those of their parents. Here he found a strong link between educational homogamy of parents and that of their offspring, resulting in a "multiplier effect" across generations. If "homogamy begets homogamy," then propensity to marry alike reflects not just couples' characteristics at the time of marriage, but their social-class backgrounds as well.

Another driver for class homogamy that provides a barrier to marriage mobility is the increasing importance of dual-working couples, specifically the additional reliance on women's earnings for maximizing household financial well-being. Similar to studies on education, one reason for high homogamy in recent decades relates to opportunity to marry someone like yourself. A recent comprehensive study of married couples between 1970 and 2013 by sociologists Pilar Gonalons-Pons and Christine Schwartz (2017) provides evidence of increasing income homogamy. Their findings suggest that the increase in income homogamy is due less to changes in assortative mating—in which couples select mates of similar income levels—than changes in the division of paid labor between spouses over the course of their marriages. Between 1970 and 2013, rates of female participation in the paid labor force greatly increased. This coincided with a change from the husband-breadwinner / wife-homemaker households to an increasing number of dual-earner households. Moreover, married women in the later years were less likely to drop out of the paid labor force if they had children than in prior periods. This, along with decreasing gender pay gaps, increased the level of income homogamy over time.

In other words, married women have increasingly become more engaged in the labor force, which is narrowing differences between married men's labor force activities, while the income gap is further decreased by the narrowing gender pay gap. Looking at both newlyweds and prevailing marriages, Gonalons-Pons and Schwartz estimate that only 16 percent of the increase in economic homogamy between 1970 and 2013 can be attributed to changes in assortative mating at the time of marriage, whereas 78 percent of the change is due to income convergence after marriages took place. The longer the couple remained married, the greater the degree of convergence. Pons and Schwartz also looked at couples' perceptions of their spouses' earning potential at the time of marriage, and found no evidence of increasing sorting based on earnings potential.

Despite a greater reliance on women's income for the overall socioeconomic standing of a household, evidence suggests that gender asymmetry in marrying up remains. Using US Census and American Community surveys, sociologist Yue Qian (2017) compared cohorts of married working-age couples in 1980 and 2008–2012. Qian found that rates of both educational and income homogamy increased between the two time periods. Using four categories of educational attainment (less than high school, high school, some college, and college and above), consistent with prior research, Qian found relatively high rates of educational homogamy. In the recent cohorts, for instance, 56 percent of both newlyweds and those in prevailing marriages had the same level of educational attainment. With regard to education, more women married up in the earlier time cohort than men, but in the latter time period, the pattern was reversed, with more women marrying down than men. This finding is consistent with women as a whole exceeding men with regard to educational attainment, beginning in the 1990s.

With respect to couples' incomes, however, women by a substantial degree married up in both time periods compared to men, although the rate at which women married up in income decreased considerably over time. To access instances of income homogamy, Qian used income deciles of husbands and wives. Education can be considered a marker for earning potential, but as the age of first marriage has increased, partners can be assessed on actual earnings rather than estimated earning potential, making income a more salient indicator of homogamy. Income homogamy matchings were measured as incomes of both husbands and wives falling into the same decile; all others were income-heterogamous. Using this measure, Qian found that 86 percent of women in prevailing marriages married up in income in the 1980 cohort, while 68 percent of women in prevailing marriages married up in income in the more recent cohort. The tendency for women to marry up in income was especially pronounced among couples in which the wife's education level equaled or exceeded her husband's. Further, where marrying outside one's education or income level does exist for couples, women are now slightly more likely than men to marry down in education, but substantially more likely to marry up in income, although to a somewhat lesser extent than in the past. This could reflect gender inequalities in the labor market for wages, or a persistent cultural norm that ties masculinity to being the primary breadwinner.

DIVERGENT DESTINIES

The overall effect of increased concentration of income and wealth at the top of the system, increased female participation in the paid labor force, decreased fertility, and greater gender equality is the consolidation of pooled capital for married, affluent, and college-educated "power couples."

Poor and working-class adults, on the other hand, are much less likely to be married, much more likely to have children outside of marriage, and much more likely to experience familial disruption through divorce—all of which have adverse economic consequences (Carlson and England 2011; Cherlin 2014). Moreover, all of these trends have accelerated in the past several decades. Some have argued that the increase in familial instability, especially among the poor and working class, is related to a moral breakdown, which then is seen as a cause of economic instability in and of itself (Murray 2012). Those who take this position often call for a "marriage agenda" that encourages marriages among the poor as a means to achieve economic stability.

Others (Cherlin 2014; Wilson 1987; Carbone and Cahn, 2014), however, point to the opposite direction of influence; that is, how economic instability creates familial instability. Research, for instance, indicates that even among poor and working-class populations in which marriage rates are low and out-of-wedlock births are high, marriage is still highly valued and preferred (Edin and Kefalas 2005; Cherlin, Cross-Barnet, Burton, and Garrett-Peters 2008). The reduction of good-paying manufacturing and construction jobs (see chapter 6) has increased economic instability among the poor and working class, and has resulted in a shortage of "marriageable men" with secure-enough economic prospects who are not otherwise unemployed, underemployed, or incarcerated (Wilson 1987; Oppenheimer et al. 1997, Carbone and Cahn 2014).

These trends not only reduce the prospects for initial marriage, but also result in higher rates of divorce and familial disruption for those who do marry. For those who adopt this view, the effective solution to the problem of familial instability among the poor is not a "marriage agenda," but better economic prospects and opportunity.

These trends have not only contributed to greater economic inequality between affluent and poor adults, but "diverging destinies" for their children as well (McLanahan 2004; Lundberg et al. 2016; Putnam 2015; Carbone and Cahn 2014). Sociologists Shelly Lundberg, Robert Pollak, and Jenna Stearns (2016) suggest that high-resource men and women have responded to increased returns on human capital available to them by entering into marriage as a "commitment device" that encourages child rearing as a "joint economic investment." The poor and less educated, on the other hand, face uncertain or bleak economic prospects that discourage long-term commitment; they have less capacity for such investments; and the return on those investments is less effective.

Social demographer Sara McLanahan (2004) analyzed the impact of demographic changes associated with the "second demographic transition" on well-being and the prospects of children. The first demographic beginning in Western societies around the time of the Industrial Revolution was associated with declines in mortality and fertility. The first demographic revolution generally improved the fates of children overall. Fewer children died in childhood, and fewer of their parents died while they were growing up. As work rapidly moved from the family farm to the paid labor force, society as a whole also made greater investments in children's futures through rapid expansion of public schools. Trends associated with the second demographic transition—delays in fertility and marriage, increases in maternal employment, cohabitation, divorce, and nonmarital childbearing—have resulted in more uneven and divergent outcomes for children.

In general, children of affluent and highly educated parents are much more likely to be born and reared in economic and social circumstances that advance their futures, whereas children of the poor and less-educated are much more likely to be born and reared in economic and social circumstances that disadvantage their futures. That is, affluent couples are much more likely to be employed, to be married, to delay childbearing, and to invest heavily in their children's future. Well-off parents have always been better positioned to transfer advantages to offspring than the less affluent, but changes in family arrangements associated with the second demographic transition have exacerbated and accelerated divergent outcomes for children.

SUMMARY

Through most of human history, people have married people like themselves and marriages were largely arranged by parents. Social-class divisions did not emerge until the beginning of the agricultural revolution. Since there were no social-class divisions before then, all marriages were essentially economically homogenous. With the development of economic surplus beyond subsistence, some managed to get more than others, and social-class divisions developed. Marriages, however, remained largely economically homogenous, with rich marrying rich and poor marrying poor. Marriages in preindustrial societies were largely economic arrangements between families and kinship groups, complete with bride price and dowries.

Romantic love as a prime criterion for marriage and freedom of choice in mate selection did not become widespread until the beginning stages of the Industrial Revolution. While cross-class marriages at least became possible under these conditions, people still mostly married people of roughly equivalent social standing. In the contemporary mate-selection process, the field of potential marriage partners is narrowed through a filtering process that increases the likelihood for homogamy along a number of social dimensions, including class, race, religion, age, and attractiveness. Even with freedom of choice in mate selection, homogamy along these dimensions is still more likely to occur than not since the mate-selection process is mediated by geographic and social proximity, as well as socially defined expectations and preferences.

Where marriage across social groups does occur, women have historically been more upwardly mobile through marriage than men. This partly reflected an exchange of female youth, beauty, and fertility with male wealth, power, and status. It also reflected a greater probability that women will marry up in income because men in general had higher incomes and greater wealth than women. Women in recent decades, however, have entered the paid labor force in greater numbers, and the income gap between men and women has narrowed, lowering their probability of marrying up in income. In terms of education, it is increasingly more likely that women will marry down, as women's levels of educational attainment overall have exceeded those of men.

While rates of marriage endogamy have increased for affluent, college-educated, dual-income "power couples" at the top of the system, those at the bottom of the system are less likely to marry at all, more likely to divorce after marriage, and much more likely to have children outside of marriage. This bifurcation of family circumstances has resulted in increasing "divergent destinies" for children born and reared in these different social settings. Affluent parents at the top of the system are better able to consolidate economic resources, invest more heavily in their children's futures, and have higher returns on those investments. By doing so, affluent parents are able to pass on nonmerit economic, social, and cultural advantages to their children, further expanding existing levels of economic inequality across generations.

The following chapter examines the effects of discrimination on economic outcomes, a blatantly nonmerit factor that in its various forms may be experienced throughout the life course.

REFERENCES

Abbott, Elizabeth. 2010. *A History of Marriage: From Same-Sex Unions to Private Vows and Common Law, the Surprising Diversity of a Tradition.* New York: Seven Stories Press.

Abramova, Olga, Annika Baumann, Hanna Krasnova, and Peter Buxmann. 2016. "Gender Differences in Online Dating: What Do We Know So Far? A Systematic Literature Review." In *2016 49th Hawaii International Conference on System Sciences (HICSS)*, 3858–67. IEEE.

Burgess, Ernest W., and Harvey J. Locke. 1945. *The Family: From Institution to Companionship.* New York: American Book.

Buss, David. 2016. *The Evolution of Desire: Strategies of Human Mating.* New York: Basic Books.

Carbone, June, and Naomi Cahn. 2014. *Marriage Markets: How Inequality Is Remaking the American Family.* New York: Oxford University Press.

Carlson, Marcia J., and Paula England. 2011. "Social Class and Family Patterns in the United States." In *Social Class and Changing Families in an Unequal America* , ed. Marcia J. Carlson and Paula England, 1–20. Stanford, CA: Stanford University Press.

Cherlin, Andrew J. 2009. *The Marriage-Go-Round: The State of Marriage and the Family in America Today.* New York: Vintage Books.

———. 2014. *Labor's Love Lost: The Rise and Fall of the Working-Class Family in America.* New York: Russell Sage Foundation.

Cherlin, Andrew, Caitlin Cross-Barnet, Linda M. Burton, and Raymond Garrett-Peters. 2008. "Promises They Can Keep: Low-Income Women's Attitudes toward Motherhood, Marriage, and Divorce." *Journal of Marriage and Family* 70(4):919–33.

Choi, Kate H., and Marta Tienda. 2017. "Marriage-Market Constraints and Mate-Selection Behavior: Racial, Ethnic, and Gender Differences in Intermarriage." *Journal of Marriage and Family* 79(2):301–17.

Collins, Randall. 1982. *Sociological Insight: An Introduction to Non-Obvious Sociology.* New York: Oxford University Press.

Coontz, Stephanie. 2005. *Marriage, a History: How Love Conquered Marriage.* New York: Penguin Books.

Edin, Kathryn, and Maria Kefalas. 2005. *Promises I Can Keep: Why Poor Women Put Motherhood Before Marriage.* Los Angeles: University of California Press.

Elder, Glen H., Jr. 1969. "Appearance and Education in Marriage Mobility." *American Sociological Review* (34)4:519–33.

Fisher, Helen. 2009. *Why Him? Why Her? Finding Real Love by Understanding Your Personality Type.* New York: Henry Holt.

Fu, Xuanning, and Tim B. Heaton. 2008. "Racial and Educational Homogamy: 1980 to 2000." *Sociological Perspectives* 51(4):735–58.

Fugere, Madeleine A., Jennifer P. Leszcanski, and Alita J. Cousins. 2015. *The Social Psychology of Attraction and Romantic Relationships.* New York: Palgrave.

Gonalons-Pons, Pilar, and Christine R. Schwartz. 2017. "Trends in Economic Homogamy: Sorting into Marriage or Changes in the Division of Paid Labor?" *Demography* 54(3):985–1005.

Hiscock, Rosemary, Linda Bauld, Amanda Amos, Jennifer A. Fidler, and Marcus Munafò. 2012. "Socioeconomic Status and Smoking: A Review." *Annals of the New York Academy of Sciences* 1248(1):107–23.

Hitsch, Günter J., Ali Hortaçsu, and Dan Ariely. 2010a. "What Makes You Click? Mate Preferences in Online Dating." *Quantitative Marketing and Economics* 8(4):393–427.

———. 2010b. "Matching and Sorting in Online Dating." *American Economic Review* 100(1):130–63.

Kalmijn, Matthijs. 1998. "Intermarriage and Homogamy: Causes, Patterns, Trends." *American Review of Sociology* 24:395–41.

Kalmijn, Matthijs, and Hendrick Derk Flap. 2001. "Assortative Meeting and Mating: Unintended Consequences of Organized Settings for Partner Choices." *Social Forces* 79:1289–1312.

Kreager, Derek A., Shannon E. Cavanagh, John Yen, and Mo Yu. 2014. " 'Where Have All the Good Men Gone?' Gendered Interactions in Online Dating." *Journal of Marriage and Family* 76(2):387–410.

Levi-Strauss, Claude. 1969. *The Elemental Structures of Kinship*. Trans. James Harle Bell and John Richard von Sturmer. Boston: Beacon Press.

Lewis, Kevin. 2015. "Studying Online Behavior: Comment on Anderson et al. 2014." *Sociological Science* 2.

———. 2016. "Preferences in the Early Stages of Mate Choice." *Social Forces* 95(1):283–320.

Lin, Ken-Hou, and Jennifer Lundquist. 2013. "Mate Selection in Cyberspace: The Intersection of Race, Gender, and Education." *American Journal of Sociology* 119(1):183–215.

Livingston, Gretchen, and Anna Brown. 2017. "Intermarriage in the U.S. 50 Years after *Loving v. Virginia*." Pew Research Center. http://assets.pewresearch.org/wp-content/uploads/sites/3/2017/05/19102233/Intermarriage-May-2017-Full-Report.pdf (accessed September 12, 2017).

Lundberg, Shelly, Robert Pollak, and Jenna Stearns. 2016. "Family Inequality: Diverging Patterns in Marriage, Cohabitation, and Childbearing." *Journal of Economic Perspectives* 30(2):79–102.

Mare, Robert D. 2016. "Educational Homogamy in Two Gilded Ages: Evidence from Intergenerational Social Mobility." *Annals*, AAPSS 663.

McLanahan, Sara. 2004. "Diverging Destinies: How Children Are Faring under the Second Demographic Transition." *Demography* 41(4):607–27.

Murray, Charles. 2012. *Coming Apart: The State of White America, 1960–2010*. New York: Crown Forum.

Oppenheimer, Valerie, Matthijs Kalmijn, and Nelson Lim. 1997. "Men's Career Development and Marriage Timing during a Period of Rising Inequality." *Demography* 34(3):311–30.

Pew Research Center. 2015. "America's Changing Religious Landscape." http://assets.pewresearch.org/wp-content/uploads/sites/3/2017/05/19102233/Intermarriage-May-2017-Full-Report.pdf (accessed September 12, 2017).

Putnam, Robert D. 2015. *Our Kids: The American Dream in Crisis*. New York: Simon & Schuster.

Qian, Yue. 2017. "Gender Asymmetry in Educational and Income Assortative Mating." *Journal of Marriage and the Family* 79:318–36.

Reardon, Sean F., and Kendra Bischoff. 2011. "Income Inequality and Income Segregation." *American Journal of Sociology* 116(4):1092–1153.

Rosenfeld, Michael J. 2008. "Racial Educational and Religious Endogamy in the United States: A Comparative Historical Perspective. *Social Forces* 87(1):1–31.

Rosenfeld, Michael J., and Reuben J. Thomas. 2012. "Searching for a Mate: The Rise of the Internet as a Social Intermediary." *American Sociological Review* 77(4):523–47.

Sanderson, Stephen K. 2001. *The Evolution of Human Sociality: A Darwinian Conflict Perspective*. Lanham, MD: Rowman & Littlefield.

Schwartz, Christine, and Robert D. Mare. 2005. "Trends in Educational Assortative Marriage from 1940 to 2003." *Demography* 42(4):621–46.

Slater, Dan. 2013. *Love in the Time of Algorithms: What Technology Does to Meeting and Mating*. London: Penguin.

Streib, Jessi. 2015. *The Power of the Past: Understanding Cross-Class Marriages*. New York: Oxford.

Toffler, Alvin. 1980. *The Third Wave*. New York: Morrow.

US Census Bureau. 2017. Table MS-2. Estimated Median Age at First Marriage: 1890 to Present. www.census.gov/data/tables/time-series/demo/families/marital.html (accessed September 12, 2017).

Walker, Robert S., Kim R. Hill, Mark V. Flinn, and Ryan M. Ellsworth. 2011. "Evolutionary History of Hunter-Gatherer Marriage Practices." *PLoS ONE* 6(4):e19066.

Wilson, William J. 1987. *The Truly Disadvantaged: The Inner City, the Underclass, and Public Policy*. Chicago: University of Chicago Press.

9

An Unlevel Playing Field

Racism, Sexism, and Other Isms

> The arc of the moral universe is long, but it bends toward justice.
>
> —Martin Luther King Jr., Speech at Ebenezer Baptist Church in
> Atlanta, Georgia, March 30, 1967

According to the ideal of the American Dream, America is a land in which merit is the sole basis for vast and limitless opportunity. Discrimination, however, invalidates the American Dream. Discrimination not only interferes with, but is the antithesis of, merit. By excluding entire segments of the American population from equal access to opportunity, discrimination reduces competition and increases the chances that members of some groups will get ahead on what they often presume to be exclusively their own merit.

DISCRIMINATION: INDIVIDUAL
AND INSTITUTIONALIZED

Discrimination refers to exclusionary practices that create unequal access to valued social resources such as education, jobs, housing, income, wealth, and so on, based on nonmerit characteristics (often ascribed) that would otherwise be irrelevant to the acquisition of those resources. Individuals may discriminate because they are openly bigoted toward others. Discrimination, however, can also occur unintentionally and without malice. Giving preference to people you know (social capital) or people who share your way of life (cultural capital), for instance, necessarily excludes others and is therefore discriminatory.

Individuals can and do discriminate, but the most consequential discrimination occurs at the group, organizational, community, and institutional levels. This latter form, which is the consequence of cumulative individual acts of discrimination over time, is sometimes called *institutional discrimination*, and does not refer to isolated individual acts of discrimination but to actions, practices, and policies systematically embedded in the organization of society itself. Legalized slavery, Jim Crow laws, and laws prohibiting interracial or same-sex marriage are examples of institutional discrimination.

Individual and institutional discrimination involve unequal treatment of individuals based on group characteristics that have little, if any, relation to what could conventionally be considered individual merit. Furthermore, discrimination can easily become reinforcing and self-perpetuating. Over time, individuals and groups affected by discrimination become as unequal as they have been treated. By depriving people of access to opportunities, for instance, discrimination often leads to lack of qualifications for them. The involuntarily ascribed and negatively evaluated categorical status that emerges from discrimination not only takes precedence over any achieved status, but also reduces the probability of such achievement, thereby lowering all life chances. Put quite simply, discrimination makes it more difficult for the objects of discrimination to develop merit and reduces the likelihood that their merit will be recognized and rewarded.

RACIAL AND ETHNIC DISCRIMINATION IN AMERICA

The long history of deliberate discrimination against racial and ethnic groups in America belies the American ideology of individual freedom and equality of opportunity. From the near-genocide of Native Americans and the banishment of survivors to reservations, to the importation and enslavement of Africans, to the subsequent Jim Crow legislation that legalized racial segregation and unequal opportunity in the South, to exclusionary acts and discriminatory immigration quotas, to land displacement of Mexican Americans, to the internment of Japanese Americans during World War II, to current forms of residential, occupational, educational, and political discrimination against various minorities, the American experience has for many been more of an American *Nightmare* than an American *Dream*.

While most Americans acknowledge historical forms of discrimination, many insist that discrimination against racial and ethnic minorities is a thing of the past. Many assert that we have moved beyond this sordid past, and that this is, in itself, a testimony to the American Dream. The election and reelection of America's first black president, Barack Obama, is often heralded as evidence that America has moved to a "postracial" era. Indeed, great strides to reduce discrimination have been made, especially since the civil rights movement of the 1960s. Unfortunately, it is also abundantly clear that discrimination has not been eliminated. Discrimination in America is down but not out. Since most forms of discrimination are now illegal and overt bigotry is no longer considered socially acceptable, today's discrimination is either more tacit or more elaborately cloaked, and thus more difficult to detect. Instead, there is a "new racism" that is disguised through various codes and denials (Bonilla-Silva 2017). To put it another way, discrimination has been driven underground. Scratching just below the surface, however, reveals a pattern of declining but ongoing forms of political, occupational, educational, housing, and consumer discrimination.

Not only is there a continued pattern of discrimination, but the effects of past discrimination continue to have a long reach into the present. This is sometimes referred to as lagged or past-in-present discrimination (Feagin and Feagin 2007). For instance, if a person of color went to inferior, segregated schools in the South during the 1960s and was subjected to subsequent employment discrimination, that now-middle-aged person is at a current competitive disadvantage, even if the schools he or she went to are now equal and integrated, and even if he or she is no longer being actively discriminated against. Prior discrimination not only likely hampered prospects for that person's own career advancement, but it also likely resulted in unequal starting points for subsequent generations.

ECONOMIC AND OCCUPATIONAL DISCRIMINATION

There are a variety of ways that social scientists measure ongoing occupational discrimination. One way is through self-report surveys indicating the percentage of workers who report having been discriminated against in employment. Another way is by keeping track of how many workers file official discrimination complaints. Yet another way is through the use of field audit studies in which researchers send out applicants of different race or sex with similar qualifications to answer job applications and see who gets callbacks or interviews. In addition, there are a variety of ways to measure outcomes that would imply the likely cumulative effects of discrimination, such as systematic lower pay, or how segregated jobs are by various social categories, controlling for strictly merit factors. Using these various methods, overwhelming evidence demonstrates that while there has been progress since the civil rights era, income and employment discrimination based on race in America lingers and is still pervasive (cf. Anderson 2017; Iceland 2017; Stainback and Tomaskovic-Devey 2012; Massey 2007; Shapiro 2017; Feagin and Ducey 2017; Bonilla-Silva 2017).

Lack of sustained progress is most clearly reflected in trends in racial economic inequality. Many Americans assume that in the "postracial era" since the civil rights movement of the 1960s and 1970s, economic gaps between whites and people of color have narrowed substantially. However, that is not the case. In 1972 the median household income for blacks, for instance, was 56 percent that of whites; by 2015 the median household income for blacks had increased to only 61 percent of whites (US Census Bureau 2016). A similar lack of progress is evident with Hispanics. In 1972, the median household income of Hispanic households was 75 percent that of whites; in 2015 the median income for Hispanic households remained at 75 percent of white households (US Census Bureau 2016).

Gaps in wealth accumulation are even more unequal and in many ways even more consequential. Moreover, racial gaps in wealth accumulation have increased in recent decades. In 1983, black households had only 12 percent of the net worth of whites, and Hispanics had 9 percent of the net worth of whites (Pew Research Center 2016). By 2013, blacks held only 8 percent of the wealth of white households, or were thirteen times less wealthy than whites. By 2013, Hispanic households had only 10 percent of the wealth of white households, or were about ten times less wealthy than whites. Moreover, blacks and Hispanics on average have rates of unemployment and poverty that are about double those of whites, again similar to pre–civil rights era numbers. Some of these differences reflect the current effects of past discrimination, including unequal access to educational opportunity and unequal access to asset-building opportunities, which in turn produced housing discrimination and unequal access to housing in areas with quality schools. But current discrimination also continues to contribute to these huge and stubborn economic deficits.

Blatant discrimination on the basis of race is no longer legal or considered socially acceptable. Most Americans denounce racial discrimination and proclaim to be against it. Few would publicly condone it, much less admit to engaging in it. Discrimination persists, however, often in indirect, subtle, or implicit ways. Such ongoing discrimination has been found in recruitment, hiring, promotion, layoff, and discharge practices. It may take the form of selective placement of job advertisements, the use of word-of-mouth and informal recruitment networks, or recruitment limited to local areas. Discrimination has also been found in screening practices, where it may take the form of discriminatory hiring standards and procedures. Credential requirements, including educational and physical requirements, can be discriminatory when, for instance, such requirements are irrelevant to the demands of a particular job. Nonvalidated credentials—those that cannot be demonstrated to measure what they purport to measure, or cannot be demonstrated to be necessary for satisfactory job performance—continue to be used to the disadvantage of minorities and women.

Employment interviews may be used to screen out candidates who have unwanted characteristics unrelated to merit. Presumptions of inferiority and use of negative stereotypes that lead to constant scrutiny and overly close supervision are discriminatory. Promotion practices that give high consideration to subjective evaluations and supervisors' recommendations can be discriminatory. Segregative tracking into "job ghettos"—dead-end jobs in departments or units with short mobility ladders, as well as organizational rules that do not permit movement out of such units—can be discriminatory. Assignments to "fast-track" jobs are often based on nonmerit criteria. Informal workplace relations can create a "hostile workplace environment." Selective mentoring, sponsorship, and exclusion from insider networks can be discriminatory.

DISCRIMINATION IN THE
POLITICAL AND LEGAL SYSTEMS

Today, government at all levels, at least formally, has taken an antidiscrimination position; yet problem areas remain. Past discrimination by government policy has led to minority disadvantage, and current government inaction and unwillingness to undo the effects of past discrimination perpetuate minority disadvantage.

Minorities are underrepresented in major elected and appointed offices at the state and federal levels. Historically, voting and political participation have been directly correlated with socioeconomic status. Minority overrepresentation among the less privileged partially explains minorities' lower political participation. Thus, the political power of minorities is limited by their numbers, geographical concentrations, residential segregation, and overrepresentation among the less privileged, as well as by continuing individual and institutional discrimination.

One form of ongoing institutional political discrimination is with recent "voting suppression" measures that effectively reduce voting opportunities and participation among racial minorities. In 2010, the Republican Party gained control of the US House of Representatives, as well as achieving widespread gains in state and local elections. This was also a census year, in which voting districts are reapportioned. Following the 2010 midterm elections, newly Republican-dominated legislatures in many states reconfigured voting districts that advantaged Republican candidates and limited voting among groups that are more likely to vote Democratic, including racial minorities. State-sponsored voting-suppression efforts included restricting times and locations when votes could be cast, especially in areas with heavy concentrations of minority voters, and requiring approved forms of voter identification, which were especially burdensome for the poor and people of color to secure.

Opponents viewed these "voter-suppression" actions as discriminatory. Defenders argued that such measures were justified on the basis of concerns of supposed widespread voter fraud, although no credible empirical evidence exists for such claims. Several of these provisions have been challenged in the courts as racially discriminatory, and some have been subsequently delayed or overturned.

In addition to voting restrictions that disproportionately exclude or discourage minority voters, abundant research documents a continuing pattern of racial discrimination throughout the American criminal justice system. Discrimination is well documented at each step in the criminal-justice process, from police scrutiny and detection of crime to the severity of sentencing (Reiman and Leighton 2017). Racial stereotypes and negative expectations can lead to elevated police scrutiny and racial profiling, which in turn lead to racial discrimination in crime detection. Varying degrees of racial discrimination have been documented in all of the following: police decisions to follow up on observations of possible violations, to apprehend, and to arrest suspects; decisions about whether to prosecute, to refer a case to the court system, and, if so, to what type of court; the setting and administration of bail for the accused; decisions made by judges, judicial panels, or juries about whether an accused is guilty or innocent (conviction decisions); and decisions regarding the nature and severity of penalties for crimes (sentencing decisions). Minorities receive longer and more severe sentences (controlling for criminal record and severity of crime).

Evidence of these discriminatory processes reveals that a highly disproportionate number of persons imprisoned in state and federal correctional facilities in the United States are people of color. In 2015, rates of imprisonment for whites were 5.6 times less than those for blacks and 2.6 times less than those for Hispanics (US Department of Justice 2016). At any given step of the criminal-justice process, the bias may be large, small, or even nonexistent, but enough bias exists in enough places at each step that, even though the effect at any one step may be small, the cumulative effect over the entire course of the criminal-justice process can be substantial. Former convicts often face reduced employment and credit opportunities, and in many states are permanently denied the right to vote, even after they have paid their debt to society. Since minorities are disproportionately arrested and convicted of crimes, a lower percentage of minorities as a whole are eligible to vote.

Blacks and other minorities have long complained of various forms of inadequate police protection—from inadequate patrol of their neighborhoods to inadequate response to calls for assistance. Minorities have also complained, sometimes bitterly, of police brutality, of the lack of respect shown them by police, and of the inability of police to distinguish law-abiding minorities from minority criminals. Following the acquittal of George Zimmerman in the shooting death of African-American teen Trayvon Martin in 2013, and several subsequent high-profile fatal shootings of unarmed black suspects by police, a loosely organized social movement, Black Lives Matter, emerged. Activists in the movement want to draw attention to inequities in the criminal-justice system, especially with regard to police brutality and the use of lethal force on suspects of color.

DISCRIMINATION IN EDUCATIONAL SYSTEMS

Chapter 5 is devoted to a discussion of the relationship between education and the American Dream. Briefly, the American education system is viewed as the basic mechanism through which the American Dream can be achieved. Thus, the education system is seen as a means to produce, measure, and certify merit. Discrimination in educational systems, however, erodes the very foundation of the American Dream because it invalidates this basic assumption of meritocracy.

Throughout American history, access to education has varied by class, race, and gender. The history of American education has been one of increasing access to education for previously excluded groups. While access has been expanded, discrimination continues.

One form of educational discrimination is continuing segregation of schools by race and socioeconomic status. Although *Brown v. Board of Education of Topeka*

(1954) signaled the end of blatant de jure segregation, de facto segregation continues. More than sixty years after the *Brown* court ordered desegregation of public schools, public schools remain highly segregated. According to a recent federal study by the US Government Accountability Office (2016), 16 percent of public K–12 schools in 2014 had enrollments of more than 90 percent of low-income students and students of color, an increase from 9 percent of public schools with that profile in 2001. The study found that such schools were less likely to offer as complete a range of math and science courses as other schools, and had higher rates of expulsion and disciplinary problems. Other research shows that students who attended integrated schools are much more likely to graduate, attend college, and earn higher incomes as adults, and that whites who attend integrated schools have no negative impacts (Feagin and Ducey 2017). In short, the overwhelming evidence is that students who attend highly segregated schools do not have the same opportunities as students who attend integrated schools.

Much of the recent trend toward resegregation of schools is due to the abandonment of integration measures such as school busing. In addition, the rise of charter schools, magnet schools, and other alternate school choice settings have accelerated the trend toward resegregation, as white families seek alternatives to sending their children to school districts with high minority enrollments. Finally, official segregation figures often underestimate the actual amount of segregation because calculations are typically based only on public school data. Private schools, except for some inclusive Catholic schools in large cities in the Northeast, remain overwhelmingly white.

Unequal access to educational opportunity is partially due to the fact that at every class level, however social class is measured, blacks and Hispanics have only a small fraction of the wealth of whites. The repercussions of these staggering levels of wealth inequality are clear: Economically disadvantaged blacks and Hispanics cannot provide what sociologist Thomas Shapiro (2017) has called "transformative assets" to their offspring for crucial financial support for higher education, down payments for a first house in a good neighborhood, or other opportunities at crucial junctures in their children's lives. This lack of financial assistance in turn requires minorities to come up with their own resources. This often limits them to the purchase of houses in neighborhoods with low-quality schools. In turn, these lower-quality schools enroll larger proportions of students from minority and other lower-income groups, reducing the possibility of equality of educational opportunity.

According to the American Dream, there is a strong correlation between educational achievement and occupational success; doing well in school is seen as the ticket to a good job. But educational discrimination against minorities reduces their chances for academic achievement, and occupational discrimination reduces their chances for occupational success. Even if minorities manage to transcend educational discrimination and become academically successful, research consistently shows that minorities receive much lower income and occupational returns on equivalent amounts of educational attainment than whites.

SEGREGATION IN HOUSING AND EVIDENCE OF
CONTINUING DISCRIMINATION

The impacts of housing discrimination are severe. Minorities, especially African and Mexican Americans, pay more and get less for their housing dollar, and are underrepresented as homeowners at every income level. They are thus disproportionately denied a major means of wealth accumulation, and this jeopardizes their ability to transmit wealth to their children. Minorities end up living in neighborhoods with fewer resources, services, and amenities, poorer schools, and higher rates of poverty than whites of similar socioeconomic status. Stores in poor and minority areas tend to have poorer selection, lower quality, and higher prices (Walker et al. 2010). Further, residential segregation contributes to school segregation, which as we have seen tends to perpetuate existing inequalities across generations. Residential segregation of groups with high proportions of poverty leads to concentrated poverty and the additional problems it creates (Massey 2007; Wilson 1987). Residential segregation often limits its victims to areas of declining job opportunities. Finally, the racial residential segregation produced by housing discrimination isolates and marginalizes people, denying them full and equal participation in American society.

A major component of the American Dream is home ownership. Equity in a home is the major form of asset accumulation for the large majority of Americans. Home ownership and socioeconomic status are positively related; almost all of the privileged are homeowners, while much less than half of the poor own their own homes. This is reflected in highly unequal rates of home ownership by race. In 2017, the rate of home ownership for whites was 72 percent, but the corresponding figures for blacks and Hispanics were 42 and 46 percent, respectively (US Census Bureau 2017a). Yet the issue is not simply owning or not owning a home. Inequalities in home ownership are much greater if one considers the value of real estate held. Here again, there are also large disparities by race. The median equity value of homes for whites in 2013 was $90,000, compared to only $56,000 for blacks and $50,000 for Hispanics (US Census Bureau 2017b). These differences partly reflect how elaborate houses are and the percentage of total market value held as equity, but also where homes are located, with homes of equivalent size and scope worth much less in communities with high percentages of people of color (Thomas et al. 2017).

Residential segregation by race is one of the legacies of a long history of racial discrimination with effects that reach into the present. That is, even if further housing discrimination ceased altogether, most people would continue to live in already highly segregated neighborhoods and communities. The simplest and most commonly reported measure of residential segregation is the index of dissimilarity. Ranging from 0 (no segregation) to 1 (complete segregation), it indicates the proportion of one group that would have to move to a different census tract to reproduce the residential pattern of the other group. The residential dissimilarity index for blacks fell from 79 in 1970 to 59 in 2010; rates for Hispanics fell from 77 to 55 over the same period (Iceland 2017). Although this represents a clear reduction, over half of all blacks and Hispanics (or whites) would have to move to a different census tract to reproduce the residential pattern of the other group.

Discrimination in the sale and rental of housing became illegal with the Civil Rights Act of 1968 and subsequent fair housing laws. Discrimination persists in the post–civil rights era, but it is expressed in more subtle and clandestine ways that are not readily observable and are unlikely to trigger legal action or invite public disapproval. Government officials and social scientists nevertheless have developed powerful and convincing techniques to measure discrimination unobtrusively. Using field audit studies, for instance, units being marketed for sale or rent are randomly selected, and separate teams of white and nonwhite auditors posing as home seekers are sent to inquire about the availability of the advertised unit, the number of other units available, and the terms under which units might be obtained. Auditors are assigned similar personal, social, and economic characteristics by the researcher and carefully trained to present themselves in a neutral fashion and to ask standard questions about the housing being marketed. Afterward, each auditor fills out a form describing the nature and outcome of the encounter without knowing what happened to the other auditor. These studies and others continue to find significant discrimination against minorities in the rental and sale of housing in which whites and people of color are "steered" by real estate agents and others toward specific neighborhoods and communities based on their racial profiles (Massey 2007, 76–100).

Minorities are also subjected to discrimination in securing loans and property insurance. Blacks and Hispanics, for instance, are more likely to be turned down for mortgage loans and more likely to pay higher rates when they are approved than can be accounted for by black–white differences in income and other relevant characteristics (Bocian et al. 2010). The practice by which banks and insurance companies would identify neighborhoods or communities in which they would not do business became known as "redlining," based on the practice of drawing red lines on maps for such purposes. Redlining and racial profiling in extending loans and insurance is illegal and has been greatly curtailed, but still occurs.

Finally, there is the related phenomenon of voice discrimination (Feagin and Sikes 1994), which also contributes to housing discrimination. Segregation itself makes linguistic profiling possible. One consequence of historical segregation in the United States is that a large proportion of African Americans speak a distinctive version of English, with different rules for pronunciation, diction, grammar, and syntax from that ordinarily spoken by whites. Research has shown that white Americans are capable of making accurate racial attributions on the basis of very short speech fragments (Feagin and Sikes 1994; Massey 2007). Not only are whites quick to identify the race of someone speaking black English and to discriminate accordingly, based, for instance, on initial phone inquiries regarding housing availability and pricing, but they are able to identify the race of a *code-switching* black—one who speaks mainstream English but with a "black" pronunciation of certain words (Doss and Gross 1994).

A NOTE ON ASIAN AMERICANS

Asian Americans are often described as "the model minority." One reason for this depiction is that Asian Americans as a whole have higher rates of income and educational attainment than not only other minorities, but whites as well. The assumption is often made that if Asian Americans can succeed, then other minorities should be able to as well. However, these generalizations overlook important differences and distinctions related to Asian Americans. First, Asian Americans, like Hispanic Americans, make up a broad category comprised of people from many different countries and subcultures, including China, India, Japan, Korea, Vietnam, Pakistan, Cambodia, Nepal, and the Philippines, to name a few. These different groups have fared differently depending on their unique experience in America as immigrants, or descendants of immigrants. Factors contributing to the overall success of Asian Americans include the recent influx of high numbers of highly skilled and educated immigrants from some of these countries, greater emphasis on communal values in Asian cultures resulting in higher levels of social capital, high emphasis on educational attainment in some of these groups, and less discrimination faced by Asian Americans than for blacks or Hispanics (Iceland 2017). Nevertheless, Asian Americans have faced historical discrimination in America, and continue to experience ongoing differential treatment.

SEX DISCRIMINATION

Women experience many of the forms of employment discrimination discussed above for racial and ethnic minorities, as well as several that are unique to women. But unlike racial and ethnic minorities, women as a whole are not systematically disadvantaged by social-class background. As a result, since the civil rights era of the 1960s and the resurgence of the women's movement in the 1970s, women have more quickly closed the gaps between themselves and men than nonwhites have closed gaps with whites. Once artificial barriers to achievement were lifted, women from privileged social backgrounds were poised to take immediate advantage, especially in educational attainment. For instance, once Ivy League universities opened admissions to women beginning in the 1970s, women from privileged backgrounds with high-quality preparatory education and abundant parental resources could immediately take advantage of these new admission policies. Following the civil rights struggles of the 1960s, by contrast, racial and ethnic minorities generally did not have the social, economic, or cultural capital available to take as much advantage of expanding opportunities.

The closing of the gender gap is most apparent in educational attainment, where women as a group have caught up to, and largely surpassed, men. As recently as the 1990s, men exceeded women in almost all areas of educational attainment. By 2014, however, women earned 57 percent of all bachelor's degrees, 60 percent of all master's degrees, and 52 percent of all doctoral degrees conferred that year (US Department of Education 2016). Women have achieved parity or near parity in earning professional degrees in fields such as law (47 percent), medicine (48 percent), osteopathic medicine (47 percent), and dentistry (46 percent). Women have also achieved near parity in the traditionally male-dominated arena of business education, earning 47 percent of all bachelor's degrees, 43 percent of master's degrees, and 43 percent of doctoral degrees in business. Women far exceed men in earning degrees in some professional fields, such as pharmacy (61 percent), optometry (65 percent), clinical psychology (77 percent), and veterinary medicine (79 percent). While women are closing educational gaps in general, they still lag considerably behind in some traditionally male-dominated professional fields, such as engineering (earning 24 percent of bachelor's, 24 percent of master's, and 23 percent of doctoral degrees), computer science (earning 29 percent of bachelor's, 11 percent of master's, and 22 percent of doctoral degrees), and theology (earning 32 percent of bachelor's, 35 percent of master's, and 28 percent of doctoral degrees) (US Department of Education 2016).

Despite the women's movement, rapidly increased educational achievement and labor-force participation, and continuing social, economic, and cultural change, the power structure of the United States remains heavily male-dominated. In both the public and private sectors, the vast majority of positions at the top, such as those held by corporate officers, members of boards of directors, top-level professionals, and high elected officials, are held by males. Men continue to dominate socially, politically, and economically. In short, gender, a factor with no demonstrable independent effect on individual merit, conditions access to opportunity, and women have been denied full participation in the American Dream.

THE PINK-COLLAR GHETTO

Historically and cross-culturally, the degree of male dominance in society is directly related to the kind and extent of female participation in economic production. That is, the more women participate in economic production—and the more *equally* they participate in economic production—the less the degree of male dominance. Since the 1970s, female labor-force participation has steadily increased. In 1950, women made up just 29 percent of the US labor force; by 2015, women made up 47 percent of the total labor force, achieving near parity with men (US Department of Labor 2017). Although the level of female participation in the labor force is now almost equivalent to that of men, women are not equally spread out within the labor force. In particular, women are highly concentrated in the low-wage service sector of the economy. While there has been a decline in occupational segregation since the 1970s, there is still a substantial amount of sex-based occupational segregation in the labor force (Blau et al. 2013; Stainback and Tomaskovic-Devey 2012; Levanon and Grusky 2016). For instance, in 2015, women comprised 97 percent of preschool and kindergarten teachers, 96 percent of dental hygienists, 95 percent of secretaries and administrative assistants, 95 percent of child-care workers, 91 percent of receptionists and information clerks, 89 percent of registered nurses, and 85 percent of personal care workers, just to name a few (US Department of Labor 2017).

Although there has been some sex desegregation in the labor force in the past several decades, the movement of men and women into and out of job categories has been uneven. Women, for instance, as we have seen, have been rapidly moving into traditionally male-dominated professions, especially as lawyers, doctors, professors, veterinarians, and pharmacists. Men, however, have not been moving as quickly into traditionally female-dominated professions, such as social work, nursing, and elementary school teaching. Likewise, there is very little movement of women into traditionally male-dominated blue-collar trades such as construction, and there has not been much movement of men into the lower-white-collar service jobs, such as secretary. Collectively, the jobs in which women remain highly concentrated have come to be called the pink-collar occupational ghetto.

Some occupations in which women are highly concentrated, such as nursing, teaching, and social work, require postsecondary training and pay moderately well, conferring moderate levels of prestige. Nevertheless, they are often lower in pay and prestige than "men's jobs" that require equivalent levels of skill and training. The jobs in which women are concentrated also tend to be "order-taker" rather than "order-giver" positions, located in an occupationally defined chain of command; for instance, nurses take orders from doctors, secretaries take orders from bosses, and so on. Often these are "dead-end" jobs with limited prospects for promotion; that is, they have short mobility ladders with few rungs available for advancement. A nurse, for instance, may aspire to be head nurse, but there are few rungs on the advancement ladder beyond that. Even if one is an especially skilled and competent nurse, the head nurse on the floor may also be competent, forty years old, and going nowhere.

Many pink-collar jobs are disproportionately located in the low-wage service sector of the economy. The jobs themselves are insecure, and those who hold them face higher-than-average risks of irregular employment, involuntary part-time work, and layoffs or firing. These jobs typically carry limited fringe benefits, and some require shift work. Pink-collar jobs and the industries in which they are located are typically not unionized; therefore, workers do not benefit from protections won by the collective power of unions. Change has occurred in a few of the female-dominated professions, such as social work, teaching, and nursing, which have formed more powerful professional associations. But most pink-collar jobs in the low-wage service sector are unrepresented by either unions or professional associations. Finally, pink-collar jobs are often extensions of traditional domestic female sex roles: nurses and nursing aides taking care of the sick and the elderly, teachers and day-care workers taking care of children, and so on. These nurturing tasks are critical to any civilized society, but as paid labor they are grossly underappreciated, undervalued, and underrewarded.

THE GENDER INCOME AND WEALTH GAPS

In 2015, the median earnings of full-time, year-round female workers were 81 percent of the median hourly wage of their male counterparts, whereas in 1979 they were only 62 percent (US Department of Labor 2017). In a comprehensive study of the gender wage gap, Cornell economists Francine Blau and Lawrence Kahn (2016) show that differences in the occupational distributions of men and women—occupational segregation of women into "women's jobs," which are lower-paying and centered around low-wage industries—explain the bulk of the aggregate male–female wage gap. Other factors include interrupted careers due to marriage and childbearing, lower rates of unionization for women, and interactions of race and gender. Taking these factors into account, the adjusted wage gap is reduced from roughly 80 percent to about 92 percent. Blau and Kahn speculate that the remaining 8 percent of "residual" difference is likely due to unmeasured gender discrimination.

While pay gaps have narrowed and discrimination has been reduced, efforts to eliminate employment discrimination against women have not been entirely successful. Since men and women tend to do different kinds of work, the call for "equal pay for equal work" did not fully address pay equity issues for women. During the 1980s, pay equity, or comparable worth, was proposed as a means to address the tendency for the paid work that women perform in the labor force to be undervalued. Comparable worth calls for equal pay for different types of work that are judged to be comparable in value by measuring such factors as employee knowledge, skills, effort, responsibility, and working conditions. In terms of the actual skills needed to do the job, for instance, the female office secretary might score higher than the male truck driver working in the same firm who earns more. Except for some local initiatives mostly in government employment, comparable-worth programs have not been widely implemented.

Although such proposals make sense from an equity and merit standpoint, one of the problems with implementing them is that people do not ordinarily get paid on the basis of merit in the first place. According to market principles, people get paid on the basis of whatever the market will bear (e.g., "the going rate"), which may not be directly related to what workers think their labor is "worth" based on how demanding their jobs are, or what their skills are, or how hard they work, or how productive they are, or the actual contributions they make to their employing organizations or to society as a whole.

In addition to having less income than men, women also typically have less wealth (Chang 2010, 2015). Although men and women have an equal chance of being born poor or wealthy, women tend to accumulate less wealth in a lifetime. Single women, for instance, have only 32 percent of the median wealth of single men, never-married women have only 21 percent of the median wealth of never-married men, and divorced women have only 25 percent of the median wealth of divorced men (Chang 2010). Although married couples nominally share assets, research shows that men tend to have greater control of those assets. Finally, at the very top of wealth echelons, women are especially underrepresented. Among the 2016 *Forbes* list of the wealthiest four hundred Americans, only fifty-one (or roughly 13 percent) were women, 80 percent of whom inherited the bulk of their wealth (*Forbes* 2017). A number of factors contribute to these wealth discrepancies, including lower lifetime earnings, greater tendency to have custody of children and related predominant or exclusive financial responsibility for them, and less access to government benefits, tax breaks, and fringe benefits favorable for asset accumulation (Chang 2010, 2015).

THE GLASS CEILING

The phrase *glass ceiling*, another form of employment discrimination, refers to discriminatory policies that limit the upward mobility of qualified women and minorities, keeping them out of top management positions. As previously noted, many of the jobs in which women are concentrated have short mobility ladders. Secretaries rarely become bosses. Even though many secretaries *could* do the work of their bosses—and, indeed, many often do—they do not get the credit, the salary, or the opportunity to move up, regardless of their level of competence. The glass ceiling operates so that although all applicants may be welcomed by a firm at entry levels, when it comes to powerful managerial and executive positions, women are much less represented.

Part of this overall differential is due to lag effects of women's more-recent entry into the professions in particular, and into the labor force in general. It often takes twenty or thirty years in a company or a profession to ascend to the highest levels of management. For example, though women now are graduating from law schools at rates comparable to men, few women occupy judgeships or senior partnerships in major law firms, in part because few women graduated from law schools twenty or thirty years ago, and those who did were often subjected to much more severe discrimination than occurs now, derailing their prospects for career advancement. The same pattern is reflected in other professions in which women have more recently approached parity with males at the entry level, including medicine and the professoriate. On top of these lag effects, however, discrimination continues. Even among younger cohorts, research shows that women do not ascend as often or as quickly as men.

OLD BOY NETWORKS

Regardless of where women are located in the labor force (i.e., be they doctors or secretaries), women as a group face unique nonmerit impediments that make it more difficult to compete evenly with men. One of these impediments is lack of sponsorship—one form of social capital. Since the most powerful and influential positions are usually held by men, women are at a critical disadvantage. Mentor–protégé relationships are crucial for advancement, especially in the professions. After all, it is the senior partners in the law firm, the full professors in the department, and the top-level executives in the corporation who have the most experience and the most knowledge to impart to aspiring protégés. Mentors take their protégés under their wings, show them the ropes, and when the time comes, go to bat for them.

Women are less likely to receive these benefits: They receive far less informal support, inclusion in networks, mentoring, and sponsorship than men (McDonald et al. 2009; Lutter 2015). Men seem to be less willing to mentor and sponsor women than men, partially because climates of sexual tension or appearances of sexual harassment may make cross-gender mentorship and sponsorship seem dangerous or uncomfortable for both men and women. In the business world, for example, women have been denied equal access to male-dominated "inner sanctums": Many deals are cut on the golf course, on the racquetball court, over drinks at the men's club, "at the game," or at other sites not fully open or accessible to women.

FAMILY VERSUS CAREER

Women experience a greater degree of perceived role conflict between family and career than men do. Role conflict occurs when the expectations and requirements associated with one position that an individual occupies interfere or conflict with those of another position. Although males can act as homemakers and caretakers for children, women have customarily performed these roles. Men are far less likely to feel that they must make an either-or choice (homemaker or caretaker versus paid employment) or to attempt to "burn the candle at both ends." It has been said that we will know that the women's liberation movement has fully arrived when men routinely ask themselves if they can combine family and career.

Research further shows that even though fertility has declined and having children no longer keeps most women out of the labor force—and it is illegal to discriminate on the basis of marital or family status—some employers still assume that women are temporary workers in the labor force whose careers will be derailed by childbirth. As a result, such employers may be reluctant to hire women in the first place, and, if they hire them, may invest less in their training and career development. This precludes eligibility for top-level positions and forces women into a career trajectory with lower chances for advancement.

Related to the issue of child care is the issue of reproductive freedom. A rapid decline in fertility has coincided with the increased participation of women in the labor force. As women have fewer children, they are freer to participate in the labor force. And as women participate in the labor force, they choose to have fewer children. By increasing control over their reproductive lives, women are more able to compete as equals in the public domains from which they were previously excluded. In concrete terms, reproductive freedom means freedom to pursue educational and occupational goals, unconstrained by unplanned or unwanted pregnancies.

Another type of role conflict for women has sometimes been referred to as the "fear of success syndrome." This is actually a misnomer because women do not fear success. Instead, some women are understandably leery of being stigmatized for exhibiting behaviors associated with a formula for success defined in male terms. The formula for success for the successful business*man*, for instance, includes being assertive and aggressive. Business talk often mimics athletic or military jargon: "beating the enemy at his own game," "hitting a home run," "coming on board," and the like. Men who exhibit these behaviors and orientations are perceived as "self-starters" and "go-getters" on the fast track to success. Women who exhibit these same behaviors, however, risk being labeled as "pushy," "bitchy," or "cold." Such double standards and stigmatizing labels are clearly discriminatory against women.

THE SECOND SHIFT

When men and women in the same household are both working, men and women spend about equal time in paid and unpaid work combined, although a larger share of unpaid work typically is done by women (Offer and Schneider 2011; Pew Research Center 2015). Although differences are narrowing, there continues to be an inequitable division of domestic labor. Women are much more involved in labor-intensive routine chores than men and in the invisible mental labor associated with taking care of children and planning for their activities (Offer and Schneider 2011). Women also do the bulk of the "emotional work" that sustains relationships—between husband and wife, between parents and children, and between the immediate and extended families and friends (Hochschild 1989, 1990). For instance, women typically make the phone calls, send birthday and anniversary cards, buy and send gifts, plan special family events, and the like. Moreover, women are more likely than men to multitask in performing paid and unpaid labor. Multitasking, in turn, produces higher levels of stress and work–family conflict (Offer and Schneider 2011).

Sociologist Arlie Hochschild (1989, 1990) has used the term *second shift* to describe this double burden—work outside the home followed by child care and housework. These extra duties off the job may affect performance on the job. Despite the image of the "24/7" woman who can have it all and do it all, the reality is that any one person has only a finite amount of time, energy, and attention available. One way to reduce the burdens of the second shift is to outsource domestic labor to others. Research shows that the gender gap in household labor is lower for affluent women, who can better afford to pay others to perform domestic labor (Schneider and Hastings 2017). To whatever extent women carry these additional burdens more than men, they are at a collective nonmerit disadvantage in the labor force competing with men. In this way, unequal division of household labor creates severe handicaps for women who bear these additional responsibilities, and a distinct nonmerit advantage for men who do not.

SEXUAL HARASSMENT

Prior to women's recent surge into the labor force, men and women mostly operated in separate social worlds: The home was women's domain, and the workplace was men's domain. As women have entered the labor force in larger numbers, and as they have become less concentrated in a limited number of jobs, non-family-related men and women are working in the same social space more often. A spate of recent allegations of sexual harassment and sexual misconduct against prominent entertainment, media, and political figures has heightened national attention on the problem of sexual harassment in the workplace and prompted the development of the #MeToo social movement in which women victims are encouraged to support each other and share their stories. Sexual harassment is another nonmerit impediment that women face in the labor force in far greater proportion than men, and that has detrimental effects for women victims both on the job and in terms of long-term career advancement (McLaughlin et al. 2012, 2017).

Social scientists know that opposite-sex social interaction is different from same-sex social interaction. Opposite-sex interaction is more sexually charged, often resulting in an element of flirtation that is missing in same-sex interaction. Most of this casually flirtatious behavior is innocent enough and falls outside the realm of sexual harassment. The line is crossed when flirtatious behavior turns into unwelcome sexual advances that interfere with a person's ability to perform a job and enjoy its benefits. Sexual harassment may include everything from blatant demands for sex, to subtler pressures regarding sexual activity, to a panoply of behaviors that create a hostile workplace environment, including sexual taunts, intimidation, and threats. Sexual harassment is not only an indicator of the continuing dominance of men in the workplace, but a form of discrimination that jeopardizes women's chances for occupational success and impinges upon their pursuit of the American Dream.

POLITICAL ACTIVITY AND OFFICE HOLDING

Women constitute over half of the voting population and about half of the labor force, but only a relatively small percentage of women hold high governmental positions. While percentages of women holding political office has increased in recent decades, women are still severely underrepresented in these positions. In 2017, women comprised 20 percent of the US House of Representatives, 21 percent of the US Senate, 17 percent of presidential Cabinet positions, and one-third of the seats on the US Supreme Court. Women held 12 percent of state governorships and 25 percent of state legislative seats, and comprised 20 percent of the mayors of the largest one hundred cities in the United States (Center for American Women and Politics 2017). To date, there have been no women presidents or vice presidents, although Hillary Clinton was the Democratic nominee for president in 2016, Sarah

Palin was on the Republican ticket for vice president in 2008, and Geraldine Ferraro was on the Democratic ticket for vice president in 1984.

As sociologist Deborah Carr (2008) has pointed out, there are several possible explanations for the continuing underrepresentation of women in political office, including perceived familial role conflict; fewer available economic resources; the power of incumbency and name recognition, which favor males already holding office; and voter stereotypes regarding women as less suited to positions of power. Also, most political careers evolve out of training, experience, and leadership in law, the military, and business, areas from which women were largely excluded until the last few decades.

To summarize, while women's political office holding is increasing, women remain severely underrepresented in major elected and appointed offices at the state and federal levels. In short, gender inequality continues in the political system. The continued denial of full and equal political participation also denies women equal access to the American Dream and deprives women of the full potential for political clout to reduce gender inequalities in other spheres of social life.

OTHER ISMS

When we discuss discrimination and its victims, we are not talking about a few people. More than half of the population is female, roughly a third of the population are members of a racial or ethnic minority, and a sizable proportion are both. Although race and gender discrimination in America have historically been the most visible and prevalent, they are not the only forms of discrimination. Other, often less visible forms of discrimination continue to operate in ways that deny equal opportunity to their victims. While these other forms of nonmerit discrimination may involve fewer overall victims, it is small comfort to those who are victimized. For them, the rate of victimization is 100 percent.

COMING OUT BUT OFTEN STILL
SHUT OUT: HETEROSEXISM

Homophobia and heterosexism—individual and institutionalized prejudice and discrimination against gays and lesbians—are present in every facet of life: the family, organized religion, the workplace, official policies, and the mass media. Throughout most of American history, gays and lesbians, fearing hostility and discrimination, generally hid their sexual orientation from public view, remaining "in the closet." Efforts were made to prevent, control, and "correct" it.

More recently, issues of institutional discrimination regarding sexual orientation have focused on military service and marriage. The military has often been seen as a vanguard institution in overcoming discrimination. The military was largely racially segregated until 1948 when President Harry Truman signed an executive order to desegregate the military, long before the height of the civil rights movement and deseg-regation of other major social institutions. The US military, however, did not permit homosexuals to openly serve. President Bill Clinton's attempt in 1993 to end this dis-criminatory policy met with severe opposition in Congress and from some segments of the general population. In the end, the discriminatory law was retained, modified by the "don't ask, don't tell" compromise. Under this compromise policy, military recruits no longer had to state their sexual orientation and the military was not supposed to inquire about it, but the policy still permitted investigations and dismissals of military personnel if evidence was found that they had engaged in homosexual acts. Finally, in 2011, with increasing public tolerance toward homosexuality, although with still-strong pockets of resistance, a new policy was put into effect allowing homosexuals to serve openly in the military. In 2017, however, President Donald Trump announced a new policy that bans transgender persons from entering the military.

Another form of discrimination against gay and lesbian couples is the withholding of legal recognition of their relationships. Legal recognition of what has come to be called domestic partnerships provides numerous benefits and protections for gay and lesbian couples with respect to inheritance, parenting, pensions, taxation, housing, immigration, workplace fringe benefits, and health care. In 1996, the US Congress enacted the Defense of Marriage Act (DOMA), which denied federal recognition of same-sex marriages. Under the "equal protection" clause of the US Constitution, court challenges to the denial of gay marriage began to bubble up in lower courts. In 2003, Massachusetts became the first state to legalize gay marriage through court order. After thirty failed state public referenda to allow same-sex marriage, for the first time in 2012 public referenda in Maine, Maryland, and Washington passed, allowing same-sex marriages to take place. In 2015, the US Supreme Court ruled in a close 5–4 decision that gay marriage is a constitutional right, meaning that all fifty states must allow it, and all bans against it are invalid.

In response to a combination of change in military policy, successful court chal-lenges to marriage restrictions, and a more-vocal and -organized "gay pride" social movement, public sentiment has shifted in favor of more tolerant attitudes regarding homosexuality, especially among younger cohorts.

Despite these gains, gays and lesbians still face discrimination in most areas of life, including employment, which severely jeopardizes their access to opportunity and their pursuit of the American Dream. For instance, there is especially strong resis-tance to hiring those known to be gay, lesbian, or transgender in certain occupations, such as teaching and the clergy. Open avoidance, stereotyping, name-calling, physi-cal threats, and violence against gays and lesbians continue to occur (Meyer 2015).

Finally, it has become clear that those who are transgender—individuals whose gender identity does not "match" their sexual identity in conventional ways—face much of the same stereotyping, hostility, discrimination, violence, and exclusion as that encountered by gays and lesbians. A recent example of ongoing institutional discrimination of transgender persons is the passage and belated partial repeal of the so-called "bathroom" bill in North Carolina. The state bill enacted in 2015 made it illegal for persons to use public bathrooms that did not correspond to the sex listed on their original birth certificate. It also prohibited municipalities within the state to pass antidiscrimination ordinances or set minimum wages. The bill further defined classes of people who could sue the state for discrimination, excluding LGBT persons and therefore making it legal to discriminate against them. The controversial bill was met by immediate resistance, including boycotts from entertainers, businesses, and the National Collegiate Athletic Association. In a "compromise" measure and under intense public and national pressure, state legislators partially repealed the bill in 2017, including the "bathroom" provision. The compromise measure, however, prevented municipalities from adopting antidiscrimination ordinances for three years, and reverts all policies regarding use of multistall public restrooms to the state.

WHERE THE HANDICAPPED GET PARKED: ABLEISM

Americans with disabilities have long been the victims of prejudice and stereotypes and the objects of various forms of discrimination, which have denied them equal opportunity to pursue the American Dream. Disabilities may result from congenital defects, injury, or disease, and include a wide range of impairments and limitations (Thomason et al. 1998).

Nearly 19 percent of the population have some level of disability, and 12.6 percent have a severe disability (Brault 2012). The most common types of disability include hearing, vision, and cognitive impairments, arthritis, back or spine problems, and heart trouble. All told, over fifty-six million Americans report some level of disability. The number of workers with disabilities continues to increase. In 2016, 8.8 million workers received federal disability payments, up by 60 percent since 2002 (US Social Security Commission 2017). Because of advances in medicine, many people who once would have died from an accident or illness now survive. Disabilities are found in all segments of the population, but racial and ethnic minorities are disproportionately more likely to experience them and have less access to assistance.

Employers have been reluctant to hire people with disabilities even when the disabilities do not keep them from doing the job. Stigmas attached to many forms of disability have become the basis of stereotypes and discriminatory treatment. For example, individuals with physical disabilities must deal with those who assume that they have mental limitations as well. People with disabilities are often viewed unidimensionally as disabled, so that the single characteristic of their disability comes to define their identity. Stigmas attached to disability and the discrimination imposed on people with disabilities are widely institutionalized, and often become a greater handicap than the disability itself.

World War II and the Korean, Vietnam, Gulf, Iraq, and Afghanistan wars have produced thousands of disabled veterans. Increases in the number of disabled veterans have produced a growing effort to ensure people with disabilities the same rights as enjoyed by others. By the early 1970s, a strong social movement for disability rights had emerged in the United States, and legislation and labor–management contracts have forbidden discrimination on the basis of disabilities not related to job performance. Discrimination against the disabled was forbidden by the Rehabilitation Act of 1973, but only for federal employment and private employers with federal contracts.

In 1992, the Americans with Disabilities Act (ADA) went into effect and greatly extended these protections. This law broadens protections for people with disabilities against discrimination, requires that employers accommodate them, and requires that public facilities be accessible. Among the specific provisions is a ban on discrimination against people with physical and mental disabilities in hiring and promotion. This ban applies to all employers with more than twenty-five employees, and allows people to directly sue the organizations that discriminate. It also outlaws tests that have the effect of screening out job applicants with disabilities unless it can be shown that the tests relate to a worker's ability to perform the job. In addition to strengthening the ban on discrimination, the ADA requires that workplaces and public accommodations be made accessible to people with disabilities. Restaurants, colleges and universities, transportation systems, theaters, retail stores, and government offices are among the kinds of public facilities that must now be accessible. Finally, employers are required to make "reasonable accommodations" for employees with disabilities. The word *reasonable*, however, is subject to various, often self-serving, interpretations.

It is difficult to quantify gains that those with disabilities may have made because of this legislation. Formal complaints of violations filed with the US Equal Employment Opportunity Commission (US EEOC 2017) regarding disabilities nearly doubled, from 15,894 cases in 2000 to 28,073 cases in 2016, second in number only to complaints regarding race discrimination. In 2015, the number of complaints regarding disability discrimination for the first time exceeded the number of complaints regarding gender discrimination.

OLD DOGS AND NEW TRICKS: AGEISM

Most but not all age discrimination is directed toward older Americans who are subject to stereotypes, prejudice, harassment, and various forms of discrimination that jeopardize their chances to fulfill important parts of the American Dream. Older Americans constitute a significant segment of the population—15 percent of the US population was over sixty-five in 2015, and this number is projected to increase to 25 percent by 2060 (US Census Bureau 2017c), increasing the percent of the population who could be subject to age discrimination. Moreover, as people are now living longer, they are subject to age discrimination for more years and a larger proportion of their lives. In a 2013 nationwide survey conducted by the American Association of Retired Persons (AARP), 64 percent of workers aged forty-five to seventy-five report that they have seen or experienced age discrimination; 16 percent, or roughly one in six, also report that they have been treated worse by their employer because of their age (American Association of Retired Persons 2014).

Negative stereotypes of old age are strongly entrenched in our youth-oriented society. Age discrimination has been increasingly evident in the disproportionate firing of older employees during layoffs, and older employees in long-term jobs lose work at a higher rate than their younger counterparts. It is often difficult for older workers to find work after being displaced by layoffs, automation, or downsizing. Once conditions improve, employers often prefer to hire younger workers at less pay who might be available for continued employment over longer periods, independent of the ability of applicants to do the job. As a result, the number of age-discrimination complaints received by the US Equal Employment Opportunity Commission typically increases when layoffs increase. The peak number of age-discrimination complaints, for instance, occurred in 2008, at the beginning of the Great Recession (US EEOC 2017).

Employers may discriminate against older workers using coded language, such as saying that the organization "needs new blood," or referring to older workers or job applicants as "overqualified" or "set in their ways." Age discrimination has led to protective and advocacy efforts by groups who are the objects of such discrimination. Although the American Association of Retired Persons is the best known of such organizations, numerous other organizations have developed in response to age discrimination.

Older workers are not the only age group to be subject to age discrimination independent of their level of merit or capacity to do the job. The major way this occurs is by conflating "merit" with "experience." Younger workers or job applicants typically have less experience than older workers and typically start out in "entry-level" positions that pay less. Experience, in itself, however, does not necessarily reflect individual merit or actual productivity. As many recently trained or youthful aspirants are painfully aware, jobs that require "X" years of experience exclude them categorically and present them with the frustrating dilemma of how to acquire experience if employers regularly require it as a precondition for employment.

Other "reverse forms" of age discrimination are compensation or other employment perks based strictly on seniority alone. Like experience, seniority in itself is not a direct reflection of individual merit, capacity to do the job, or actual work productivity. One way this commonly occurs are pay increases based on percentage increases rather than absolute dollar amounts, which favors already higher-paid workers who tend to be older. Employers may wish to reward longtime employees for their loyalty and commitment to the employing organization with other various perks and privileges, including better parking privileges, fancier offices, better work assignments, and so on, but to do so is itself a violation of strictly meritocratic principles.

GETTING STUNG BY THE WASP: RELIGIOUS DISCRIMINATION

One might argue that an important component of the American Dream is freedom of religious belief and practice. However, even during colonial times, instances of religious intolerance and discrimination were not uncommon. Throughout the eighteenth, nineteenth, and early twentieth centuries, religious minorities—Catholics, Jews, and Mormons, for example—were victims of severe discrimination, persecution, and even violence.[1] These groups and others were subjected to vicious literature of all sorts, hostile political-party platforms, Know Nothing and Ku Klux Klan demonstrations and violence, and American Protective Association activities.

Even today, severe competition, intolerance, and hostility among various religious groups surfaces sporadically. For instance, anti-Muslim stereotypes and hostility surfaced following the terrorist attacks of September 11, 2001, subsequent US military intervention in the Muslim countries of Afghanistan and Iraq, and ongoing international tensions in much of the Middle East. Islam has been stereotyped as a fundamentally flawed and intolerant faith that sanctions violence and terrorism. In 2016, presidential candidate Donald Trump called for a ban on all Muslim immigrants, who he suggested posed a security risk to the United States. A form of religious profiling, such a ban would likely not have survived judicial scrutiny and was subsequently revised to an immigration ban from select Muslim-dominated countries associated with terrorist activities.

Notwithstanding these and similar occurrences, religious pluralism, the privatization of religion, and other aspects of continuing secularization have largely eliminated institutionalized forms of religious discrimination in America. Individual-level religious bigotry where it occurs, however, continues to deny full participation in the American Dream to the unchurched and those of nondominant faiths. For example, Pentecostal and Holiness groups, Jehovah's Witnesses, Seventh-Day Adventists, and other nondominant Christian groups, as well as non-Christian groups like Jews, Muslims, Hindus, Rastafarians, and Sikhs, continue to suffer hostility and discrimination. Finally, the merely *non*religious (agnostics and atheists) have also been subject to individual acts of prejudice and exclusion.

Compared to other forms of discrimination today, religious discrimination appears to be less common. In 2016, for instance, there were more than eight times as many race-discrimination charges and seven times as many sex-discrimination charges filed with the EEOC (US EEOC 2017). However, there is evidence of increases in cases of religious discrimination. In 1997, charges of religious discrimination represented 2.1 percent of all charges filed with the EEOC; by 2016, the percentages of religious discrimination cases filed doubled to 4.2 percent (US EEOC 2017).

A major problem in estimating the extent of religious discrimination is its highly contested definition. The US Constitution formally protects the "free exercise of religion" and forbids the government itself from establishing or favoring one religion over any other. But these religious freedoms are not unlimited. The government does not, for instance, permit members of religious groups to use violence against its members or others as part of their religious beliefs, no matter how strongly held. On the other hand, should religious "conscientious" exemptions or "carve outs" be made, for instance, for government-paid employees to refuse to be party to issuing same-sex marriage licenses, or for private vendors to refuse to provide goods or services for a legal same-sex wedding? Or should pharmacists licensed by the state be able to refuse to fill legally prescribed medications for birth control or "morning-after" abortion pills on the basis of personal religious objections? Religious liberty for some may result in discrimination for others. These are not easily resolved issues that have spawned a considerable amount of nuanced case law and vigorous public debate (Corvino et al. 2017).

SURVIVAL OF THE PRETTIEST: LOOKISM

Physical attractiveness is a pervasive yet often overlooked nonmerit factor that affects getting ahead in America. *Lookism*—favoritism for the attractive and discrimination against the unattractive—creates a structure of unequal opportunity, providing unearned advantages to the attractive and disadvantages to the unattractive.

"Good looks" for both men and women provide decided advantages in almost every aspect of life. For nearly twenty years, University of Texas at Austin economist Daniel S. Hamermesh studied the effects of physical appearance on economic outcomes. His conclusions are summarized in his book, *Beauty Pays: Why Attractive People Are Successful* (2011). Hamermesh estimates that, apart from other factors, attractive people earn on average about 5 percent more in income than average-looking people, and as much as 10 percent more compared to below-average-looking people. Hamermesh's research shows that the penalty for being below-average-looking is greater than the premium for being above-average-looking. Although the income premium for being above-average-looking is greater for women than men, somewhat surprisingly, the income penalty for being below-average-looking is substantially greater for men than women. Hamermesh estimates that for the average paid worker, the economic premium for being above-average-looking compared to below-average-looking is about $230,000 over a lifetime of earnings.

Attractiveness matters not just for income but for other economic outcomes as well. Hamermesh points to research that shows that above-average-looking people are more likely to obtain loans even with the same demographic characteristics and credit histories as less-attractive applicants. Moreover, better-looking borrowers get lower interest rates on loans than other borrowers. The ability to secure loans as investment capital, in turn, is a critical factor in starting a business and establishing equity for wealth accumulation.

In another thorough examination of the effects of attractiveness, Harvard psychologist Nancy Etcoff notes in her book, *Survival of the Prettiest* (1999), "Beauty is howlingly unfair. It is a genetic given. And physical appearance tells us little about a person's intelligence, kindness, pluck, sense of humor, or steadfastness, although we think it does" (1999, 242). Americans seem to know that the link between beauty and goodness is spurious; yet attractive people tend to be the beneficiaries of positive stereotypes and unearned opportunities. Etcoff shows that preferential treatment of beautiful people is extremely easy to demonstrate, as is discrimination against the un-attractive. From infancy to adulthood, beautiful people are treated preferentially and viewed more positively. This is true for men as well as women. Beautiful individuals, for instance, are more likely to receive leniency in the courts and to elicit cooperation from strangers. Beauty conveys modest but real social and economic advantages, and equally importantly, ugliness leads to major social disadvantages and discrimination.

Etcoff reviewed a large body of research and cataloged the numerous advantages of attractiveness. Lookism affects us all from an early age: Parents respond more af-fectionately to physically attractive newborns. Attractive schoolchildren differentially benefit from positive teacher expectations. People are more likely to help attractive individuals, and this holds true even if they don't like them. People are less likely to ask good-looking people for help. Efforts to please good-looking people with no expectation of immediate reward or reciprocity are clear evidence of the unearned rewards of beauty, which are not unlike those of being born into the nobility or inheriting wealth. Attractive people are expected to be better at everything, and such expectations at school and work can be self-fulfilling. People presume that at-tractive people of both sexes are more, not less, intelligent than unattractive people. Good-looking people are more likely to get away with anything from shoplifting, to cheating on exams, to committing serious crimes.

The rhetoric of proponents of the American Dream is that the advantages that accrue to the attractive are legitimate because they are achieved. That is, meritocracy applies to considerations of beauty because it is argued that beauty is attainable through hard work and effort. But just *how* does one "achieve" attractiveness? A vast and complex multibillion-dollar beauty industry (cosmetics, plastic surgery, diets, drugs, vitamins, herbs, potions, creams, ointments, food supplements, physical fit-ness and exercise, and fashion) supposedly levels the playing field, providing equal opportunity to achieve a socially constructed and mythical ideal of beauty (Wolf 1991). Despite this expense, research suggests that only minor increments to others' perceptions of attractiveness occur as a result of these efforts (Hamermesh 2011). The "opportunities" to improve attractiveness offered by the beauty industry, how-ever, are not equal. Natural variation in beauty creates different starting points and makes the most difference, but "working hard" to be attractive usually takes money, sometimes lots of it.

Stanford University law professor Deborah Rhode in her book, *The Beauty Bias: The Injustice of Appearance in Life and Law* (2010), further points out that appearance discrimination is treated differently in the law than other forms of discrimination. Discrimination against race, sex, and age is based on ascribed characteristics that are typically recognized in the law as "protected classes." Attractiveness, however, is not a category but a continuum, and is often perceived as an individually achieved char-acteristic as opposed to an ascribed group characteristic. As a result, appearance dis-crimination generally gets less attention and less opportunity for remedy in the courts.

To sum things up, one can hardly doubt the considerable advantages that at-tractiveness provides in pursuit of the American Dream. What is more, there is no level playing field, since attractiveness and the opportunities to "earn" it are distributed unequally. While attractiveness does not guarantee happiness any more than money does, having either is considered good, and having either helps in getting the other.

MULTIPLE JEOPARDY: A NOTE ON INTERSECTIONALITY AND THE MATRIX OF DOMINATION

It is harmful for any one individual to be subject to discrimination along any one of the various dimensions of discrimination discussed above. But it is exponentially harmful to be subject to discrimination along multiple dimensions simultaneously (Collins 1990; Weber 2001). For instance, on average there is a "cost" to being black in America in terms of the likely loss of opportunity and income; there is also a "cost" to being a woman in America. Social scientists have further identified an additional "cost" associated with the *combination* of factors, such as the cost of being both black *and* a woman. The combination of sources of discrimination along multiple axes of inequality represents what sociologist Patricia Collins (1990) calls a "matrix of domination." Within a matrix of domination, several axes of inequality can overlap for any one person, placing them at added risk at the points where those various axes intersect.

SUMMARY

Although race and sex discrimination are the most visible and damaging forms of discrimination in America, other forms of discrimination also interfere with the pursuit of the American Dream. Indeed, discrimination is not only inconsistent with meritocratic principles; it is the antithesis of merit. Although heterosexism, ageism, ableism, religious bigotry, and lookism may not victimize as many Americans as sexism and racism, they routinely operate in addition to sex and race discrimination, and often in combination. We have seen that discrimination in most of its forms has declined in the sweeping history of American society, especially in recent decades and among younger cohorts. Although discrimination is down, it is not out. In most cases, the most public and overt forms of discrimination have become socially unacceptable, driving remaining discrimination underground in more tacit forms, but with often equally devastating effects. Even as some forms of discrimination have been reduced, the effects of prior discrimination continue to reach into the present, both in the form of permanent and cumulative costs of lost opportunity for its victims, and in the creation of unequal starting points for successive generations.

REFERENCES

American Association of Retired Persons. 2014. "Staying Ahead of the Curve 2013: The AARP Work and Career Survey—Older Workers in an Uneasy Job Market." www.aarp.org/content/dam/aarp/research/surveys_statistics/general/2014/Staying-Ahead-of-the-Curve-2013-The-Work-and-Career-Study-AARP-res-gen.pdf (accessed August 25, 2017).

Anderson, Margaret L. 2017. *Race in Society: The Enduring American Dilemma*. Lanham, MD: Rowman & Littlefield.

Blau, Francine D., and Lawrence M. Kahn. 2016. "The Gender Wage Gap: Extent, Trends, and Explanations." Institute for the Study of Labor Discussion Papers, No. 9656.

Blau, Francine D., Peter Brummund, and Albert Yung-Hsu Liu. 2013. "Trends in Occupational Segregation by Gender, 1970–2009: Adjusting for the Impact of Changes in the Occupational Coding System." *Demography* 50:471–92.

Bocian, Debbie Gruenstein, Wei Li, and Keith S. Ernst. 2010. *Foreclosures by Race and Ethnicity: The Demographics of a Crisis*. Durham, NC: Center for Responsible Lending.

Bonilla-Silva, Eduardo. 2017. *Racism without Racists: Color-Blind Racism and the Persistence of Racial Inequality in the United States*, 5th ed. Lanham, MD: Rowman & Littlefield.

Brault, Matthew W. 2012. "Americans with Disabilities: 2010." *Current Population Reports*, 70–131. Washington, DC: US Census Bureau.

Brown v. Board of Education of Topeka. 1954. 347 US 483.

Carr, Deborah. 2008. "Gender Politics." *Contexts* 7(4):58–59.

Center for American Women and Politics. 2017. "Women in Elective Office 2017." www.cawp.rutgers.edu/women-elective-office-2017 (accessed August 21, 2017).

Chang, Mariko Lin. 2010. *Shortchanged: Why Women Have Less Wealth and What Can Be Done about It*. New York: Oxford.

———. 2015. "Women and Wealth: Insights for Grantmakers." Asset Funders Network. www.mariko-chang.com/AFN_Women_and_Wealth_Brief_2015.pdf (accessed August 19, 2017).

Collins, Patricia. 1990. *Black Feminist Thought: Knowledge, Consciousness, and the Politics of Empowerment*. Boston: Unwin Hyman.

Corvino, John, Ryan T. Anderson, and Sherif Girgis. 2017. *Debating Religious Liberty and Discrimination*. New York: Oxford University Press.

Doss, Richard C., and Alan M. Gross. 1994. "The Effects of Black English and Code-Switching on Intraracial Perceptions." *Journal of Black Psychology* 29:282–93.

Etcoff, Nancy. 1999. *Survival of the Prettiest: The Science of Beauty*. New York: Doubleday.

Feagin, Joe R., and Clairece Booher Feagin. 2007. *Racial and Ethnic Relations*, 8th ed. Englewood Cliffs, NJ: Prentice Hall.

Feagin, Joe R., and Kimberly Ducey. 2017. *Elite White Men Ruling: Who, What, When, Where, and How*. New York: Routledge.

Feagin, Joe R., and Melvin P. Sikes. 1994. *Living with Racism: The Black Middle-Class Experience*. Boston: Beacon.

Forbes, 2017. *Forbes* 400 2016 List. www.forbes.com/forbes-400/list/ (accessed August 19, 2017).

Hamermesh, Daniel S. 2011. *Beauty Pays: Why Attractive People Are More Successful*. Princeton, NJ: Princeton University Press.

Hochschild, Arlie. 1989. *The Second Shift: Working Parents and the Revolution at Home*. New York: Viking.

———. 1990. "The Second Shift: Employed Women Are Putting in Another Day of Work at Home." *Utne Reader* 38 (March–April):66–73.

Iceland, John. 2017. *Race and Ethnicity in America*. Berkeley: University of California Press.

Levanon, Asaf, and David B. Grusky. 2016. "The Persistence of Extreme Gender Segregation in the Twentieth Century." *American Journal of Sociology* 122(2):573–619.

Lutter, Mark. 2015. "Do Women Suffer from Network Closure: The Moderating Effect of Social Capital on Gender Inequality in a Project-Based Labor Market, 1929–2010." *American Sociological Review* 80(2):329–58.

Massey, Douglas S. 2007. *Categorically Unequal: The American Stratification System*. New York: Sage.

McDonald, Steve, Nan Lin, and Dan Ao. 2009. "Networks of Opportunity: Gender, Race, and Job Leads." *Social Problems* 56(3):385–402.

McLaughlin, Heather, Christopher Uggen, and Amy Blackstone. 2012. "Sexual Harassment, Workplace Authority, and the Paradox of Power." *American Sociological Review* 77(4):625–47.

———. 2017. "The Economic and Career Effects of Sexual Harassment on Working Women." *Gender and Society* 31(3):333–58.

Meyer, Doug. 2015. *Violence against Queer People: Race, Class, Gender and the Persistence of Anti-LGBT Discrimination*. New Brunswick, NJ: Rutgers University Press.

Offer, Shira, and Barbara Schneider. 2011. "Revisiting the Gender Gap in Time-Use Patterns: Multitasking and Well-Being among Mothers and Fathers in Dual-Earner Families." *American Sociological Review* 76(6):809–33.

Pew Research Center. 2015. "Raising Kids and Running a Household: How Working Parents Share the Load. www.pewsocialtrends.org/2015/11/04/raising-kids-and-running-a-household-how-working-parents-share-the-load/ (accessed August 21, 2017).

———. 2016 "On Views of Race and Inequality, Blacks and Whites are Worlds Apart." http://assets.pewresearch.org/wp-content/uploads/sites/3/2016/06/ST_2016.06.27_Race-Inequality-Final.pdf (accessed August 15, 2017).

Reiman, Jeffrey, and Paul Leighton. 2017. *The Rich Get Richer and the Poor Get Prison: Ideology, Class, and Criminal Justice*, 11th ed. New York: Routledge.

Rhode, Deborah L. 2010. *The Beauty Bias: The Injustice of Appearance in Life and Law*. New York: Oxford University Press.

Schneider, Daniel, and Orestes P. Hastings. 2017. "Income Inequality and Household Labor." Forthcoming, *Social Forces*.

Shapiro, Thomas M. 2004. *The Hidden Cost of Being African American: How Wealth Perpetuates Inequality*. New York: Oxford University Press.

———. 2017. *Toxic Inequality: How America's Wealth Gap Destroys Mobility and Deepens the Racial Divide and Threatens Our Future*. New York: Basic Books.

Stainback, Kevin, and Donald Tomaskovic-Devey. 2012. *Documenting Desegregation: Racial and Gender Segregation in Private-Sector Employment since the Civil Rights Act*. New York: Sage.

Thomas, Melvin E., Richard Moye, Loren Henderson, and Heywood Derrick Horton. 2017. "Separate and Unequal: The Impact of Socioeconomic Status, Segregation, and the Great Recession on Discrepancies in Housing Values." *Sociology of Race and Ethnicity*, 1–6. 2332649217711457.

Thomason, Terry, John F. Burton Jr., and Douglas E. Hyatt. 1998. "Disability and the Workplace." In *New Approaches to Disability in the Workplace*, ed. Terry Thomason, John F. Burton, and Douglas E. Hyatt, chap. 1. Madison: University of Wisconsin, Industrial Relations Research Association.

US Census Bureau. 2016. "Income and Poverty in the United States: 2015." www.census .gov/content/dam/Census/library/publications/2016/demo/p60-256.pdf (accessed August 15, 2017).

———. 2017a. "Housing and Vacancies and Homeownership: Current Population Survey." Table 16. Quarterly Home Ownership by Race and Ethnicity of Householder: 1994 to Present. www.census.gov/housing/hvs/data/histtabs.html (accessed August 16, 2017).

———. 2017b. "Wealth, Asset Ownership and Debt of Households: Detailed Tables 2013. Table 1. Median Value of Households by Type of Asset Ownership and Selected Character-istics 2013. www.census.gov/data/tables/2013/demo/wealth/wealth-asset-ownership.html (accessed August 16, 2017).

———. 2017c. "Facts for Features: Older Americans Month, May 2017." www.census.gov/ newsroom/facts-for-features/2017/cb17-ff08.html (accessed August 23, 2017).

US Department of Education. 2016. *Digest of Education Statistics*. Table 318.30. "Bachelor's Master's, and Doctor's Degrees Conferred by Postsecondary Institutions, by Sex of Student and Discipline Division." https://nces.ed.gov/programs/digest/d15/tables/dt15_318.30.asp (accessed August 16, 2017).

US Department of Justice. 2016. "Prisoners in 2015." www.bjs.gov/content/pub/pdf/p15.pdf (accessed August 16, 2017).

US Department of Labor. 2017. *Women in the Labor Force: A Databook*. www.bls.gov/opub/ reports/womens-databook/2016/home.htm (accessed August 18, 2017).

US Equal Employment Opportunity Commission (US EEOC). 2017. "Charge Statistics FY 1997 through FY 2017." www.eeoc.gov/eeoc/statistics/enforcement/charges.cfm (accessed August 22, 2017).

US Government Accountability Office. 2016. "K–12 Education: Better Use of Information Could Help Agencies Identify Disparities and Address Racial Discrimination." www.gao .gov/assets/680/676745.pdf (accessed August 16, 2017).

US Social Security Commission. 2017. "Disability Worker Beneficiary Statistics by Calendar Year, Quarter, and Month." www.ssa.gov/oact/STATS/dibStat.html (accessed August 25, 2017).

Walker, Renee E., Christopher R. Keane, and Jessica G. Burke. 2010. "Disparities and Access to Healthy Food in the United States: A Review of Food Deserts Literature." *Health and Place* 16:876–84.

Weber, Lynn. 2001. *Understanding Race, Class, Gender and Sexuality: A Conceptual Framework*. Boston: McGraw-Hill.

Wilson, William Julius. 1987. *The Truly Disadvantaged: The Inner City, the Underclass, and Public Policy*. Chicago: University of Chicago Press.

Wolf, Naomi. 1991. *The Beauty Myth: How Images of Beauty Are Used against Women*. New York: William Morrow.

10

Growing Inequality in the Twenty-First Century

What Can Be Done?

> All animals are equal but some animals are more equal than others.
>
> —George Orwell, *Animal Farm*

This book has challenged widely held assertions about meritocracy in America. According to the American ideology of meritocracy, individuals get out of the system what they put into it. The system is seen as fair because everyone is assumed to have an equal, or at least "fair," chance of getting ahead. Getting ahead is ostensibly based on merit—on being made of the right stuff. Being made of the right stuff means a combination of being talented, working hard, having the right attitude, and playing by the rules. Anyone made of the right stuff can seemingly overcome any obstacle or adversity and achieve success. In America, the land of opportunity, the sky is presumed to be the limit: You can go as far as your individual talents and abilities can take you.

While it helps to have more merit than less in most regards, the effects of merit are limited. Although innate capacity matters, for instance, there is a large reservoir of potential talent in America that is never recognized and remains largely untapped and underutilized. The talent that is recognized, much less cultivated to an elite level, represents only the tip of the talent iceberg. To be successful in most pursuits, it is not necessary to be the most talented, but to be talented enough, and the minimum thresholds required to be successful in most jobs are relatively modest. Although working hard is often considered the most crucial merit factor in getting ahead, there is simply not enough variation in either the amount of hours individuals work or the intensity of effort per unit of time expended to account for the highly skewed level of income and wealth inequality in American society. Compensation is more directly related to what people do than how "hard" they are

201

working while doing it. The most physically demanding jobs, for instance, often get paid the least. Although the actual activities that people engage in are probably more important than their attitudes in getting ahead, it probably also helps to have the "right set of attitudes," if that can be determined—or at least an appropriate match of attitudes to the specific tasks that one is engaged in. Finally, while virtue may be its own reward, there is no compelling case that says the rich are any more virtuous than anyone else; indeed, there is some evidence that being virtuous may be inversely related to getting ahead, since the virtuous are more restricted in the means they are willing to employ to do so.

Even with these restrictions, merit is only part of the story. Despite the pervasive rhetoric of merit in America, merit is in reality only one factor among many that influence who ends up with what. Nonmerit factors are also at work. These nonmerit factors not only coexist with merit, blunting its effects, but also act to suppress merit, preventing individuals from realizing their full potential based on merit alone.

Chief among the nonmerit factors is inheritance, broadly defined as the effect of where one starts on where one finishes in the race to get ahead. If we had a true merit system, everyone would start in the same place. The reality, however, is that the race to get and stay ahead is more like a relay race in which we inherit starting positions from our parents. The passing of the baton between generations profoundly influences life outcomes. Indeed, the most important factor in getting and staying ahead in America is where one starts in the first place. Most parents wish to maximize the futures of their children by providing them with every possible advantage. To the extent that parents are successful in transferring these advantages to their children, their children's life outcomes are determined by inheritance and not merit.

Social capital (whom you know) and cultural capital (what you need to know to fit into the group) are also nonmerit factors that affect life outcomes. These factors, in turn, are related to inheritance. It helps to have friends in high places, and the higher up one starts in life, the greater the probability that one will travel in elite social circles. One must also have the cultural wherewithal to be fully accepted within high-echelon social circles. Those who are born into these circles have a nonmerit cultural advantage over those not born into them; the latter group has the difficult task of learning the ways of life of the group from the outside in.

If not born into wealth and privilege, the primary pathways to upward social mobility in America have historically been through education or entrepreneurial activity. Education is widely perceived as the preeminent merit filter, sifting and sorting on the basis of demonstrated individual achievements. Education, however, is both a merit and nonmerit factor in getting ahead. Although individuals "earn" diplomas, certificates, and degrees based on demonstrated individual competence (merit), the nurturing of individual potential and opportunities to earn these credentials are unevenly and unequally distributed (nonmerit). Research overwhelmingly confirms that the amount and quality of education children are likely to acquire are highly mediated by children's socioeconomic background. In this way, educational attainment is largely reproduced across generations.

An alternate means of upward mobility in the United States has been through entrepreneurial activity. In many ways, the greatest expression of the ideals of rugged individualism, meritocracy, and the American Dream has been to start your own business and become your own boss. This pathway to upward mobility, however, has been severely compromised for recent generations of Americans. High rates of market concentration of increasingly large corporations and national chains have created barriers of entry for the lone entrepreneur, reducing business dynamism and compromising the entrepreneurial pathway to upward mobility.

Another nonmerit factor in getting ahead in America is the random effect of luck, both good and bad. Just plain dumb luck also plays a significant role in the race to get ahead. Apart from the discrete characteristics of individuals, being in the right place at the right time matters. Factors such as the number and types of jobs available, the number of people chasing those jobs, where one lives, where one works, and the vicissitudes of domestic economic cycles and the global economy profoundly factor into individual life chances—above and beyond individual merit or the lack of it. The imperfections and ultimate uncertainty of both the stock market on Wall Street and the labor market on Main Street add an undeniable element of luck into the mix of who "wins" and who "loses."

Although most people marry or partner with persons of similar socioeconomic background and status, it is possible to become upwardly (or downwardly) mobile indirectly through a relationship with another. Being able to attract a person of higher social standing might be considered as having an element of merit attached to it, but most Americans would not consider an intentional strategy to marry up a legitimate part of the American Dream. On the other hand, if love is the primary motivation for marriage and marrying up in social standing is incidental to the relationship, then mobility through a relationship with another could be considered legitimate. To the extent that the rich marry the rich and the poor marry the poor, economic, social, and cultural advantages or disadvantages are consolidated and passed on to future generations.

Finally, discrimination is another nonmerit factor that compromises equality of opportunity based on merit. Discrimination is not just a nonmerit factor; it is the antithesis of merit. In a pure merit system, the only thing that would matter would be the ability to do the job—irrespective of any non-performance-related criteria. To the extent that discrimination affects life outcomes, meritocracy does not exist. At the beginning of the twenty-first century, race and sex discrimination are clearly on the decline, and certainly less blatant than during earlier periods, Nevertheless, the lingering effects of past discrimination persist into the present, and although less visible and more subtle, its remaining, contemporary forms continue to be damaging. The "underground" nature of modern forms of discrimination makes them especially damaging because it has enabled the emergence of an aggressive and popular denial of the persistence of discrimination and its continuing damaging effects. In addition to race and sex discrimination, heterosexism, ageism, ableism, religious discrimination, and "lookism" are forms of discrimination that continue to create differential access to opportunity and rewards independent of individual merit.

Americans desperately want to believe in the ultimate fairness of the system and its ability to deliver on its promises. To a great extent, this is the basis of the strength and durability of meritocratic notions and the American Dream. But as they strive to achieve it, they have found that it has become more difficult simply to keep up and make ends meet. Instead of "getting ahead," many Americans find themselves working harder just to stay in place, and despite their best efforts, many find themselves "falling behind"—worse off than they were earlier in their lives, or compared to their parents at similar points in their lives.

INDIVIDUAL COPING STRATEGIES

Over the past several decades, there has been growing economic inequality in America. Those at the top of the system, deriving most of their income from investments, have done very well. Average wage earners, on the other hand, have experienced flat or declining wages in what amounts to a long wage recession extending as far back as the 1970s. During this period, rates of upward mobility have slowed. In response to growing economic pressures and the lack of opportunity, Americans have resorted to a variety of coping strategies to try to make ends meet, or at least to maintain a lifestyle to which they have become accustomed. Among these strategies are having multiple family wage earners and fewer children, delaying retirement, and borrowing more.

Relying on Multiple Wage Earners

In 1950, women made up just 29 percent of the US labor force; by 2015, women made up 47 percent of the total labor force, near parity with men (US Department of Labor 2017a). There are many reasons for the dramatic increase in female labor-force participation, including declining fertility; increasing divorce rates; growth of the service sector, in which women have been historically overrepresented; increasing levels of educational attainment among women; and the changing role of women in society. Another generally acknowledged factor is that women work for the same reason men do: to make ends meet. As costs of living have increased and wages have remained stagnant, more women have been drawn into the labor force to help make ends meet. Besides a sharp rise in female labor-force participation, there has also been a sharp increase in dual-income families. Among all married couples with children under eighteen, those in which both husband and wife worked increased from 25 percent of the total in 1960 to 60 percent by 2012 (Pew Research Center 2015). Related to the increase in dual-income families, working wives' contributions to median family income increased from just 2 percent in 1970 to 30 percent in 2015 (Golan and Kerdnunvong 2016). Having married couples both work as a strategy to offset increased costs of living, however, has an upper limit. That is, except in cases of bigamy, an already-working husband or wife has only one spouse who can also enter the labor force.

The next line of defense would presumably be children, especially adult children working while going to school. This, too, is occurring as higher proportions of college students work while going to college, and work longer hours. In 1970, among full-time college students, 34 percent were employed (US Department of Education 2012); by 2015, 43 percent of full-time college students were employed (US Department of Education 2017a). Of full-time college students employed in 1970, 14 percent worked more than twenty hours per week, and 4 percent worked more than thirty-five hours per week (US Department of Education 2012); by 2015, 17 percent of employed full-time college students worked more than twenty hours, and 10 percent worked more than thirty-five hours (US Department of Education 2017a).

Having Fewer Children

Another potential strategy to offset increased costs of living is to reduce family size. For whatever combination of reasons, it is clearly the case that American women have sharply reduced rates of fertility in the past half century. A standard measure of fertility is the total fertility rate (TFR), which is an estimate of the average number of children that would be born to a woman over her lifetime. This rate has fallen from an average of 3.7 children born to American women in a lifetime at the height of the baby boom in 1957, to 1.8 in 2016 (US Census Bureau 2017), which is below the replacement threshold of 2.1 that would be required to maintain current population size over time, assuming no net in-migration. According to the demographic transition theory, as countries industrialize, rates of fertility are reduced primarily because the economic incentives for higher fertility are reduced. That is, in agrarian societies it makes sense to have large families in order to have more potential workers available to work on the family farm. But as societies shift to industrial economies, children become net economic liabilities instead of potential economic assets. In a reinforcing pattern, reduced fertility is also associated with increased labor-force participation among women. That is, as more women work outside the home, they tend to have fewer children, and as women have fewer children, they tend to increase their rates of labor-force participation.

While reduced fertility rates have many potential causes, demographers generally agree that economic factors are paramount. According to the US Department of Agriculture (2017), the estimated cost of raising one child to age eighteen without college in 2015 for middle-income husband-wife families was $233,610.[1] Adding the average cost of tuition, fees, and room and board for a four-year public college education for in-state residents in the 2013–2014 academic year of $72,440 (US Department of Education 2017b) brings the total tab per child to $306,050. The extent to which parents or potential parents limit fertility in the face of such large potential expenditures is unknown, but no doubt factors into reproductive decisions.

Reduced fertility as a strategy to reduce total household expenses also has upper limits. Obviously a woman cannot reduce her fertility below zero. As noted above, the US TFR, now less than replacement level, has in recent years flattened, suggesting that fertility levels are approaching a probable effective ceiling below which couples who want children are unwilling to go, despite the costs.

Delaying Retirement

Americans are increasingly working past traditional retirement ages (Clark and Morrill 2017; Bosworth et al. 2016; Toossi 2015). For persons over sixty-five years of age, rates of labor-force participation increased from 12.4 percent in 1994 to 18.8 percent in 2014 (Toossi 2015). In addition, a higher proportion of workers over sixty-five are working full-time. In 1995, less than half of workers over sixty-five were working full-time, but by 2014, nearly 60 percent were working full-time (Bosworth et al. 2016). Moreover, these trends are likely to continue into the future. Labor-force participation rates for workers over sixty-five are projected to increase from 18.6 percent in 2014 to 21.7 percent in 2024 (Toossi 2015).

The trends toward working at older ages and working more at older ages are likely due in part to longer life expectancies. As Americans live and attend school longer, the proportion of their total life spans spent working will also need to increase to be equivalent to prior generations. Many older workers choose to work to stay active as long as they remain in good health. However, older workers are also postponing retirement for financial reasons; for example, as full Social Security benefits have been made available only at older ages, and as employers have cut back on health-care and pension benefits to retirees. Delaying retirement in order to make ends meet, however, obviously has its upper limits, since older workers will eventually reach a point at which they are physically or cognitively unable to continue working.

Going into Debt

Another strategy to make up for shortfalls in income is to go into debt. In 2017, total household debt in the United States reached a to-date peak of $12.8 trillion (Federal Reserve Bank of New York 2017). Household debt as a percent of the gross national product increased steadily throughout the second half of the twentieth century, peaking at the beginning of the Great Recession and ticking down somewhat since then, but still at historically high levels. In 1960, household debt as a percent of GDP was 30 percent, rising to a peak of 98 percent in 2008, and falling somewhat to 80 percent in 2016 (Federal Reserve Bank of St. Louis 2017a). Over the same period, with some year-to-year fluctuation, rates of personal savings have declined overall from around 10 percent in 1960 to 3.5 percent in 2017 (Federal Reserve Bank of St. Louis 2017b). Borrowing as a means of making ends meet obviously has its upper limits for many Americans, ultimately leading to financial insolvency. Overextended in debt and without much of a safety net of savings, life in the middle class for many Americans has become increasingly precarious.

In short, in response to the increased financial insecurity of the past several decades, Americans who have fallen behind have resorted to a variety of strategies in attempts to cling to at least the outward appearance of maintaining a middle-class lifestyle and living out the American Dream: increasingly relying on multiple wage earners, having fewer children, delaying retirement, and going into debt. Each of these individual coping strategies, however, obviously has its upper limits, which are quickly being realized: There are only two spouses who can work, fertility cannot be reduced below zero, retirement cannot be postponed indefinitely, and a spiral of borrowing and spending eventually results in financial collapse.

WHAT CAN BE DONE?

These individual coping strategies, although responses to societal-level imperatives, will not, in and of themselves, change social institutions, larger organizational forms, or the ways that resources are distributed. In short, they will not change America's social-class system, nor will they make America more equal, more meritocratic, or more just. Changes of this magnitude would require reductions in socially structured inequality, especially inequalities of wealth and power. How could such change be brought about? There are several policy options, all of which depend on the will of those in charge. In the final analysis, policy is determined by the outcome of political contests. These contests reflect competing visions regarding what kind of society people think we ought to have, or what is desirable.

In the book *The Spirit Level: Why Greater Equality Makes Societies Stronger* (2009), epidemiologists Richard Wilkinson and Kate Pickett provide compelling cross-cultural evidence showing that countries with high levels of economic inequality are associated with a variety of what most would agree are undesirable outcomes, such as poor physical health (including lower levels of life expectancy and higher rates of infant mortality), higher rates of stress and mental illness, higher rates of drug abuse, lower levels of overall childhood well-being (as well as higher rates of childhood obesity, lower levels of student math and literacy scores, and higher teenage rates of pregnancy), higher levels of violence (including homicide rates), higher rates of incarceration, and lower levels of social mobility.

Assuming that it is desirable to reduce levels of economic inequality and to make the system operate more like a meritocracy (an assumption that will be examined at the end of this chapter), several policy options could be considered.

Tax Policy

One way to reduce the gap between the top and the bottom of the system is to impose a more heavily progressive system of taxation on income, wealth, or both.

Progressive taxes are those in which the tax rate increases as taxable income increases. In other words, progressive taxation operates on an ability-to-pay principle; that is, those who have higher incomes and can presumably afford to pay more get taxed at higher rates. Progressive taxation does not necessarily result in simple redistribution of income or wealth from the rich to the poor. Revenue from more progressive taxation, for instance, rather than funding transfer payments to lower-income individuals, could be invested in public projects in ways that would provide more equal access to education, health care, public transportation, and other critical services, thereby reducing the nonmerit effects of cumulative advantages in these areas that higher incomes and wealth provide. In this way, the gap in opportunities between the rich and the poor would be reduced, and a more level playing field could be established.

Progressive taxation in itself, however, does not increase the prospects for equality of opportunity. Indeed, if income and wealth were entirely accrued based on individual merit, and if there were no advantages in opportunity to achieve based on one's current economic standing, then progressive taxation could create a disincentive for individuals to achieve. On the other hand, to the extent that income and wealth are acquired or augmented through nonmerit advantage, then the progressive taxation of such nonmerit advantage would help to establish more equality of opportunity.

Two types of taxes aimed specifically at nonmerit forms of wealth accumulation are estate taxes and gift taxes. These are aimed at nonmerit forms of wealth accumulation, since recipients of such largess do not technically "earn" them in the marketplace based on their own individual merit (although one may argue that recipients could potentially "earn" these forms of largess informally through demonstration of familial loyalty or friendship, by rendering services such as caring for elderly parents, or as a return for prior favors). Resistance to wealth taxation has most recently coalesced around the push to eliminate federal estate taxes, renamed the "death tax" by opponents, because they seem to tax the dead. Of course, it is not possible to tax the dead. Instead, the estate itself is taxed, and its inheritors receive the remainder.

Exclusions have historically been generous, so only the very largest estates have been subject to the tax. With the passage of the 2017 Tax Cuts and Jobs Act, the thresholds for the amount at which estates would be subject to federal estate taxation essentially doubled from $5.49 million for individuals and $10.98 million for married couples to $11.2 million for individuals and $22.4 million for married couples. Prior to the 2018 tax year when the new law comes into effect, an estimated 99.8 percent of all estates did not pay any federal estate tax (Huang and Cho 2017). With the passage of the new bill, less than .1 of all estates are likely to be subject to any federal estate tax. Moreover, assets left to a surviving spouse or charitable organizations are not generally subject to estate taxation. In addition, estate taxation can be avoided or drastically reduced through a combination of exclusions, qualified deductions, inter vivos giving, and careful estate planning. States can also level estate taxes independent of federal estate tax, but only eighteen states and the District of Columbia have some form of an estate or inheritance tax, at rates much lower than the federal levels (Scarboro 2017).

In short, existing estate taxes are currently not large enough and do not affect enough of the total amount of wealth transferred intergenerationally to make much difference in reducing the nonmerit effects of inheritance on who gets what, and how much. Higher estate taxes could potentially help to "reshuffle the deck" between generations to create more equal starting points by both reducing the total amount of inequality and providing more resources for the government to allocate in ways to create more opportunity for those who start further behind.

Estate taxes are only one way of taxing wealth. Tax on wealth could also be based on its possession (assets tax), its use (consumption tax), or its exchange (transfer tax) (Wolff 2002; Scheve and Stasavage 2016). Those who oppose such taxes often label them "confiscatory" and argue that they discourage work, savings, and investment. Supply-side advocates argue that taxing wealth in any form discourages investments that would otherwise create more jobs and a "trickle-down" effect of wealth creation. They contend that excessive taxation of wealth encourages the wealthy to flee to other countries that tax wealth less, thereby depriving American society of investment and spending that the wealthy would otherwise provide. Supply-siders argue that the sum of individual decisions with regard to the stewardship of resources is collectively more productive, efficient, and efficacious than collective decisions that emerge from the political process. Those who advance this position tend to view inheritance as a natural rather than a civil right, which should not be limited or abridged by the state.

The argument in favor of progressive wealth taxation suggests that unchecked accumulation of wealth increases social inequality to an unacceptable level. According to this view, taxes should be based on an ability-to-pay principle, with the wealthiest being taxed the most. The case in favor of estate taxation argues that inheritance rights are not natural but civil rights granted by the state, which has the power to both regulate and tax wealth in all its forms. According to this view, the state is coheir to claims of private property, the individual accumulation of which was made possible, protected, and promoted by the state.

Many forms of taxes tend to be regressive; that is, lower-income groups pay more as a proportion of total income than higher-income groups. While state income taxes are generally progressive, other forms of state taxes are highly regressive, such as sales taxes and excise taxes. In a comprehensive study of the net effect of state and local taxes, the Institute on Taxation and Economic Policy (2015) showed that in 2015, on average, the poorest one-fifth of Americans paid an average of 10.9 percent of their income in state and local taxes, whereas the middle fifth paid 9.4 percent, while the top 1 percent of earners paid only 5.4 percent.

Similarly, income taxes at the federal level are progressive, with almost half of Americans not paying any federal income taxes. But other forms of federal tax are regressive, such as the federal tax on gasoline, and Social Security and Medicare taxes (known as FICA or payroll taxes). With FICA taxes, employees and employers pay a percentage of employee income into Social Security and Medicare. Unlike the Medicare tax, the tax base for Social Security taxes is capped. In 2017, the cap for the Social Security tax was a taxable income of $127,200; that is, income over that amount was not subject to the Social Security tax. As taxable income exceeds $127,200, the percentage of total income paid in Social Security tax goes down. Thus, the higher the income above $127,200, the more the tax is regressive. Social Security taxes are capped because Social Security benefits are also capped at a maximum amount.

To the extent that Medicare and Social Security benefits exceed that which individuals pay in over a lifetime, additional benefits received are being subsidized by the general revenue, mostly through contributions of current workers. That is, both low-income and high-income individuals are eligible for these benefits, regardless of need. One proposal for reform is to make Social Security tax more progressive by increasing or eliminating the income cap subject to this tax. Another proposal is to means-test the benefits (as in the case of Medicaid), which would make them essentially "welfare" programs based on need rather than "entitlement" programs available to all regardless of need. That is, everyone would pay into the system as a kind of destitution insurance, available only if you became destitute. A concern, however, is that this would create a disincentive to save or be frugal into old age, and that the recipients would be stigmatized for receiving such benefits.

Another form of federal regressive tax is based on the source of income. Unearned income from capital gains (income gained from selling stock at a higher price than it was originally purchased) is taxed in the United States for most Americans at about half the rate of earned income from salary and wages. The top statutory federal tax rate in 2017 is 40 percent, for earned income over $444,550, but the top rate for unearned income from capital gains is 20 percent. That is, income from investments is taxed at about half the rate of income from labor. The higher one's total income, the more likely it is that a higher proportion of it comes from investments, rather than wages or salary. The substantial difference in tax rates between earned and unearned income, however, seems inconsistent with the work ethic associated with the American Dream. Lower tax rates on investment income are justified on the assumption that capital gains taxes discourage investments, and investments stimulate the economy in ways that generate both jobs and total income. These tax breaks, however, are not tied to these outcomes; instead, companies increasingly use their tax savings to merge with other companies, buy back stock in their own companies, increase dividends for shareholders, or invest in foreign markets, all of which typically result in loss of jobs and reductions of income for ordinary workers.

Government Spending

Like tax policy, government spending is determined by the outcome of political contests. And like tax policy, government spending has a major impact on both the extent of inequality and the prospects for mobility within society. As with all modern states, the United States has what economists refer to as a "mixed" economy. That is, part of the economy is produced by market forces, and part is administered by governments. There are no "pure" capitalist or socialist economies; instead, national economies are aligned on a continuum according to whether they are more or less capitalist (market-driven) or socialist (government-administered).

Even in highly capitalist societies such as the United States, segments of the economy are "set aside" from the marketplace because they are deemed either too important or too impractical to be left to the vicissitudes of market forces. One prominent example is public education. Public education is administered by governmental units (usually local municipalities or states). Public schools operate on essentially socialist principles; that is, they are not-for-sale, not-for-profit entities whose services are administered by the government and are available to all citizens regardless of ability to pay. Since providing basic education to all of its citizens regardless of ability to pay is seen as being in the public interest, this segment of the economy is set aside from the market. In an ideal democracy in which everyone presumably has an equal say in what happens, it is in the best interest of society for citizens who are making decisions to make informed decisions. It is also seen as in the public interest to have a skilled labor force, which further justifies access to education regardless of the ability to pay. Likewise, it is considered in the interest of fostering democracy and an informed public to have access to information in the public domain. Most communities in the United States, for instance, have not-for-profit public libraries (as well as school libraries and government offices) in which individuals can "look it up" without payment or fees.

It is important to point out, however, that there are mixed entities even within education, such as private schools—which are generally, but not always, not-for-profit, though they do operate on ability-to-pay principles—or public universities that are not-for-profit, but are not available to all (most have competitive rather than open admissions policies), and not entirely free (although usually subsidized). Other sectors of the economy, such as police and fire protection, waste disposal, public parks, and so on, are similarly set aside from the market. And still others operate on modified market principles, such as for-profit utility companies, which typically operate as government-sanctioned but regulated monopolies, or private defense contractors, which often have no competitors or operate for security reasons on no-bid, cost-plus contracts.

Economies vary, then, by the extent to which segments of them are, for various reasons, set aside from market forces. These are ultimately political decisions. In Western European democracies, for instance, much greater portions of their economies are set aside from market forces compared to the United States. Among advanced industrialized democracies, the United States until recently was unique in not having some form of government-guaranteed health care. With the passage of the Affordable Care Act in 2010, a step was made in that direction with a model for government-guaranteed access to health insurance for most Americans, but one that is still mostly market-driven and organized through private insurance companies. The passage of this act was intensely contested not only in its particulars, but in the role of government in providing access to health care, and essentially to what extent, if any, health care should be set aside from ability-to-pay market principles.

There are a variety of ways in which government spending could result in a society that operates on more strictly meritocratic principles. To the extent that access to opportunity to achieve is based on ability to pay, meritocracy is compromised. The most obvious case is education. To the extent that access to opportunity is mediated through education, and to the extent that educational opportunities are unequally distributed, meritocracy is compromised. More centralized funding and standards of quality for public schools set by states and the federal government instead of local governments could reduce inequities in educational opportunity. To the extent that government-funded schools were as "good" as private alternatives, the incentive for private retreats from the public school system would be reduced. However, there is great resistance to such proposals because parents want to retain "local control of local schools," and wealthier families often have a vested interest in retaining the advantage of "better" schools located in "better" neighborhoods.

Government could also extend "free" public education beyond secondary schools to include university and professional education. Likewise, opportunities for vocational or trade schools could be publicly funded. The government could also more aggressively fund preschool and after-school programs aimed at making up cultural or social-capital deficits among low-income or at-risk children. All of these measures would reduce the nonmerit access to opportunity predicated on ability to pay, and thereby foster a more genuinely meritocratic society.

Beyond education, government could provide or improve infrastructure (roads, bridges, sewer and water supply, electrical grids, telecommunication systems, airports, and so on) and other basic services such as health care, available to the general public. This would reduce the expenses of lower-income groups in particular who would otherwise have to expend limited resources to gain market access to such services and would deflect time and resources that could be directed toward investment in their own human-capital potential. This principle is illustrated by Abraham Maslow's well-known "hierarchy-of-needs" concept. According to Maslow, individuals have a hierarchy of needs that begins with basic subsistence such as food, clothing, and shelter. Maslow further notes that individuals cannot attend to higher-order needs, much less "self-actualization," the highest-order need, until the more basic needs are met. Poor people are essentially "stuck" at lower-order needs and are therefore at a personal-development disadvantage regardless of their individual capacities or potential. Government could intervene in the market by providing such critical basic needs, which would allow lower-income groups to compete with others based more on individual capacities than individual circumstance.

While some forms of government spending could promote meritocracy, other forms violate meritocratic principles. A purely meritocratic society would operate on strict survival-of-the-fittest social Darwinist principles. In such a society, individuals who, for whatever reasons, were "unfit" would not get ahead, and in many cases would not even survive. Children, the disabled, the infirm, the elderly, and others with no viable means of support would be on their own. Most modern industrial countries, however, furnish some form of "safety net" to provide for the basic necessities of citizens if they cannot provide for themselves. Such individuals are often referred to as "the deserving poor," since their inability to provide for themselves is beyond their control.

What about individuals who are willing and able to work but are poor nevertheless because they do not have jobs, or do not have jobs that provide a living wage? Individuals may be unemployed or underemployed because they are less fit than others (assuming that "fitness" can be determined), or they may be unemployed or underemployed simply as the result of market forces. If the market itself does not provide enough jobs that pay at least a subsistence wage for all those who are able and willing to work, governments could intervene in the market by providing direct financial assistance to such individuals, or by becoming "the employer of last resort," putting people to work, presumably on public works projects that could benefit society as a whole.

Government's spending is limited by the amount of revenue it can raise or borrow. In this way, government tax and spending policies are inextricably linked. How government revenue is expended affects both the extent of inequality in society and prospects for mobility. In general, societies with more progressive tax systems, along with more extensive welfare programs, have lower levels of inequality and higher rates of social mobility, while those with more regressive tax systems, along with less-extensive welfare programs, have higher levels of inequality and less social mobility (Dreier 2007).

Affirmative Action

Discrimination remains a major source of nonmerit inequality. For America to extend true equality of opportunity to all, discrimination would have to be eliminated, or at least significantly reduced. Several specific reform strategies could be pursued to this end. Antidiscrimination laws could be strengthened and more effectively enforced. Additional resources could be made available for individuals to pursue complaints. Punishments for demonstrated acts of discrimination could be made more certain and consequential. Beyond mere passive nondiscrimination, more proactive measures designed to reduce the effects of past discrimination and prevent future discrimination could be more aggressively pursued. Such proactive measures generally fall under the label of what has become known as affirmative action.

Like antidiscrimination laws, the goal of affirmative action policies is to make equal opportunity a reality for members of groups that have historically been the objects of discrimination. Unlike antidiscrimination laws, which provide remedies to which individuals can appeal after they have suffered discrimination, affirmative action policies aim to keep discrimination from occurring and compensate for injustices incurred in the past. Affirmative action can prevent discrimination by replacing practices that are discriminatory, either by intent or default, with practices that safeguard against discrimination. Rather than a single policy that involves the same procedures, affirmative action comprises a set of policies and practices, including admission standards for schools and universities, guidelines for hiring practices, and procedures for the granting of government contracts, each with its own complex and contentious history (Alon 2015; Reskin 1998; Wise 2005; Waters 2012).

In a series of affirmative action cases, the US Supreme Court has limited the scope of affirmative action policies and practices. The most extreme and controversial form of affirmative action, using quotas or set-asides as a means to increase diversity in schools and workplaces, was ruled unconstitutional in 1978 by the US Supreme Court in the landmark *Regents of the University of California v. Bakke* case regarding admission practices at the UC Davis Medical School. Quotas or set-asides were in practice rarely used. More typically, affirmative action programs have sought to promote efforts to include members of groups that have been historically excluded from consideration for school admissions, jobs, and promotions. With such efforts, there are no requirements or quotas to hire members of certain "protected classes" or disadvantaged groups. Instead, in the context of proactive affirmative action, efforts are made to make the admission, hiring, or promotion processes as open as possible to encourage members of disadvantaged groups to apply. For instance, many jobs were formerly filled without public advertisement through word-of-mouth networks, which favor the already privileged and reproduce the demographic and social profile of existing occupants of such positions (social capital). To counter these exclusionary tendencies, the Equal Employment Opportunity Commission put requirements in place for some jobs that job notices be posted in widely publicly accessible outlets before positions can be filled. Job listings may specifically invite members of disadvantaged groups to apply (using language such as "women and minorities are encouraged to apply"), and other extra recruitment efforts (e.g., advertising in outlets targeted to such groups) may be used to encourage such applicants to apply.

In a precedent-setting case involving admission procedures in use at the University of Michigan, *Gratz v. Bollinger* (2003), the US Supreme Court reasserted the ban against quotas but condoned the use of race as a factor in admission decisions. Specifically, race may be used to pursue a legitimate institutional goal of diversity of access—not exclusively or in any across-the-board fashion, but in conjunction with other factors. All of these efforts are intended to ensure that members of formerly excluded groups are given full consideration for educational and occupational positions, but there is no requirement to hire and no quota to fill. In a series of subsequent court challenges, *Fisher v. University of Texas* (2013) and *Fisher v. University of Texas* (2016), the US Supreme Court upheld the principle of affirmative action to achieve the educational goal of racial diversity, but with the provision that such policies be "narrowly tailored" and adopted only after other race-neutral solutions prove unworkable.

Opponents of affirmative action argue that such programs constitute "reverse discrimination." Affirmative action has been characterized as a set of highly discriminatory policies and practices in hiring and promotion decisions, resulting in the selection of less qualified minorities over more qualified white males. Such reverse discrimination, if and when it occurs, does indeed violate strict meritocratic principles. In order to have a strictly meritocratic society, *all* forms of discrimination and nonmerit preference "reversal" would need to be eliminated. In addition to the race-based considerations discussed above, for instance, commonly used nonmerit preferences for such categories as seniority, legacy status, geographic balance, or veteran preference would also be disallowed. Preference based on seniority is not in itself a measure of merit, although organizations may consider such privileges of rank as reward for prior service. Similarly, legacy preference in admissions often used in elite universities (preference given to those whose relatives previously attended) is nonmerit-based, and indeed tends to reproduce existing social and demographic profiles. Although a grateful nation may want to extend preference in hiring to veterans for prior service rendered, veteran status in itself does not qualify as a merit consideration.

Although Americans are generally in favor of the ideal of equality of opportunity, they are often opposed to affirmative action attempts to achieve that outcome. The objection is not so much against affirmative action in principle but against specific provisions of some forms of affirmative action, especially those that target minorities and women. This is further complicated in the case of race-based programs by increasing rates of racial intermarriage, increasingly blurred racial boundaries, and increasing multiracial identities (Winant 2012).

One potential for reform, then, is to develop affirmative action programs for the economically disadvantaged, regardless of race or sex (Alon 2015). Such an essentially class-based affirmative action program may be more politically palatable and overcome many of the objections related to charges of reverse discrimination. Racial minorities, disproportionately represented among the economically underprivileged, would therefore disproportionately, but not exclusively, benefit from such arrangements. Such programs, however, would not fully take into account the uniquely damaging effects of the cumulative combination of class and racial disadvantage, and it's therefore unlikely that these programs, if used exclusively, would lead to an overall result of greater racial diversity in educational or employment settings (Alon 2015).

Asset Accumulation

To lack capital in a capitalist society is to be at a distinct economic and social disadvantage. As we have seen, compared to income inequality, the extent of wealth inequality in the United States is much greater, involves much higher total sums, persists much more both intra- and intergenerationally, and is ultimately more consequential for economic well-being. Because so much wealth is transferred intergenerationally either through bequests or inter vivos gifts, the distribution of wealth in American society compared to income is also much more related to inheritance and much less related to merit.

Sociologists Dalton Conley (1999) and Thomas Shapiro (2004, 2017) have presented persuasive evidence that the basic and persisting economic problem for minorities especially is their continuing inability to accumulate wealth. They point out that African Americans may have improving educational and occupational opportunities but have not made much economic progress because at every educational, income, and occupational level, they have fewer assets than white Americans. Asset-building policies, such as government assistance for home purchases or starting and expanding businesses, as well as tax incentives targeted at those of modest means to encourage savings and investments, could help to stimulate wealth creation. Shapiro, for instance, proposes government-subsidized children's savings accounts, individual-development accounts, and down-payment accounts as means to build assets for low-income populations. Shapiro proposes the establishment of an initial $1,000 childhood savings account for every child born in the United States, provided by government funds. Additional payments into these accounts by families could be matched by government funds. Account holders could use accumulated funds to defray college costs, make down payments for first-time home buyers, start businesses, or, if still active, supplement retirement or pass on to the next generation. Similar accounts could be set up for low-income adults as individual-development accounts aided by tax credits or matching public or private funds. Shapiro further suggests programs to stimulate home ownership, the major form of wealth equity for most Americans. For asset-poor families, government-backed low-interest mortgages could be provided, and savings from tax credits on rate payments could be set aside along with personal savings to be used for down payments for first-time home buyers.

Shapiro points out that government policies and programs such as the Homestead Act, the GI Bill and Veterans Administration home loans, mortgage deductions, tax deductions for IRA accounts, and other policies helped middle-class families accumulate assets but were largely unavailable to the poor, and especially, poor minorities. As with other government-sponsored programs, societal investment in these programs would likely come largely from public sources. Alternatively, or in combination, funds for such programs could also come from private philanthropic sources, to which we now turn our attention.

Noblesse Oblige

Noblesse oblige has its roots in feudal Europe, where it referred to the sense of obligation that the nobility had toward the peasantry. The difference between slave societies and estate societies is that slaves had no rights, but peasants did. Although the peasantry did not own land in its own name and had to forfeit to the nobility all but a meager portion of their crops, the nobility, in exchange for the loyalty of their subjects, were expected to provide the peasants with land to work, protection from thieves and invaders, and occasional collective celebrations, especially at harvest. These expectations were implicit rather than explicit—a set of moral obligations embedded in the culture of the group. These felt obligations of the rich toward the poor became known as *noblesse oblige*, a term that has its modern-day equivalent in the view that "to whom much is given, much is expected."

In modern times, noblesse oblige essentially means a combination of philanthropy and a desire to "give something back" through public service or service to humanity. Both philanthropy and progressive taxation are possible ways to reduce levels of inequality and restore more equity to the system—that is, to reduce the nonmerit effects of inheritance across generations. The primary difference between the two is that the former is voluntary, and those who benefit are selected by the giver, whereas the latter is nonvoluntary, and the objects of beneficence are not chosen by the giver. Through charitable giving, the wealthy can control who receives their largesse, the purposes for which they might receive it, the amounts given, and the pace at which amounts are given.

Philanthropy, particularly that provided by the superwealthy, has the potential to promote meritocracy in several ways. First, the extent to which the wealthy give their fortunes away to charity instead of leaving their fortunes to heirs determines how much the overall gap between the rich and the poor is reduced, making it easier for those at the bottom of the system to reach the top. Second, the concentration of nonmerit dynastic wealth at the top of the system is diminished, reducing the transfer of nonmerit advantage across generations. Third, if donated funds are directed in ways that reduce nonmerit disadvantage for those at the bottom of the system, merit-based equality of opportunity is expanded.

In 2010, Bill and Melinda Gates started the "Giving Pledge," which encourages billionaires like themselves to commit to giving away more than half of their fortunes to charity. As of 2017, over 170 billionaires from twenty-one countries have signed on (Giving Pledge 2017). The trend in philanthropy in recent years shows that small donations are down and large donations are up, reflecting the increase in societal inequality overall (Herzog and Price 2016; Callahan 2017). In 2016, Americans donated a total of $390 billion to charities, with 72 percent coming from individuals and the remainder from foundations (15 percent), charitable bequests (8 percent), and corporations (5 percent) (Giving USA 2017). Among funds allocated, religious organizations received 32 percent; education, 16 percent; human services, 12 percent; health organizations, 9 percent; public-society benefit organizations, 8 percent; international charities, 6 percent; arts, culture, and humanities, 5 percent; and environmental and animal organizations, 3 percent (Giving USA 2017).

Research shows that roughly 60 percent of Americans within a given year donate money to charitable organizations; of those who do donate to charities, most donations are relatively small, with 80 percent of Americans giving less than $500 annually (Herzog and Price 2016). It is difficult to assess the total impact of such giving on assisting the poorest segments of society, reducing inequality, and increasing the prospects for equality of opportunity. Many charitable dollars are given to very worthy causes but are not targeted to the poor, such as donations to cure diseases or to advance the arts. The vast portion of donations to religious organizations—by far the largest recipient of charitable funds—goes to support the internal operations of such organizations. Religious groups vary in the degree to which their resources are otherwise directed toward social services and "outreach" ministries, with traditional conservative churches and denominations providing the least, and more liberal churches and denominations the most (Hall 2005). Other charitable donations can be made by the wealthy directed toward upper-class institutions, such as donations to elite private schools and Ivy League colleges, or for support of "highbrow" culture, thereby extending rather than reducing inequality in society.

Increasingly, major donors are using their great wealth to advance political agendas and affect public policy through political campaigns, lobbying, media, and think tanks (Callahan 2017). In a recent in-depth analysis of these trends, David Callahan points out that great wealth has been amassed at the top of the system in recent decades, amplifying the voice and impact of a small group of elite private donors in society. Much of this impact occurs through the expenditure of "dark money," whose source is not identified and is not accountable to the general public, and is often directed to advancing the economic interest of the already wealthy.

Despite these concerns, at least some of this largesse eventually makes its way to the truly needy in ways that expand opportunity for the less fortunate. Since these donations are voluntary, they can be directed toward either expanding or limiting opportunities of the less fortunate, depending on the inclinations and motivations of donors. If philanthropy is directed toward expanding opportunities for the less fortunate in significant-enough amounts, then it has at least the potential to reduce both the distance from the top to the bottom of the system, and the nonmerit advantages of inheritance. One potential "solution" to the problem of inequality, then, is to encourage a greater sense of noblesse oblige among the wealthy in ways that would help level the playing field, simultaneously increasing the potential for meritocracy while decreasing the nonmerit intergenerational advantages of inheritance.

Labor Unions and Workers' Movement

The United States has a long and noteworthy history of social reform movements. The country itself was born in "revolution" as a movement against a dominant colonial power. Since then, other reform movements have helped to bring about more equality of opportunity, including the labor movement of the 1930s, the civil rights movement, the women's liberation movement, and the LGBT movement. Each of these movements, with varying degrees of success, has reduced discrimination and exclusion and has made the system more meritocratic than it was previously.

While these movements in the United States have been ascendant in the past several decades, the labor movement has been in decline. Union membership as a proportion of the labor force has fallen off sharply, from a peak of 35 percent during the mid-1950s to a low since then of 10.7 percent in 2016 (US Department of Labor 2017b). This is significant because the labor movement has been responsible for a variety of reforms that have reduced inequality and enhanced the quality of life for workers that we now take for granted, such as the eight-hour workday, the two-day weekend, paid holidays, minimum wage, and restrictions on child labor. During the height of industrialization in America in the middle of the twentieth century, labor unions in the United States helped to check the power of corporations over workers in what was sometimes described as a "countervailing" force. Without strong worker unions, it is much easier for employing organizations to "divide and conquer" individual workers and take a larger portion of productivity in the form of profits, dividends, and management salaries.

Several factors have accelerated the decline of unions in the United States, especially deindustrialization and globalization. In the United States, unions have not represented workers as a whole as much as workers in specific industries and trades. The most heavily unionized segment of the labor force was manufacturing, and as manufacturing declined, so did unions. Globalization has also weakened unions, giving corporations alternative sources of cheap and unorganized labor overseas. Finally, corporations have aggressively resisted unions, forcing concessions and givebacks and systematically trying to eliminate or weaken unions where they do exist, and discouraging the formation of new unions. More recently, unions have increased representation in arenas of the labor force not traditionally highly unionized, such as public-sector workers and service workers. Public-sector workers, for instance, now have a rate of union membership (35.9 percent) more than five times higher than that of private-sector workers (6.6 percent) (US Department of Labor 2017b). However, it is illegal for most public workers to strike, and the right of public unions even to collectively bargain has been challenged and is an especially contentious issue.

Reversing the decline of unions and restoring more balance to management–labor negotiations could potentially help to make the system more equal and more equitable than it is. Another version of strengthening the relative power of workers is to establish more worker-owned and -controlled businesses. This is a challenge, since most unions and workers do not have the resources to buy businesses outright; indeed, most employee-owned business are acquired as high-risk rescues when businesses are failing and workers would otherwise lose their jobs. Unions could also be strengthened by organizing across industries and work settings and contributing to global rules and guidelines for fair labor and market practices.

Other social movements in America have confronted issues of race, gender, and sexual orientation with varying degrees of success. The issue of racial inequality gained momentum with the civil rights movement of the 1960s. The issue of gender inequality gained momentum with the women's movement of the 1970s. The issue of LGBT inequalities gained momentum with the gay liberation movement of the 1990s. While not fully resolved, these social movements were nevertheless successful in bringing public attention to these forms of inequality on the political radar screen, and are now part of the mainstream political discourse. The primary justification for reform that gives these movements both their energy and their moral purpose is that discrimination unrelated to ability to do the job violates deeply held American values of fair play, equality of opportunity, and meritocracy.

What has not been fully confronted and has not become part of mainstream political discourse until very recently has been the issue of class and economic inequality. Largely because of the power of the ideology of meritocracy and the presumption of individual responsibility and the ideal of the American Dream, Americans have largely been in denial of even the existence of social classes. America appeared to be on the edge of directly confronting class issues during the buildup to the Great Depression, but ameliorative reforms of the New Deal era seemed to ease these concerns. As with heightened inequality of the first Gilded Age that preceded the Great Depression, heightened inequality of the so-called second Gilded Age that preceded the Great Recession has produced effects that reached beyond just the poor to deeply within the working and middle class, and aroused public attention to the issue. Increased inequality that violates the tenets of fair play and equality of opportunity is ultimately unsustainable. If inequality continues to increase, a growing crisis of legitimacy could spark new class and worker movements that are likely to generate enhanced grassroots pressure for reform.

Growing public concern about the fundamental economic fairness of the system was displayed by the Occupy Wall Street (OWS) movement. Starting in September 2011, protesters convened and occupied Zuccotti Park, located in the Wall Street financial district, drawing attention to economic inequality, and specifically the banks and investors whose reckless speculation had triggered the onset of the Great Recession. The OWS slogan, "We are the 99 percent," referred to the top 1 percent of the population in which wealth is highly concentrated compared to everyone else. The nascent movement was intentionally nonhierarchical, depriving it of formal leadership and hindering its long-term effectiveness. It did have the effect, however, of bringing national attention to class issues in a public forum.

Economic fairness and inequality were also directly addressed in the 2016 presidential election campaign. From the political left, Bernie Sanders's energized campaign for the Democratic presidential nomination was centrally organized around a theme of class inequality, directly challenging corporate power and the privilege of the upper 1 percent. From the political right, Republican candidate Donald Trump also attacked what he identified as a rigged economic system that was hurting ordinary working Americans, but placed most of the blame on immigration and globalization. Hillary Clinton took a less strident approach in her campaign, but also emphasized economic fairness and equality of opportunity. That these issues are entering the political arena is a hopeful sign for reform in the future.

A Note on Other Economic and Political Reforms

In addition to the options discussed above as possible ways to decrease inequality in general and create more equitable conditions in society, other reforms in the organization of economic and political institutions themselves might also be considered. Corporations could be reformed in such a way as to make them more publicly accountable and more socially responsible. This could include changes in corporate governance that foster greater public transparency, accountability, and inclusiveness; more aggressive antitrust enforcement; more scrutiny of foreign investments; more oversight of public health and safety issues, and the long-term integrity of the environment; and greater restrictions on risk taking where the public interest or tax dollars are involved. Political institutions could also be reformed in ways that would make them more genuinely democratic. Chief among such reforms would be reducing the influence of money in politics. Measures could also be taken to make elections more genuinely competitive by eliminating political gerrymandering and by making it easier rather than harder to vote. The intent of such reforms would be to make economic and political institutions more responsive to the general public and less captive to the narrow interests of the wealthiest segments of society.

IS A MERITOCRATIC SOCIETY
NECESSARILY A FAIR AND JUST SOCIETY?

For all the reasons discussed in this book, true equality of opportunity is highly unlikely. The system, however, could be made much fairer, much more open, and much more meritocratic than it is. Most Americans, sometimes grudgingly, acknowledge that because of discrimination on the bases of sex, race, creed, or other characteristics irrelevant to individual ability, the system has not always been entirely fair or just. The assumption is, however, that these forms of discrimination are rapidly being eliminated and that their ultimate elimination will finally bring about true equality of opportunity. But, as has been demonstrated in this book, even if all such forms of discrimination and their residual effects were somehow miraculously eliminated, we would still not have genuine equality of opportunity or a system entirely based on merit. Other nonmerit factors, including inheritance and patterns of social and economic organization that are external yet constraining to individuals, operate to modify and reduce the effects of individual merit on life chances.

In the abstract at least, Americans enthusiastically embrace the principle of proportional contribution; that is, one should get out of the system what one puts into it. According to this formulation, individuals should have an equal opportunity to get ahead, and getting ahead should be exclusively based on individual merit. This would mean not only eliminating artificial nonmerit barriers to mobility for those who are behind, but also eliminating all nonmerit advantages for those already ahead.

In a purely meritocratic system, all children would have equal starting points in the race to get ahead, and parents would not be able to engage in any practice that would give any advantage to their children not available to all others. Affluent parents, for instance, would not be able to use their personal resources to locate in neighborhoods and communities with reputations for the best public schools or send their children to elite private schools. Parents would not be able to provide their children with extracurricular or enrichment activities that have educational benefit that would not be available equally to all children. Parents would not be able to pay for private tutors, or rescue children who falter because of their own incompetence or inadequacies. Parents, families, or friends would not be able to use their networks of personal contacts or social influence to assist their children in any way. And most of all, parents would not be permitted to bequeath an inheritance to children, or indeed, to provide them with any resource not equally available to all other children.

Since most parents naturally try to do everything they possibly can to provide their children with every assistance and advantage, and would never voluntarily accede to these restrictions, it is unlikely that a pure merit system could ever be established. And herein lies the great American contradiction. Americans desperately want to believe that the system is fair and that everyone has an equal chance to get ahead. At the same time, we also emphatically endorse the right of individuals, with minimal state intervention or outside restriction, to dispose freely of their property as they personally see fit. But we simply cannot have it both ways. Inheritance and meritocracy are zero-sum principles of distribution; the more there is of one, the less there is of the other.

Furthermore, for a truly meritocratic system to operate, the influence of all other nonmerit factors identified in previous chapters would also need to be reduced to zero, including luck. To the extent that valued resources are distributed by random chance, they are not distributed by merit. As we have seen, luck comes in many forms, including being in the right place at the right time. Luck could also refer to the genetic dice roll that provides individuals with whatever innate capacities they have over which they have no personal control. Even allowing genetic endowment as part of "merit," the extent to which other forces beyond one's control influence life outcomes is substantial. While genuine equality of opportunity and achievement based exclusively on individual merit is realistically not possible, what is less often acknowledged by either the Left or the Right is that such a social system would be neither entirely just, nor desirable.

British sociologist Michael Young, in his fictional satire *The Rise of the Meritocracy* (1961), envisioned a society based solely on individual merit. In this futuristic dystopian society, individuals are assigned their place in society exclusively based on a system of rigid tests. Those who score highest on the tests fill the most important positions and get the most rewards. A strict hierarchy of merit is created and maintained. What at first seems like an eminently fair and just system in practice degenerates into a ruthless regime. The meritocratic elite feels righteously superior to all those below it and holds those at the bottom of the system in utter contempt. The meritocratic elite, secure in its lofty status, exercises complete and total domination of society. Those at the bottom of the system are incapable of challenging the elite and are permanently deprived of the capacity to rise up against their oppressors. A purely meritocratic society would also operate as a brutally "survival of the fittest" society in which there would be no safety net for the sick, the infirm, the disabled, or anyone else or who could not flourish or even survive on the basis of their own individual merit.

One possible advantage of a nonmeritocratic society is that at any time, for whatever combination of reasons, at least some of those at the top of the system are less capable and competent than at least some of those at the bottom. Such discrepancies should inspire humility in those at the top and hope and dignity for those at the bottom. But this can only happen if it is widely acknowledged that inheritance, luck, discrimination, and a variety of other circumstances beyond the merit of individuals are important in affecting where one ends up in the system. This is why the *myth* of meritocracy is itself harmful: It provides an incomplete explanation for success and failure, mistakenly exalting the rich and unjustly condemning the poor. We may always have the rich and the poor among us, but we need neither exalt the former nor condemn the latter.

REFERENCES

Alon, Sigal. 2015. *Race, Class, and Affirmative Action*. New York: Russell Sage Foundation.

Bosworth, Barry, Gary Burtless, and Kan Zhang. 2016. "Later Retirement, Inequality in Old Age, and the Growing Gap in Longevity between Rich and Poor." Economic Studies at Brookings. www.brookings.edu/wp-content/uploads/2016/02/BosworthBurtlessZhang_re tirementinequalitylongevity_012815.pdf (accessed September 16, 2017).

Callahan, David. 2017. *The Givers: Wealth, Power, and Philanthropy in the New Gilded Age*. New York: Knopf.

Clark, Robert L., and Melinda Sandler Morrill. 2017. "Working Longer, Retiring Later: Are Employers Ready for the New Employment Trend?" *Employment Research* 24(2):4–6.

Conley, Dalton. 1999. *Being Black, Living in the Red: Race, Wealth, and Social Policy in America*. Berkeley: University of California Press.

Dreier, Peter. 2007. "The United States in a Comparative Perspective." *Contexts* (Summer), 38–46.

Federal Reserve Bank of New York. 2017. "Household Debt and Credit Report." www.new yorkfed.org/microeconomics/hhdc.html (accessed September 16, 2017).

Federal Reserve Bank of St. Louis. 2017a. "Total Credit to Households and Non-Profit Institutions Serving Households, Adjusted for Breaks, for United States. US Bureau of Economic Analysis." https://fred.stlouisfed.org/series/QUSHAM770A (accessed September 16, 2017).

———. 2017b. "Personal Savings Rate." US Bureau of Economic Analysis. https://fred.stlou isfed.org/series/PSAVERT (accessed September 16, 2017).

Giving Pledge. 2017. https://givingpledge.org/ (accessed September 20, 2017).

Giving USA. 2017. "Total Charitable Contributions Rise to New High of $390.05 Billion." https://givingusa.org/giving-usa-2017-total-charitable-donations-rise-to-new-high-of -390-05-billion/ (accessed September 20, 2017).

Golan, Limor, and Usa Kerdnunvong. 2016. "Home Economics: The Changing Work Roles of Wives and Husbands." Federal Reserve Bank of St. Louis. www.stlouisfed.org/ publications/regional-economist/october-2016/home-economics-the-changing-work-roles -of-wives-and-husbands (accessed September 15, 2017).

Hall, Peter Dobkin. 2005. "Religion, Philanthropy, Service, and Civic Engagement in Twentieth-Century America." In *Gifts of Time and Money: The Role of Charity in America's Communities*, ed. Arthur C. Brooks, 159–83. Lanham, MD: Rowman & Littlefield.

Herzog, Patricia Snell, and Heather E. Price. 2016. *American Generosity: Who Gives and Why?* New York: Oxford.

Huang, Chye-Ching, and Chloe Cho. 2017. "Ten Facts You Should Know About the Federal Estate Tax." Center on Budget and Policy Priorities. Washington, DC. www.cbpp .org/research/federal-tax/ten-facts-you-should-know-about-the-federal-estate-tax (accessed September 17, 2017).

Institute on Taxation and Economic Policy. 2015. *Who Pays? A Distributional Analysis of the Tax System in All 50 States*, 5th ed. https://itep.org/wp-content/uploads/whopaysreport.pdf (accessed September 17, 2017).

Pew Research Center 2015. "Rise in Dual Income Households." www.pewresearch.org/ ft_dual-income-households-1960-2012-2/ (accessed September 15, 2015).

Reskin, Barbara F. 1998. *The Realities of Affirmative Action in Employment*. Washington, DC: American Sociological Association.

Scarboro, Morgan. 2017. "Does Your State Have an Estate or Inheritance Tax?" Washington, DC: Tax Foundation. https://taxfoundation.org/state-estate-inheritance-tax/ (accessed September 17, 2017).

Scheve, Kenneth, and David Stasavage. 2016. *Taxing the Rich: A History of Fiscal Fairness in the United States and Europe*. Princeton, NJ: Princeton University Press.

Shapiro, Thomas M. 2004. *The Hidden Cost of Being African American: How Wealth Perpetuates Inequality*. New York: Oxford.

———. 2017. *Toxic Inequality: How America's Wealth Gap Destroys Mobility, Deepens the Racial Divide and Threatens Our Future*. New York: Basic Books.

Toossi, Mitra. 2015. "Labor Force Projections to 2024: The Labor Force Is Growing, but Slowly." *Monthly Labor Review* (December). www.bls.gov/opub/mlr/2015/article/labor-force-projections-to-2024-1.htm (accessed September 14, 2017).

US Census Bureau. 2017. Table R1304, "Total Fertility Rate of Women (Per 1,000 Women)—United States." American Community Survey Estimates. https://factfinder .census.gov/faces/tableservices/jsf/pages/productview.xhtml?pid=ACS_16_1YR_R1304. US01PRF&prodType=table (accessed September 15, 2017).

US Department of Agriculture. 2017. *Expenditures on Children by Families, 2015*. Center for Nutrition Policy and Promotion, Miscellaneous Publication No. 1528-2015. www.cnpp. usda.gov/sites/default/files/crc2015_March2017.pdf (accessed September 15, 2017).

US Department of Education. 2012. *The Condition of Education 2012: College Student Employment Indicator 37-2012*. https://nces.ed.gov/pubs2012/2012045.pdf (accessed September 15, 2017).

———. 2017a. "College Student Employment." https://nces.ed.gov/programs/coe/pdf/ coe_ssa.pdf (accessed September 15, 2017).

———. 2017b. "Tuition Costs of Colleges and Universities." https://nces.ed.gov/fastfacts/ display.asp?id=76 (accessed January 16, 2017).

US Department of Labor. 2017a. *Women in the Labor Force: A Databook*. www.bls.gov/opub/ reports/womens-databook/2016/home.htm (accessed August 18, 2017).

———. 2017b. "Union Members: 2016." www.bls.gov/news.release/union2.nr0.htm (accessed September 21, 2017).

Waters, Mary C. 2012. "Racial and Ethnic Diversity and Public Policy." In *The New Gilded Age: The Critical Inequality Debates of Our Time*, ed. David B. Grusky and Tamar Kricheli-Katz, 230–46. Stanford, CA: Stanford University Press.

Wilkinson, Richard, and Kate Pickett. 2009. *The Spirit Level: Why Greater Equality Makes Societies Stronger*. New York: Bloomsbury Press.

Winant, Howard. 2012. "A Dream Deferred: Toward a US Racial Future." In *The New Gilded Age: The Critical Inequality Debates of Our Time*, ed. David B. Grusky and Tamar Kricheli-Katz, 211–29. Stanford, CA: Stanford University Press.

Wise, Tim. 2005. *Affirmative Action: Racial Preferences in Black and White*. New York: Routledge.

Wolff, Edward C. 2002. *Top Heavy: Increasing Inequality of Wealth in America and What Can Be Done about It*. New York: New Press.

Young, Michael. 1961. *The Rise of the Meritocracy, 1870–2033: An Essay on Education and Equality*. Baltimore: Penguin.

Notes

CHAPTER 2

1. Between 1961 and 1969, NASA conducted a similar, but much less publicized, program for women pilots. Thirteen of these women were selected after two rounds of the same testing that the male Mercury astronauts had passed earlier. The men were put through a third round of testing, but NASA prevented the women from taking the third round of tests, and the program was suddenly dropped, essentially negating any prospect that any of the women would be included in NASA's space program regardless of their individual abilities (Ackmann 2003).

2. The phrase "the right stuff" was used by Tom Wolfe in a 1979 book of the same title in reference to flight pioneers and the selection of NASA's first American astronauts. The book became the basis of a popular 1983 movie of the same title.

3. In American sociology, for instance, three of the most famous such individuals are George Herbert Mead (1863–1931) at the University of Chicago, whose work was seen as the inspiration for the symbolic interactionist perspective in sociology; George Casper Homans (1910–1989) at Harvard University, who was a pioneer in the development of social-exchange theory; and David Riesman (1909–2002), also of Harvard, who wrote the best-selling book of all time in the history of American sociology, *The Lonely Crowd*. Not only did Mead and Riesman not have PhDs, but neither was trained as a sociologist. Mead was a philosopher whose ideas attracted the attention of sociologists. Riesman was trained as a lawyer but became interested in social issues. Homans was trained as a sociologist but never earned a PhD, which he considered nothing more than a "status symbol." Despite the lack of this journeyman's credential, Homans became an important sociologist at America's most elite university, and even served a term as president of the American Sociological Association.

CHAPTER 9

1. It is sometimes difficult to distinguish discrimination based on religious identity from that based on ethnicity because of the considerable overlap of religion and ethnicity. However, it should be clear that Mormons are not an ethnic group. Those who converted to Mormonism included immigrants from several European nations, especially England and the Scandinavian countries. Similarly, Catholics have never represented a single ethnic group, but include Germans, Irish, Italians, and other Europeans, who, while enormously different in national and cultural backgrounds, all shared one important characteristic in the eyes of the Protestant majority: They were Catholics. Jews are not really a religious group, but are best considered an ethnic group. Jews migrated from several different regions and nations of Europe. But to dominant-group Christians, it mattered little that a Jew might be a German, or a Pole, or a Ukrainian—what mattered was that Jews were not Christians. Finally, "Middle Easterners" are a diverse aggregate of numerous nationalities and religions. In Iraq alone, for example, there are Muslim Shiites, Muslim Sunnis, and Kurds, to name only the three largest groups. Of course, in Israel, there are Jews, Palestinians (Muslims), and Christians.

CHAPTER 10

1. Middle income is defined as a before-tax income of between $59,200 and $107,400.

Index

academia hiring practices: collegiality of, 34; extended interview for, 38; for internal candidates, 36–37; meritocracy and, 39; national search use of, 34; paper presentation for, 35; PhD as requirement, 35, 227n3; references for, 37–38; short list for, 35–36; social skills for, 38; for trailing practices, 37; women and, 37

achievement gap, 98

ADA. *See* Americans with Disabilities Act

Adams, James Truslow, 2

affirmative action, 101; critics of, 34; for economically disadvantaged, 215; for equal opportunity, 213; meritocracy and, 34; as reverse discrimination, 214–15

African Americans: culture-of-poverty applied to, 26; median income of, 173; wealth accumulation of, 174

age discrimination, 191; reverse forms of, 192

agricultural revolution, 155–56

Ainswoth, James, 98

Alger, Horatio, 4–5

American aristocracy, talent of, 2

American Dream: achievement of, 1; for children, 11; cultural capital for, 82; cultural origins of, 7–8; discrimination

invalidation of, 171; downsizing of, 9–14; economic origins of, 6–7; educational opportunity for, 105, 177; education for, 12, 15, 91–92; home ownership and, 178; individualism for, 3–8; inequality ideology of, 2; irregular economy and, 114; marrying up as, 162; meritocracy and, 99; opportunities diminishment of, 9–10; origins of, 2; political origins of, 5–6; religious origins of, 4–5; retirement as part of, 13–14; rugged individualism of, 7–8; sexual harassment and, 187; women and, 181

The American Occupational Structure (Blau and Duncan), 93

Americans with Disabilities Act (ADA), 191

American upper class, 47

Anglo-Saxon Protestant (WASP), 4; wealthiest Americans as, 57

appreciation, of assets, 48

The Apprentice, 84

aristocracy of talent, 92

artistic abilities, for social mobility, 24–25

Asian Americans, 180

asset accumulation, 215–16

assets, appreciation of, 48

athletic abilities, for social mobility, 24–25

average teacher salary, *144*

About the Author

Stephen J. McNamee is professor of sociology at the University of North Carolina Wilmington. He is a recipient of the University of North Carolina System Board of Governors Excellence in Teaching Award, the University of North Carolina Wilmington Distinguished Teaching Professorship Award, the University of North Carolina Wilmington Faculty Scholarship Award, and the North Carolina Sociological Association Contributions to Sociology Award.